NEW PENGUIN SHAKESPEARE
GENERAL EDITOR: T. J. B. SPENCER
ASSOCIATE EDITOR: STANLEY WELLS

WILLIAM SHAKESPEARE

∗

THE FIRST PART OF
KING HENRY THE
FOURTH

EDITED BY
P. H. DAVISON

PENGUIN BOOKS

PENGUIN BOOKS

Published by the Penguin Group
Penguin Books Ltd, 27 Wrights Lane, London W8 5TZ, England
Penguin Books USA Inc., 375 Hudson Street, New York, New York 10014, USA
Penguin Books Australia Ltd, Ringwood, Victoria, Australia
Penguin Books Canada Ltd, 10 Alcorn Avenue, Toronto, Ontario, Canada M4V 3B2
Penguin Books (NZ) Ltd, 182–190 Wairau Road, Auckland 10, New Zealand

Penguin Books Ltd, Registered Offices: Harmondsworth, Middlesex, England

This edition first published in Penguin Books 1968
23 25 27 29 30 28 26 24 22

This edition copyright © Penguin Books, 1968
Introduction and notes copyright © P. H. Davison, 1968
All rights reserved

Printed in England by Clays Ltd, St Ives plc
Set in Monotype Ehrhardt

CONTENTS

INTRODUCTION

TOWARDS the end of *The First Part of Henry IV*, Prince Hal stands over two bodies. One is his dead rival, Hotspur, and the other, Falstaff, who, having been attacked by Douglas, has fallen down 'as if he were dead'. It is for Hal a moment of triumph. He has shown himself superior in battle, made 'this northern youth exchange | His glorious deeds' for Hal's own indignities, and redeemed the promise made to his father in their scene of reconciliation.

This representation of the victorious Hal standing over the two prostrate bodies is emblematic of an important aspect of the play. To Elizabethan audiences, well aware of the myth of the regenerate Hal, it must have seemed an almost mystical moment. There was a long way to go before Agincourt, but, for an audience to whom the story was familiar, this was the moment when Hal could be seen to have triumphed not only over Hotspur but also over those characteristics of his own waywardness epitomized by the fallen Falstaff.

A loooor dramatist might have made this the last moment of the play, allowing it to linger in the memory as the audience drifted from the theatre. But this is not quite the end. Hal's two epitaphs are not fashioned to give an audience the thrill of victory.

> *No, Percy, thou art dust,*
> *And food for –*

'For worms,' adds Hal, as Percy dies before being able to complete his sentence.

> *When that this body did contain a spirit,*
> *A kingdom for it was too small a bound.*
> *But now two paces of the vilest earth*
> *Is room enough. . . .*
> *But let my favours hide thy mangled face. . . .*
>
> V.4.88–95

Hal speaks sadly, regretfully; there is no glorification of victory. But that is not all. Even before Falstaff undergoes his comic resuscitation we have speeches by Hal that subtly modify the moment of triumph. 'O, I should have a heavy miss of thee' (V.4.104), he says over Falstaff's 'dead' body. The pun is obvious and it recalls a line in the epitaph spoken over Hotspur, which might so easily have been comic if spoken over Falstaff:

> *This earth that bears thee dead*
> *Bears not alive so stout a gentleman.*

Hal, as he looks down on the two bodies, is a symbol of what he has striven for throughout the play – reformation that will glitter like bright metal on a sullen ground. He has found the mean between the two extremes that Aristotle described in the Nicomachean Ethics, that which results from excess and that which results from defect. His centrality is paramount, yet, curiously, not a single title-page of any of the early quartos, nor the title of the play in the Folio of 1623, so much as mentions Hal. Nominally the play concerns Henry IV, and it is in his reign that all the events occur, but the title-pages go to some trouble to publicize the names of Hotspur and Falstaff. Even the very first mention we have of the play, in the Stationers' Register, 25 February 1598, does exactly the same:

> *. . . a booke intituled The historye of* HENRY *the IIIJth with his battaile of Shrewsburye against* HENRY

8

HOTTSPURRE *of the Northe with the conceipted mirthe of Sir* JOHN FFALSTOFF.

The battle is rightly and historically given as Henry IV's and it is language such as this which, with slight variations, is used on the title-pages of edition after edition. Shakespeare was almost certainly not responsible for the advertising matter that appeared on the title-pages of his plays. We cannot be at all sure that the description in the Stationers' Register stemmed from him. Nevertheless, in a play in which the central character is so clearly Prince Hal, it is, at first sight, a little surprising that his name should invariably be omitted.

If Hal is central to *1 Henry IV*, Falstaff is undoubtedly the play's most attractive character. He immediately became enormously popular and there have come down to us a large number of references to him and the play in the correspondence and literature of the time. One example will show how eagerly those first audiences hung on his words. In a commendatory poem by Sir Thomas Palmer, printed in the Folio edition of the works of Beaumont and Fletcher in 1647, there appeared these lines:

> *I could praise Heywood now ; or tell how long*
> *Falstaff from cracking nuts hath kept the throng.*

During the Commonwealth, when the theatres were closed, at least one short farcical piece – a droll – was extracted from *1 Henry IV*. It was called *The Bouncing Knight, or, The Robbers Robbed* and later in the seventeenth century a second playlet was similarly extracted – *The Boaster: or, Bully-Huff catched in a trap.*

As the titles indicate, the subject of these adaptations is Falstaff. Just as the attention of audiences has been attracted to Falstaff, so has that of critics. Inevitably one is in danger of seeing the play as his, whereas it is undoubtedly the development of Hal's character which is the play's major concern.

Although Shakespeare did not write his history plays in chronological order, he did, so far as we can tell, dramatize the three successive reigns of Richard II, Henry IV, and Henry V in that order, and he probably wrote all four plays within a period of five or six years. We do not know whether, when writing *1 Henry IV*, Shakespeare had a second part in mind. It is possible he intended to write only one play on this reign but found he had too much material for a single play and thus began to prepare for a second part by building up the character of Hal's brother, John of Lancaster, and suggesting, by means of the scene with the Archbishop of York (IV.4), that though Hotspur was to be beaten, further rebellion would follow.

Perhaps the success of Part One, and of Falstaff in particular, encouraged the businessman in Shakespeare to provide a second play. Certainly the pattern of scenes of each part is remarkably similar, as if a formula were being followed, and it is curious that Hal and his father should be as estranged in Part Two as ever they were in Part One. However, when Shakespeare wrote *1 Henry IV*, probably in 1596, he was an experienced man of the theatre and it is difficult to believe that by the time he was half-way through *1 Henry IV* he did not realize he had a success on his hands. Thus, if a second part was not planned from the beginning (which at least seems possible), it was probably projected when Shakespeare came near to the completion of *1 Henry IV*.

Whether the two parts were ever performed successively in the late 1590s we do not know. From the evidence we have of actual performances of plays in two parts (such as

Marlowe's *Tamburlaine*), it is not unlikely. In Shakespeare's lifetime the two parts were rather roughly put together to make a single play and a manuscript of this, the Dering version, exists. A conflation of the two parts, at least as rough, was presented at the Edinburgh Festival in 1964. The practice of performing both parts in a single day, though still uncommon, was initiated in 1923 by Birmingham Repertory Theatre (the first company to play *1 Henry IV* in full, at least since Shakespeare's day).

There is no doubt at all – because we have the evidence of the plays themselves – that Shakespeare thought of these plays as a group. It is possible he had in mind the whole sequence of plays when he first set about writing *Richard II*. Though Shakespeare's style develops from one play to the next, the continuity of theme is so strong, and the references from one reign to another so frequent, that the four plays give a strong sense of unity.

To what extent the differences in style are a result of the development of Shakespeare's art, and to what extent they are a result of his finding a medium for the particular events he wished to dramatize, it is difficult to say. Certainly we seem to move from a medieval world in *Richard II* – medieval in its attitude to kingship, in its values, and in its style – to a world that, if very different from ours, is nevertheless one with which we seem to have much in common. It would not be possible to imagine the Gardener of *Richard II* (III.4) speaking his symbolic verse in the inn yard at Rochester. The Carriers who complain of bots and peas and beans in II.1 would seem incongruous in the earlier play. Yet the transition is nothing like as sudden as these extremes might indicate. When Worcester offers to read 'matter deep and dangerous' we are very close to the world of medieval romance:

> *As full of peril and adventurous spirit*
> *As to o'er-walk a current roaring loud*
> *On the unsteadfast footing of a spear.* I.3.189–91

When Vernon describes those who follow Hal, 'Glittering in golden coats like images', and tells how he saw young Harry with his beaver on, we are not far from the chivalric tourney that takes place in the third scene of *Richard II*:

> *His cuishes on his thighs, gallantly armed,*
> *Rise from the ground like feathered Mercury,*
> *And vaulted with such ease into his seat*
> *As if an angel dropped down from the clouds*
> *To turn and wind a fiery Pegasus,*
> *And witch the world with noble horsemanship.*
> IV.1.105–10

Yet here in *1 Henry IV*, and more obviously when Hotspur speaks of his willingness 'To pluck bright honour from the pale-faced moon', we are aware that the world of Hal is not the world of Richard and Hotspur. Hotspur's eagerness is at once captivating and out-dated. If there is a touch of high romance in Worcester's description of the dangers he unfolds, there is not an atom of romance about the speaker. Glendower, recounting the names of devils who are his lackeys, telling of the dreamer Merlin and his prophecies, and conjuring music from the air, is a high-romance figure from an age that goes back even before the medieval period. Alas, the past that is recalled by Glendower is as out-dated as Hotspur's concept of honour. Shakespeare deliberately makes a gentlemanly, if comically irascible, figure of poetry and music out of the barbarian he found in Holinshed and the crafty dreamer described by Thomas Phaer in *A Mirror for Magistrates* (1559), but in the 'jolly jar | Between the king and Percy's worthy bloods' (as Phaer puts it), Glendower is disastrously ineffective. The worlds of chivalry and romance, though they are not lost entirely from sight, are already of another age.

The divinity that attended upon King Richard is also departed. Once effective usurpation of a monarch divinely appointed was seen to be possible, then clearly the concept of divinity could no longer be maintained. What matters in a secular authority is the quality of the man, and it is for this reason that Hal's evolution was so fascinating and so important a subject for Shakespeare and his audiences. Henry IV was tainted, for he had usurped the throne. Despite his desire to rule well, he is burdened by an intolerable burden of guilt, for he took not only Richard's throne but also his life. 'The hot vengeance and the rod of heaven' punish his 'mistreadings', he says (*1 Henry IV*, III.2.10–11). In the Second Part of the play he is more open:

> *God knows, my son,*
> *By what by-paths and indirect crooked ways*
> *I met this crown . . .*   *2 Henry IV*, IV.5.184–6

And Hal himself, when Henry V, can beg,

> *Not today, O Lord,*
> *O not today, think not upon the fault*
> *My father made in compassing the crown!*
>   *Henry V*, IV.1.285–8

Henry's sin was something Shakespeare iterated at great length no fewer than four times in *1 Henry IV*. Twice Hotspur recounts the story of Henry's usurpation (I.3.158–84 and IV.3.54–92); once Henry himself tells the story (III.2.39–84); and finally Worcester, as guilty as Henry in the actual usurpation, gives his version (V.1.32–71). It is this burden of guilt that makes Henry IV seem so sick and aged in the plays of his name (though he was active enough at the end of *Richard II*) and it is partly for this reason that Shakespeare takes such care to dissociate Hal from his father (just as he dissociates Hotspur from the policy of his father and uncle). The taint of the tavern is to be preferred to that of the parent.

Shakespeare retells the fall of Richard for a purpose that was obvious to his audiences but is less apparent to us. We are inured to missing many of the puns and to being unable to follow some of the allusions in an Elizabethan play. A modern audience cannot be expected to know that there were two Edmund Mortimers alive at the same time, two kinds of Marcher Lords (Welsh and Scottish), and two Walter Blunts. As Shakespeare was confused over the Mortimers and the Earls of March, and did not bother to distinguish between the Blunts, we are in good company. Nor can we, unless we have specialized knowledge, readily see Poins's witticism at II.4.211 when Falstaff explains that the points of the swords of the nine men in buckram were broken. This kind of difficulty we expect and, although it is meat to annotators, it is usually of small account in performance.

A more serious difficulty is the difference between Elizabethan and modern conceptions of the use of history. To an Elizabethan, history was directly educative in a way which we should consider naïve. By holding up a mirror to the past it was thought possible to learn how to amend one's own life and how to anticipate events. Further, since the time when John Bale had written his play, *King John* (about 1534), drama had been a means by which subjects and their rulers might be instructed in their duties one to another.

The experience of the past made the Elizabethans fear rebellion and disorder so greatly that it was considered better to obey a tyrant than to foment civil war. It is probably this attitude rather than Shakespeare's specific political beliefs (whatever they may have been) that has led some critics to see Shakespeare's histories as politically conservative. It is as if, for many people, Shakespeare's attitude were like that of York in *Richard II* when, perhaps, they would wish it were like that of his son, Aumerle. There are two further difficulties that face us. First of all, before Shakespeare's play was performed, Hal was a legend; Falstaff – Shakespeare's Falstaff, at least – was totally unknown. Shakespeare would need to characterize Hal in such a way that the audience would accept him as the man they imagined him to be. In this apparent dis-advantage, however, lay an asset that Shakespeare used in similar circumstances in other plays – in *Troilus and Cressida*, for example, in dramatizing Ajax, Achilles, and Cressida herself. In dramatizing Hal, Shakespeare could rely on the strength of the legend – Hal's 'given person-ality' – and might, simultaneously, gently reassess Hal in a way that would pass almost unnoticed except by the most thoughtful. It was an ideal technique for pleasing a large audience of widely differing intellectual standards.

We have no such 'received opinion' of Hal and as a result our view of Hal, taken simply from what Shake-speare has given us, may become distorted. It led George Bernard Shaw to call him 'an able young Philistine' who repeatedly made it clear that he would turn on his friends later on, and that 'his self-indulgent good-fellowship with them is consciously and deliberately treacherous'. Shaw may exaggerate a modern view of Hal, but it is a view that is not uncommon. Shakespeare is a little critical of Hal, but his criticism does not amount to condemnation. Hal, as Henry V, is to represent an ideal of kingship, in so far as it is possible for human beings to create such an ideal.

The final difficulty for us springs from dramatic and not national history. Before *1 Henry IV* there was a long history of Morality drama. In Shakespeare's day, though it was old-fashioned to the relatively sophisticated Globe audience, it was still performed in country districts and was often parodied in London (as it is in *1 Henry IV*). Besides referring to a place known for the stage-plays performed at its fairs, Manningtree, Shakespeare mentions on a number of occasions figures from Morality plays. The law is Father Antic (I.2.60), and Falstaff is 'that reverend Vice, that grey Iniquity, that Father Ruffian, that Vanity in years' (II.4.441-2). The whole world and meaning of Morality drama is assumed by Shakespeare to be within the knowledge of his audience. Not only are there references that are for us oblique and often obscure, but the implications of the deceptions of Falstaff as that 'villainous abominable misleader of youth' (II.4.449), and his relationship to Hal, stem from the Morality tradition. It is not that the relationship is identical; it is not as if Falstaff *were* The Vice, or Hal were Everyman, or Magnificence, or Temporal Justice, but that they exist, as dramatic characters, in a relationship which has grown out of a tradition familiar to the original audiences.

The traditional position of man in a Morality play was between his good and evil influences. Faustus, in Marlowe's play, is flanked by good and evil angels, but these angels are not wholly and unequivocally good or evil, as their names might suggest. Shakespeare, in dramatizing Hal, Hotspur, and Falstaff, seems to have had this kind of Morality pattern in the back of his mind, but the result is very much more complex. Within the play it is plain that Hal's father is anxious that he should imitate Hotspur.

> *O that it could be proved*
> *That some night-tripping fairy had exchanged*
> *In cradle-clothes our children where they lay,*
> *And called mine Percy, his Plantagenet!*
>
> I.1.85–8

To the King, Hotspur is the epitome of all that is brave and honourable, even though they are in conflict. It is noticeable that Henry here speaks in terms of out-dated romance; 'night-tripping fairies' might be expected to be in Glendower's retinue.

Simultaneously, Hal's tavern companions seek to make him completely one of them, so that he becomes 'sworn brother to a leash of drawers' (II.4.6–7). Falstaff, for his part, expects the land to be made safe for thieves when Hal is King (I.2.58–61). The faults of Hotspur and Falstaff are plain. Both are rebels, one against the King himself, denying him prisoners, maintaining that, as a usurper, he has no right to the throne but ought to surrender it to Mortimer. Falstaff, though professing loyalty to the King's person, rebels against all authority, lacking any sense of social responsibility.

The 'education' of Hal is not simply a matter of making a choice of one or other of these 'angels'. Instead, he must realize in himself what is good in each of them and ignore what will be harmful to him as a king. It is to this end that Hal is directing himself when, upbraided by the King, he says,

> *I shall hereafter, my thrice-gracious lord,*
> *Be more myself.*　　　　III.2.92–3

Because Shakespeare's creation is capable of existing in its own right, we are able to follow and enjoy the play sufficiently even without being aware of the play's dramatic heritage, but the lack of such knowledge can lead to misunderstanding. Nowhere is this more obvious than in Hal's speech at the end of the second scene. It is this speech in particular that has given Hal a reputation for treachery and priggishness. Writing of Henry V in *Ideas of Good and Evil* in 1903, W. B. Yeats said:

> *He has the gross vices, the coarse nerves of one who is to rule among violent people, and he is so little 'too friendly' with his friends that he bundles them out of doors when their time is over. He is as remorseless and undistinguished as some natural force.* . . . *His purposes are so intelligible to everybody that everybody talks of him as if he succeeded, although he fails in the end, as all men great and little fail in Shakespeare.*

Yeats is writing of Shakespeare's complete dramatic creation but he expresses, better than Shaw, not merely opposition to Hal, but an understanding of why he is as he is. The situation demanded a ruler who would not be betrayed by human weakness – a ruler who could, despite the joys of good-fellowship, reject a Corinthian, a boon companion. But Shakespeare's presentation of Hal is much more subtle than Yeats allows and its subtlety in part depends upon the dramatic inheritance and the dramatic conventions which Shakespeare used.

Hal's speech has often been considered to be wholly in character, seeming to reveal cold, calculated treachery, but it is very much more probable that it ought to be seen as a speech of explanation, spoken by Hal, of course, but not as an expression of his character. It is as if Hal were a kind of Chorus. There is a difficulty in such an explanation. We expect a character speaking a soliloquy to say what he believes to be true and also to speak as himself.

Can we be sure that the function of this speech is, as Dr Johnson said, 'to keep the prince from appearing vile in the opinion of the audience'?

Until recently, owing to the realistic dramatic inheritance of the nineteenth and twentieth centuries that separates us from the Elizabethan age more sharply than the years themselves, audiences have found it very difficult to accept breaks in the continuity of the conventional suspension of disbelief. For a character to be himself and something other than himself (common enough in music hall and television comedy) – to have two different relationships with his audience – has been out of the question.

In Shakespeare's day it was possible for an actor to move easily and rapidly from direct appeal to an audience to seeming unawareness of its presence. Thus, in *1 Henry IV*, Falstaff seems to step outside his part in telling the story of the fight at Gad's Hill. We can see something similar in Vernon's speech at IV.1.97–110, and possibly in Hotspur's at III.1.246 (see note). When Hal describes his plans at the end of I.2, he is offering his Elizabethan audience an assurance that he will not be led astray like the prodigal child in the Morality stories with which they were so familiar. It is very difficult to be sure when Shakespeare is bending the conventions, at least as we understand them, and it is partly this that makes particularly difficult a just assessment of Falstaff's part in IV.2 and V.4, and Hal's soliloquy in I.2.

It is one thing to offer an explanation, however; it is another to remove all prejudice. Ironically, it is the very assurance that Shakespeare sought to give his own audience which makes us so unsure. Even if we accept the need to renounce Falstaff, and Bardolph and Poins, as inevitably part of Hal's responsibilities of office, can we also stomach the latter part of the speech in which Hal

designs to appear 'more goodly'? If we pause to consider
the matter it is impossible, though in the theatre the
moment passes quickly and we enter into Gad's Hill and
the tavern in Eastcheap and the speech is forgotten. But
once one *is* aware that cold calculation is implied, it is hard
not to think ill of Hal. There is one way in which Hal may
here prove acceptable to us. Furthermore, it avoids
dependence on a tradition now largely lost.

Hal's speech can be taken in much the same way as we
take Hotspur's speech on his quest for honour (I.3.199).
Just as Hotspur is over-eager for honour, so is Hal over-
anxious to pursue the course that will lead to his reformation, to being himself as he really is. Hal's pursuit of
honour (for that is what it amounts to) is as youthfully
naïve as Hotspur's. Both reveal, in these speeches, a certain
selfishness, yet both show, as the play progresses, a more
generous nature. It is mistaken to read, or perform, this
speech as if Hal were a Machiavellian schemer like Shakespeare's Richard III. He is, as Hotspur is shown to be,
young, inexperienced, but beginning to be aware of his
responsibilities.

There were available to Shakespeare a number of
accounts and legends of Hal's life, some not very reliable.
His major source was the second edition of Holinshed's
Chronicles of England, 1587. From this he obtained the
basic details for his story of Hal, though he adapted them
considerably to make the story more dramatic. He adjusted
the ages of the principal characters (making Hal and
Hotspur of the same age though Hotspur was two years
older than Henry IV), brought forward Henry's reference
to a crusade, anticipated Hal's reported attempt to depose
his father, delayed Northumberland's sickness so that
news of its occurrence arrived on the eve of the battle of

Shrewsbury, and greatly enlarged the part played by Hal in the battle.

According to Holinshed, Hal 'that day helped his father like a lusty young gentleman'. He was hurt in the face by an arrow but refused to leave the field. Hotspur appears from Holinshed to have been killed in a mêlée, but though a careless reading might make it seem that Hal was involved, there is no historical justification (though ample dramatic justification) for a confrontation between the two men. Hal was barely sixteen at the time; his brother John was only thirteen and took no part in the battle. Shakespeare amplified the parts played by Blunt and Vernon, and virtually created Lady Mortimer and Lady Percy (christening her Kate – though Holinshed called her Eleanor, and her real name was Elizabeth).

Shakespeare also used Daniel's poem, *The First Four Books of the Civil Wars between the two houses of Lancaster and York* (1595), as he had when writing *Richard II*, and he followed it where dramatically convenient (as in its report that the Welsh failed to arrive at Shrewsbury). There is some evidence that there were earlier plays on Henry V, and there might even have been one on Hotspur. One such play survives and this, and perhaps Stowe's *The Chronicles of England* (1580) and *The Annals of England* (1592), may have provided supplementary material on Hal's madcap youth, though the legend of Hal's youth was very well known.

Hotspur is a figure cast in the old heroic mould. Like Hal's, his reputation was established before Shakespeare wrote *1 Henry IV*. If the names of those who have acted the parts of Hotspur and Hal are anything to go by, then there is no doubt which character has proved more attractive to actors. Hotspur has been played by Quin (who was later to play Falstaff) and Kemble in the eighteenth century; Macready and Phelps (who also went on to play Falstaff), Bourchier and Lewis Waller, in the nineteenth century; Matheson Lang, Gielgud, Olivier, and Redgrave, in this century. Hotspur's part allows for the legitimate display of the heroic, expressed in rhetoric that, although exaggerated, is nevertheless excellent to deliver. There is also a sense of doom about Hotspur, and he has a moving death-scene, both of which demand (but do not always receive) sensitive interpretation.

Although Falstaff offers to speak in King Cambyses's vein, it is Hotspur who comes very much closer to the kind of hyperbole associated with earlier dramatists. That Hotspur's speech on honour was taken to be a deliberate exaggeration in its own day is evident from its use in Beaumont's play *The Knight of the Burning Pestle*, when a character has to speak what is described there as 'a huffing part'. Hotspur's pursuit of honour, his petulant reiteration of his complaint about his Scottish prisoners, and a lack of sensitivity towards others, can very easily lead to his being seen and presented as a boor. He will look even more ridiculous if he is made to speak ludicrously because of the too enthusiastic taking-up of a hint in the Second Part of the play about his manner of speech. Lady Percy says:

> *And speaking thick, which nature made his blemish,*
> *Became the accents of the valiant;*
> *For those that could speak low and tardily*
> *Would turn their own perfection to abuse*
> *To seem like him.*   2 *Henry IV*, II.3.24–8

Lady Percy describes her now-dead husband as a man who was a pattern for all youth:

> *He was the mark and glass, copy and book,*
> *That fashioned others.*   II.3.31–2

She is not, of course, without prejudice, but in describing how even Hotspur's fault of speech was slavishly imitated, she suggests how greatly he was admired – a characteristic not always brought out in performance. The precise nature of Hotspur's defect of speech is puzzling. The word 'thick' can mean husky, hoarse, or rapid – and 'tardily' suggests the third of these. Certainly rapid speech suits a character of such impetuosity. In 1914, however, Sir Herbert Beerbohm Tree persuaded Matheson Lang to stammer, and this was enthusiastically followed by other actors. Olivier hesitated slightly before 'w' and Redgrave spoke with a thick 'r'. Unless, however, such a performance is most carefully controlled, it gives way to guying, and this is destructive of Shakespeare's creation. Hotspur ought, above all else, to be the kind of young man who sets alight admiration in everyone, young and old.

Harry Percy is, as his nickname indicates, headstrong and wilful and this is apparent from his behaviour, his flood of language, his exaggeration, and the reputation he has with others. His very name for impetuosity will serve, says Worcester, as 'an adopted name of privilege', preventing his being taken too seriously. He is 'A harebrained Hotspur, governed by a spleen' (V.2.19). On the other hand, even if his kind of honour is self-indulgent, and though there is no place for it in the post-medieval world, his standards of integrity are far removed from the shifting expediency of Henry and Worcester. Nor is there anything morbid in his manner of facing death:

> Come, let us take a muster speedily.
> Doomsday is near. Die all, die merrily.

IV.1.133-4

The contrast here with Glendower and Douglas is sharp.

23

The Welshman's promises come to nothing, and Douglas hardly makes good the boast,

> *Talk not of dying, I am out of fear*
> *Of death or death's hand for this one half year.*
>
> IV.1.135–6

So precipitate is the flight of that 'ever valiant and approvèd Scot' (I.1.54) that, when fleeing with the rest, he falls from a hill and

> *was so bruised*
> *That the pursuers took him.*   V.5.21–2

The death of Enobarbus in a ditch, that 'master leaver' and 'fugitive' of *Antony and Cleopatra*, is much more honourable than this.

It is incorrect to interpret Shakespeare's presentation of honour in *1 Henry IV* as wholly satirical, much though that may accord with current fashion. Hotspur, like Coriolanus, is still adolescent in temperament, great though each is in courage and physical might. His view of honour is partly selfish, it is true – 'out upon this half-faced fellowship', he cries – but we are not to assume, because neither Glendower nor Douglas lives up to his words, nor because Henry and Worcester and Northumberland are all treacherous, that honour is meaningless. Hotspur's attachment to an out-dated concept of honour, and Falstaff's brilliant depreciation of what it signifies, are traps that Hal avoids but into which we often nowadays tend to fall. In the world of York and Lancaster, honour is urgently needed, but it must be a new kind of honour, an integrity, a selflessness, quite different from that chivalric honour the loss of whose titles Hotspur bemoans more than life itself.

In many ways Hotspur and Hal are closely akin. Their lack of self-management takes different forms, but it is apparent in each. Hotspur's frankness is one of his most engaging qualities; in Hal, in his speech at the end of I.2, it is equally apparent, though many critics (if not audiences) are disturbed by it. Hal's aspirations may be veiled by 'base contagious clouds' but they are as strong as those more obviously displayed by Hotspur. It is in their humour, however, that Hal and Hotspur share a particularly interesting characteristic.

It has been customary to regard Hal as at least as witty a character as Falstaff. This is to do less than justice to Shakespeare's skill in distinguishing between alacrity of mind, with which he invests Falstaff, and the modest extent of Hal's inventive capacities – less remarkable than those of Poins. With much preparation Hal arranges a joke on Francis, the drawer. We probably do not have too much sympathy with Francis, but the repetition of the joke, and, compared with the fruitfulness of Poins's Gad's Hill plot, its lack of imagination, rightly lead Poins to ask, 'come, what's the issue?' And Hal's answer is as lame as it is when he is made to confess by Falstaff that he has picked the fat rogue's pocket (III.3.167). It is not merely that Hal's inventiveness is moderate, but that he takes such delight in the skill he has revealed. He cannot forbear to tease Francis again. 'What's o'clock, Francis?' he asks, having just said it is 'this present twelve o'clock at midnight', and he receives, once again, Francis's pitiful response, 'Anon, anon, sir.'

Hotspur is made to seem just as delighted with himself at his putting down of Glendower when Glendower tells him he can teach him to command the devil.

> *And I can teach thee, coz, to shame the devil*
> *By telling truth. Tell truth, and shame the devil.*
>
> III.1.54–5

And then, a line or two later – almost, one imagines, hugging himself with delight at his clever turning of the phrase – he repeats:

> *O, while you live, tell truth, and shame the devil!*

These examples reveal Hal and Hotspur at their lowest level of wit but both are given something more imaginative. In each instance the form of humour is parody. Hal's burlesque of Hotspur (II.4.100–107) is justifiably admired. Hotspur's imitation of his wife (III.1.241–50) is, appropriately, gentler and therefore less striking. More subtle, because it is a parody that informs his manner of expression rather than being directly imitative, is Hotspur's witty description of the 'certain lord' who came to him on the battlefield to demand his prisoners (I.3.30–63). Nowhere is Hal given a speech as delightful as this.

> *When I was dry with rage and extreme toil,*
> *Breathless and faint, leaning upon my sword . . .*
> *Out of my grief and my impatience*
> *Answered neglectingly, I know not what,*
> *He should, or he should not, for he made me mad*
> *To see him shine so brisk, and smell so sweet,*
> *And talk so like a waiting-gentlewoman*
> *Of guns, and drums, and wounds, God save the mark ! . . .*

Hotspur's account, later in this scene, of Mortimer's fight with Glendower on 'gentle Severn's sedgy bank' is conscious, purple verse, appropriate to describe the single combat of medieval romance; but such poetry, from one who affects hostility to 'metre ballad-mongers', ironically suggests the quality, the *virtù*, of one too facilely interpreted as a barbarian. Such language is not to be dissociated from character in the way we separate Vernon's description of Hal and his followers in IV.1 from the speaker. Words tumble at all times too freely, too thickly, indeed, for this style to be anything but the man.

In one other respect Hotspur has the advantage of Hal. Lady Percy is Shakespeare's creation (though there was a real wife) and he gives her a name he seems to have liked, Kate. Hal's field of action is Gad's Hill; he is at home in a tavern. Action for Hotspur means Holmedon, and domesticity, Kate. The effect is obvious. Lady Percy's love for 'my heart's dear Harry', as she calls him in 2 Henry IV (II.3.12), is transparently clear and in the banter they exchange one can detect his love for her.

It would be an absurd exaggeration to speak of the tragedy of Hotspur, but there is, nevertheless, a tragic aspect to his character. In Lady Percy's talk of his night-mares, and in his and her relationship with each other, it is possible to see that Hotspur is growing up. It is his mis-fortune to be killed before he has time to reach the maturity that might have forewarned him from Shrews-bury. It is this that must not happen to Hal.

The titles that Hal wins in overcoming Hotspur are not those that Hotspur was so anxious not to lose. Hal wins something less tangible. His victory marks a coming to one kind of maturity, an acceptance of princely responsibilities and a demonstration, in a world of violence, that he is stronger than those who would oppose him. But Hal has, of course, another kind of maturity to seek.

Hal's 'education in a tavern' has often been remarked upon. In a world in which hierarchical differences were even more marked than they are now, Hal's behaviour, Elizabethan though it may be rather than medieval, is particularly fascinating. A man who is to wield supreme authority is here seen in the most easy contact with ordi-nary men and women. It is this that will prepare him, and us, for that remarkable scene in *Henry V*, the dialogue with Bates and Williams.

Whilst a part of Hal's legend was his association with commoners of the lowest orders in a society we take to be rigidly structured, most of those we see Hal meeting are hardly ordinary men and women. Shakespeare goes so far as to draw our attention to their extraordinariness by dramatizing the world of the Carriers. This is shown to be quite different from the world of Gadshill and his new associates. We cannot possibly mistake the fleas, the jordan and the chamber-lye of Rochester for the sack and anchovies of Eastcheap. Furthermore, Falstaff, though he inhabits a tavern, is not ordinary in the hierarchical sense – he is a knight – and in the dramatic sense he is quite the most extraordinary comic character that any dramatist has created. Falstaff's success was instantaneous and he has stood the test of time with astonishing ease. He has attracted many great actors – not always with the happiest results. Perhaps one of Shaw's most cutting comments was directed at Beerbohm Tree's performance of Falstaff in 1906. 'Mr Tree only wants one thing to make an excellent Falstaff, and that is to get born over again as unlike himself as possible. . . . The basket-work figure, the lifeless mask, the voice coarsened, vulgarized, and falsified, without being enriched and coloured – Mr Tree might as well try to play Juliet.'

It is very easy, in performance and criticism, to coarsen Falstaff, to make him appear even more bloated than he already is. Despite his undoubted girth, despite his habits, there is about Falstaff, paradoxically, a delicacy that demands to be realized.

Just as Falstaff has attracted actors (and audiences) so has he attracted scholars and critics. His ancestry, his characteristics, and what he stands for (as if he were an

actual Morality figure), have been discussed for genera-
tions. We can be certain that the name originally given to
this character was not Falstaff but Oldcastle, a knight of
great courage who had been a companion of Henry V in
his youth, but who later took part in a rebellion and, as a
follower of Wycliffe, was burnt. Sir William Brooke, a
descendant of Oldcastle's wife by a former marriage, was
Lord Chamberlain for a short time until his death in 1597.
It would seem that he, or his son, Sir Henry, objected to
Oldcastle's being maligned. Certainly the name was
changed and Sir Henry was mockingly referred to as Sir
John Falstaff by his enemies. It is probably no coincidence
that when the jealous Ford in *The Merry Wives of Windsor*
is given a false name it is 'Brook' – a name that also seems
to have aroused hostility for it appears as 'Broome' in the
Folio, making nonsense of one of the jokes.

Oldcastle himself was the subject of legends. He was
damned as a heretic by the orthodox (the Roman Catholics
in his time), and hailed as a hero and martyr by Protestants
such as Bale and Foxe about 150 years later. His religious
associations were well known and these are carried over
into Shakespeare's Falstaff, who has a large store of Biblical
knowledge, which he is adept at perverting.

Oldcastle also appears in a gallimaufry of a play called
The Famous Victories of Henry the Fifth. It covers the
ground of both parts of *Henry IV* and also *Henry V*, and
throughout its course Hal is called Henry V, even though
his father is alive. The version we have, which is very
short and corrupt, was published in the same year as
Shakespeare's play *1 Henry IV*, but it is likely that it is not
the earliest or only version, for a play of this name is
recorded in 1594, and it, or another, was performed a
number of times in 1595 and 1596. Sir John Oldcastle's
part is not large; one extract will suggest how abysmal is

the non-Shakespearian play and how remarkable is the transformation made by Shakespeare.

The Famous Victories of Henry the Fifth describes an incident in detail that Shakespeare virtually ignores, Hal's reputed striking of the Lord Chief Justice. In *1 Henry IV* we have only the indirect allusion, 'Thy place in Council thou hast rudely lost' (III.2.32), but the incident is dramatized in the non-Shakespearian play, then forms the subject of 'a play extempore', and, in Scene 6, it is recalled by the Prince.

HENRY V *But Ned, so soon as I am King, the first thing I will do shall be to put my Lord Chief Justice out of office, and thou shalt be my Lord Chief Justice of England.*

NED *Shall I be Lord Chief Justice? By gog's wounds, I'll be the bravest Lord Chief Justice that ever was in England.*

HENRY V *Then Ned, I'll turn all these prisons into fence schools, and I will endue thee with them, with lands to maintain them withal. Then I will have a bout with my Lord Chief Justice. Thou shalt hang none but pick-purses and horse-stealers, and such base-minded villains. But that fellow that will stand by the highway-side courage-ously, with his sword and buckler, and take a purse – that fellow, give him commendations. Beside that, send him to me and I will give him an annual pension out of my Exchequer to maintain him all the days of his life.*

SIR JOHN OLDCASTLE *Nobly spoken Harry! We shall never have a merry world till the old King be dead.*

In addition to an historic source, Shakespeare drew upon dramatic sources in creating Falstaff. He has been likened to the Vice of the old Moralities, and to a variety of other names associated with such drama. The references are direct in Shakespeare (II.4.441–2) and scholars have related him to Riot, the misleader of youth, to Misrule, Gluttony, and Monsieur Remorse (by which title he is called at I.2.111–12). His relationship to court and stage fools has been examined; he has been compared to the *miles gloriosus* of Plautine comedy, to the braggart soldier of the Italian *commedia erudita*, and to the captains of Elizabeth's armies; he has been thought to have descended from the stage parasite of Latin comedy; to be a caricature of the Puritans; and even to represent 'the supernatural order of Charity'. Although the search for Falstaff's ancestry is occasionally perverse, so rich is Shakespeare's characterization, nearly all such associations have an element of conviction about them.

He was to Dryden 'the best of comical characters'; to Dr Johnson, 'unimitated, unimitable'; his 'alacrity of mind' appealed to the man who vigorously first defended Falstaff from the charge of cowardice in the eighteenth century, Maurice Morgann; to Tolstoy Falstaff seemed 'a natural and typical character', perhaps, perversely, 'the only natural and typical character portrayed by Shakespeare'. He has seemed to one psychoanalyst to be a 'depreciated father figure', and to another, 'the personification of the wholly self-centred pleasure-seeking principle'. His warmth, his wit, his clarity of vision, his comic insight, have all been justly admired. He has, it has been said, 'a set of spiritual conceptions at once simple enough to be popular and sufficiently profound to cover the wealth of human experience'. There is, it has been explained, a Falstaff in each of us and it is this that gives him an appeal that is so widespread, despite his manifold faults, his gluttony, his irresponsibility, and his selfishness.

An even tougher battle has been waged over the matter of Falstaff's cowardice than was fought between Hotspur and Hal at Shrewsbury. One is tempted, like Falstaff at Gad's Hill, to run away, roaring. Briefly, it might be said that Falstaff's cowardice was not in dispute until Maurice Morgann published a spirited defence of Falstaff in 1777. The early critics, and actors of all periods, have considered Falstaff to be cowardly. Later critics have seen him as wily; an experienced soldier, a realist; a Bluntschli with sack instead of chocolates in his holster. It has been pointed out that he does not lose his presence of mind at Shrewsbury, but he certainly roars heartily at Gad's Hill, and Poins's scheme depends for its success on the certainty that Falstaff will run away. The puzzle is that Falstaff's cowardice should have so disturbed the critics. Our admiration for the character is not dependent upon valour. He is no Hal; he is no Hotspur. No critic castigates Douglas because he flees twice (V.4.42, stage direction, and V.5.20). Indeed, Hal, when permitting Douglas to leave ransomless, actually says:

> *His valours shown upon our crests today*
> *Have taught us how to cherish such high deeds,*
> *Even in the bosom of our adversaries.*   V.5.29–31

Falstaff's quality is quality of the imagination. He is not a mere liar but a creative genius, or, as A. C. Bradley put it, 'The bliss of freedom gained in humour is the essence of Falstaff'.

But Falstaff is not the central figure, dominate the stage and our affections though he will. He stands to one side of Hal as Hotspur does the other. Both Falstaff and Hotspur, the former in his rejection, the latter in his death, have been seen as means, actual or symbolic, whereby Hal rids himself of his urge to depose his father. In *1 Henry IV*, however, Shakespeare has toned down Hal's opposition to his father, for it is only glanced at – 'Thou ... art like enough ...' says his father, 'To fight against me under Percy's pay' (III.2.124–6). Hal's aversion to his father is much stronger in *The Famous Victories of Henry the Fifth* and Holinshed reports an attempt by Hal to usurp the throne in 1412, nearly a decade after Shrewsbury.

Hal's rejection of Falstaff does not occur until the end of the Second Part of the play but it is foreshadowed in *1 Henry IV* (and sometimes overstressed in performance). Falstaff, I think, is shown to suspect what the eventual outcome of their relationship must be as early as II.4.476–8. Given that he is meant to be as shrewd as we all take him to be, it is hard to believe that he could not tell which way the wind would blow, however much he might hope otherwise. This, surely, is one of the main marks of difference between the extract from *The Famous Victories of Henry the Fifth* quoted earlier and the corresponding passage in *1 Henry IV*.

Though the comedy of the situations protects the character of Falstaff very considerably, the satire on pressing soldiers, and the ignominious stabbing of the valiant traitor, Hotspur, are not in accord with the spirit of comedy that pervades Gad's Hill and Eastcheap. This is no miscalculation on Shakespeare's part. Just as Hal must stand a little apart from the pitch with which he is associating (II.4.405), so must we, despite our delight in Falstaff, see the implications of such gay licence. In the theatre nowadays this does not always happen. We grasp too eagerly at the Falstaff who is the expression of our own repressed irresponsibilities. We delight too single-mindedly in his wit and his capacity to undercut pretension. It is one thing to point to the worthlessness of a certain kind of 'grinning honour as Sir Walter hath' and quite another to seek such honour by the means

Falstaff employs. It is tempting to gloss over the implications of Falstaff's behaviour in IV.2 and V.4 as if it was but an extension of his attack on empty honour. Shakespeare dramatizes the need for trust and integrity as forcefully as he reveals how empty is the display of honour and its total abandonment.

This is not to say that Falstaff 'deserves' rejection. He deserves rejection no more than Hotspur deserves to be deceived by Worcester. What Shakespeare is dramatizing is the pain and sacrifice entailed in the 'education' of a successful and acceptable ruler. The price for public humanity is private humanity. The magnanimity Hal learns from Falstaff and his companions will make him a better ruler, but it requires also rejection of Falstaff. Hal has to learn when it is no longer possible that 'all the year' be 'playing holidays'. As for the rejection itself, it *ought* to be painful.

Hal's relationship to Falstaff and Hotspur, and his preparation for kingship, lead to the play's being set in a variety of contrasting spheres. We seem to inhabit at least three worlds. There is the world of the King, his court, and his camp at Shrewsbury. There is Hotspur's world – a difference in atmosphere as much as place – and thirdly there is Falstaff's world – Gad's Hill, Eastcheap, the road to Sutton Coldfield – and even his part of the battlefield. 'Place' as such is of little significance; what is telling is the atmosphere and tone of each of the worlds.

No single world can be assigned to Hal. He is physically present at Gad's Hill and Eastcheap; he comes to court and is spoken of in his absence; he is present in the King's camp and on the battlefield; he is in Percy's mouth before and at Shrewsbury; and in his challenge to Hotspur to single combat he even has about him a trace of the world of medieval romance. It has been suggested that the play is divided too sharply between its various spheres of interest, and possibly this impression has been accentuated by the alternation of comic and historic, of prose and verse, and the absence of a unifying pattern of images such as is found in *Antony and Cleopatra*. Only the language of Falstaff is at all rich in imagery, the chief sources being food (not surprisingly), the Bible, and other literature.

Nevertheless, despite these accusations, the interaction of the various parts of the play is very close. There was no formal separation of Acts and scenes in Elizabethan productions and we have experienced in recent years how exciting and rational the fluid presentation of Shakespeare can be, one scene running into the next without delay of curtain fall or lengthy change of scenery. Sometimes Shakespeare contrasts one scene with the next so that one comments on the other. After Hotspur has made his plea at the end of I.3:

> *O, let the hours be short,*
> *Till fields, and blows, and groans applaud our sport!*

we have, not a curtain, nor an empty page and the heading ACT II, SCENE I, but a great yawn, 'Heigh-ho!', from the first Carrier. No sooner has Gadshill explained to the Chamberlain that his associates are no 'sixpenny strikers', no 'mad mustachio purple-hued maltworms', but we have Falstaff bemoaning his fate. At the end of III.2 the King is eager to be off:

> *Our hands are full of business, let's away,*
> *Advantage feeds him fat while men delay.*

And we turn, at once, without intermission, to advantage in the shape of Falstaff feeding himself fat, despite his complaint that he is 'withered like an old apple-john'. Falstaff's and Hotspur's reactions are similarly contrasted at the end of IV.2 and the beginning of IV.3; and at the end of V.1, as Falstaff completes his catechism, 'Honour is a mere scutcheon', on walks Worcester:

> O no, my nephew must not know, Sir Richard,
> The liberal and kind offer of the King.   V.2.1–2

There is another kind of relationship, so manifold, so interwoven, that it forms almost the substance of the play itself. Time after time, events in one world are imitated in another. The most obvious example is the way in which Falstaff's description of honour echoes Hotspur's, but there are many of lesser magnitude.

Gadshill boasts of his confederates – Hotspur has confidence in his allies; Falstaff's bawling for his horse in II.2 is followed by Hotspur's shouting after his in the following scene. After Hotspur has fought at Holmedon, we see Hal involved in the farce of the battle of Gad's Hill; Hotspur's description of Mortimer's fight with Glendower is recounted in terms of high romance – Falstaff's fight with the men in buckram is altogether of another order; and Falstaff's ragamuffins are not in accord with the magnificent description of Hal's followers that is given by Vernon. There are many more examples, but these few may suffice to suggest that *1 Henry IV* is, in its own way, as formally patterned as *Richard II*.

A measure of Shakespeare's achievement in *1 Henry IV* is the extent to which his three principal characters seem to exist for us outside the confines of the printed page. Falstaff in particular has so seized men's imaginations that it is as if this character really lived in the very flesh about which we hear so much. Of all the legends that have come down to us about Shakespeare, none strikes us as more likely to be true than that which tells of Queen Elizabeth's demand for more of Sir John. Falstaff's zest for life is so abundant that it permeates the whole play. It is perhaps this, more than any other single quality, that has given *1 Henry IV* so wide an appeal for so long.

FURTHER READING

Editions, Editorial Problems, and Sources

SIR WALTER GREG'S facsimile of the first Quarto was reissued by The Clarendon Press, Oxford, in 1966 with an additional introduction by Charlton Hinman. The Folio version can conveniently be read in the reduced facsimile, *Mr William Shakespeare's Comedies, Histories, & Tragedies*, prepared by Helge Kökeritz (not to the entire satisfaction of all critics), and published by Oxford University Press in 1955. The principal recent editions are those of G. L. Kittredge (1940, reissued in a revised form by Irving Ribner, 1966, Blaisdell), John Dover Wilson (New Cambridge Shakespeare, 1946) and A. R. Humphreys (new Arden Shakespeare 1960, revised 1965). My debt to these editions is particularly heavy. The Norton Critical Edition, edited by James L. Sanderson, includes a lengthy and particularly well-chosen selection of essays on the play. *The Famous Victories of Henry the Fifth* can conveniently be read in the major collection of source material for *1 Henry IV*, Geoffrey Bullough's *Narrative and Dramatic Sources of Shakespeare*, volume IV (London, 1962). It is also to be found in the Signet edition of *1 Henry IV* (1965), which contains a helpful introduction by the editor, Maynard Mack.

A comprehensive survey of the text is to be found in the New Variorum Edition, edited by S. B. Hemingway (Philadelphia, 1936). This has been admirably brought up to date by G. Blakemore Evans in the summer issue of *Shakespeare Quarterly*, 1956. A brief but useful annotated list of some later criticism is given by James Sanderson in his edition of the play.

The whole sequence of Shakespeare's history plays has been considered in recent years by E. M. W. Tillyard (*Shakespeare's History Plays*, 1944, reprinted by Penguin Books, 1962); Lily B.

Campbell (*Shakespeare's 'Histories'*, San Marino, 1947); D. A. Traversi (*Shakespeare from Richard II to Henry V*, Hollis and Carter, 1957); and M. M. Reese (*The Cease of Majesty*, Arnold, 1961). Harold Jenkins surveyed work on the history plays between 1900 and 1951 in *Shakespeare Survey 6*, 1953, and *1 Henry IV* is selected for study by Cleanth Brooks and Robert B. Heilman in *Understanding Drama* (New York, 1948).

Criticism

Critical comment on Falstaff is as enormous in bulk as the character himself – and as varied. Quite the most useful summary is 'Gadshill Revisited' (*Shakespeare Quarterly*, IV, 1953, reprinted in the Norton edition) by Arthur C. Sprague, who is also the author of an excellent account of *1 Henry IV* on the stage in his *Shakespeare's Histories, Plays for the Stage* (Society for Theatre Research, London, 1964). The most influential studies of Falstaff have been those of Maurice Morgann (1777), available in *Eighteenth Century Essays on Shakespeare* (edited by D. Nichol Smith, Glasgow, 1903); A. C. Bradley ('The Rejection of Falstaff', in *Oxford Lectures on Poetry*, 1909); E. E. Stoll (in *Shakespeare Studies*, New York, 1927); and John Dover Wilson, whose book *The Fortunes of Falstaff* (Cambridge, 1943) deals with more than 'that reverend Vice'. Falstaff and Hotspur, as well as Hal, are discussed in the chapter 'Henry of Monmouth' in John Palmer's *Political Characters of Shakespeare* (Macmillan, 1945). An interesting and vigorously hostile view of Hal is expressed by John Masefield in his *William Shakespeare*, 1911.

The imagery of the play is examined by Caroline Spurgeon in *Shakespeare's Imagery and what it tells us* (Cambridge, 1935) and, more comprehensively, by Madeleine Doran in 'Imagery in *Richard II* and in *Henry IV*' (*Modern Language Review*, XXXVII, 1942). The language of the play, and the ironic relationship of court, tavern, and rebel camp, are discussed by William Empson in *Some Versions of Pastoral* (1935). M. A. Shaaber argues forcibly that the unity of the two parts of *Henry*

IV is 'a theatrical impossibility' in 'The Unity of *Henry IV*' (*Joseph Quincy Adams Memorial Studies*, Washington, 1948) but Harold Jenkins, in *The Structural Problem in Shakespeare's 'Henry IV'* (Methuen, 1956), argues that the two parts are complementary yet also 'independent and even incompatible'. Professor Jenkins's study is reprinted in *Shakespeare's Histories: An Anthology of Modern Criticism*, edited by William A. Armstrong (Penguin Shakespeare Library, 1972), and in *Discussions of Shakespeare's Histories*, edited by R. J. Dorius (Boston, 1965), which also includes four essays on Falstaff and A. P. Rossiter's illuminating discussion of the juxtaposition of opposed value-judgements in *I Henry IV* – 'Ambivalence: the Dialectic of the Histories', first published in *Angel with Horns* (London, 1961).

The play is interpreted as a satire on war and policy by L. C. Knights in 'Notes on Comedy', originally published in *Scrutiny* in 1933, and reprinted the following year in *Determinations* (edited by F. R. Leavis). Knights's interpretation is challenged by C. L. Barber as 'obviously an impossible, anachronistic view' in the essay 'From Ritual to Comedy: an examination of *Henry IV*', first published in *English Stage Comedy* (edited by W. K. Wimsatt, New York, 1955) and reproduced as chapter eight of his book *Shakespeare's Festive Comedy* (Princeton, 1959). In this study the play, and Falstaff in particular, are related to the saturnalian tradition. A more sombre view of the play is taken by J. F. Danby in *Shakespeare's Doctrine of Nature* (London, 1949). He argues that those who see the world of *Henry IV* 'as some vital, joyous Renaissance England must go behind the facts Shakespeare presents'.

There are two interesting psychological studies of the play to which reference is made in the Introduction: Franz Alexander's 'A Note on Falstaff' (*Psychoanalytic Quarterly*, 1933), and, in that same journal in 1948, Ernst Kris's 'Prince Hal's Conflict' (which is reprinted in *Approaches to Shakespeare*, edited by Norman Rabkin, New York, 1964). The merging of Falstaff's identity, for a few instants, 'with that of a typical vaudeville comedian' was suggested by A. J. A. Waldock in 'The Men in Buckram' (*Review of English Studies*, 1947).

A useful collection of essays is *King Henry IV Parts 1 and 2: A Casebook* (Macmillan, 1970), edited by G. K. Hunter, whose introductory essay is particularly helpful.

THE FIRST PART OF
KING HENRY THE FOURTH

THE CHARACTERS IN THE PLAY

The King's Party

KING HENRY IV, formerly Henry Bolingbroke, son of John of Gaunt

HENRY (or HAL), Prince of Wales, the King's eldest son

LORD JOHN OF LANCASTER, a younger son of King Henry IV

EARL OF WESTMORLAND, kinsman by law to Henry IV

SIR WALTER BLUNT

The Rebels

HENRY PERCY, Earl of Northumberland

HARRY HOTSPUR, his son

LADY PERCY (KATE), Hotspur's wife, sister of Mortimer

THOMAS PERCY, Earl of Worcester

EDMUND, LORD MORTIMER

LADY MORTIMER, Mortimer's wife, daughter of Glendower

OWEN GLENDOWER

EARL OF DOUGLAS

SIR RICHARD VERNON

RICHARD SCROOP, Archbishop of York

SIR MICHAEL, a member of the household of the Archbishop

Hal's Companions

SIR JOHN FALSTAFF

POINS

BARDOLPH

THE CHARACTERS IN THE PLAY

PETO
MISTRESS QUICKLY, hostess of the Tavern in Eastcheap
FRANCIS, a drawer
Vintner

At Rochester
GADSHILL
Two Carriers
Chamberlain

Sheriff and Officers
Ostler
Messengers
Travellers
Lords and Attendants
Soldiers

Enter the King, Lord John of Lancaster, Earl of I.1
Westmorland, Sir Walter Blunt, with others

KING HENRY _uncomfortable on throne_

So shaken as we are, so wan with care,
Find we a time for frighted peace to pant,
And breathe short-winded accents of new broils
To be commenced in strands afar remote.
No more the thirsty entrance of this soil
Shall daub her lips with her own children's blood,
No more shall trenching war channel her fields,
Nor bruise her flowerets with the armèd hoofs
Of hostile paces. Those opposèd eyes,
Which, like the meteors of a troubled heaven,   10
All of one nature, of one substance bred,
Did lately meet in the intestine shock   _Go into battle_
And furious close of civil butchery,
Shall now, in mutual well-beseeming ranks,   CRUSADE
March all one way, and be no more opposed
Against acquaintance, kindred, and allies.
The edge of war, like an ill-sheathèd knife,
No more shall cut his master. Therefore friends,
As far as to the sepulchre of Christ –
Whose soldier now, under whose blessed cross   20
We are impressèd and engaged to fight –
Forthwith a power of English shall we levy,
Whose arms were moulded in their mother's womb
To chase these pagans in those holy fields
Over whose acres walked those blessèd feet,

47

Which fourteen hundred years ago were nailed
For our advantage on the bitter cross.
But this our purpose now is twelve month old,
And bootless 'tis to tell you we will go.
30 Therefor we meet not now. Then let me hear
Of you, my gentle cousin Westmorland,
What yesternight our Council did decree
In forwarding this dear expedience.

WESTMORLAND
My liege, this haste was hot in question,
And many limits of the charge set down
But yesternight, when all athwart there came
A post from Wales, loaden with heavy news,
Whose worst was that the noble Mortimer –
Leading the men of Herefordshire to fight /welsh wizard
40 Against the irregular and wild Glendower –
Was by the rude hands of that Welshman taken,
A thousand of his people butcherèd,
Upon whose dead corpses there was such misuse,
Such beastly shameless transformation
By those Welshwomen done, as may not be
Without much shame retold or spoken of.

KING HENRY
It seems then that the tidings of this broil Cancel crossed
Brake off our business for the Holy Land. because of
                                             trouble on
WESTMORLAND   welsh
This matched with other did, my gracious lord, border
50 For more uneven and unwelcome news
Came from the north, and thus it did import.
On Holy-rood day, the gallant Hotspur there,
Young Harry Percy, and brave Archibald, – Douglas
That ever valiant and approvèd Scot,
At Holmedon met, where they did spend
A sad and bloody hour –

48

As by discharge of their artillery,
And shape of likelihood, the news was told;
For he that brought them, in the very heat
And pride of their contention did take horse,   60
Uncertain of the issue any way.

KING HENRY
Here is a dear, a true industrious friend,
Sir Walter Blunt, new lighted from his horse,
Stained with the variation of each soil
Betwixt that Holmedon and this seat of ours,
And he hath brought us smooth and welcome news.
The Earl of Douglas is discomfited.
Ten thousand bold Scots, two-and-twenty knights,
Balked in their own blood, did Sir Walter see
On Holmedon's plains. Of prisoners Hotspur took   70
Mordake, Earl of Fife and eldest son
To beaten Douglas, and the Earl of Atholl,
Of Murray, Angus, and Menteith:
And is not this an honourable spoil?
A gallant prize? Ha, cousin, is it not?

WESTMORLAND   In faith,
It is a conquest for a prince to boast of.

KING HENRY
Yea, there thou makest me sad, and makest me sin
In envy that my Lord Northumberland
Should be the father to so blest a son:
A son who is the theme of honour's tongue,   80
Amongst a grove the very straightest plant,
Who is sweet Fortune's minion and her pride –
Whilst I by looking on the praise of him
See riot and dishonour stain the brow
Of my young Harry. O that it could be proved
That some night-tripping fairy had exchanged
In cradle-clothes our children where they lay,

> And called mine Percy, his Plantagenet!
> Then would I have his Harry, and he mine.

(margin note: envious of northumberland because of sons.)

90 But let him from my thoughts. What think you, coz,
Of this young Percy's pride? The prisoners
Which he in this adventure hath surprised
To his own use he keeps, and sends me word
I shall have none but Mordake, Earl of Fife.

WESTMORLAND

This is his uncle's teaching. This is Worcester,
Malevolent to you in all aspects,
Which makes him prune himself, and bristle up
The crest of youth against your dignity.

KING HENRY

But I have sent for him to answer this,

100 And for this cause awhile we must neglect
Our holy purpose to Jerusalem.

(margin note: Related in royalty not necessarily family)

Cousin, on Wednesday next our Council we
Will hold at Windsor, so inform the lords.
But come yourself with speed to us again,
For more is to be said and to be done
Than out of anger can be utterèd.

WESTMORLAND

I will, my liege.

Exeunt

1.2   *Enter Prince of Wales and Sir John Falstaff*

FALSTAFF Now Hal, what time of day is it lad?

PRINCE HAL Thou art so fat-witted with drinking of old

(margin note: Drink food brothels)

sack, and unbuttoning thee after supper, and sleeping
upon benches after noon, that thou hast forgotten to
demand that truly which thou wouldst truly know.
What a devil hast thou to do with the time of the day?
Unless hours were cups of sack, and minutes capons,

(margin note: Reinforces Ling's thoughts about son)

and clocks the tongues of bawds, and dials the signs of leaping-houses, and the blessed sun himself a fair hot wench in flame-coloured taffeta, I see no reason why 10 thou shouldst be so superfluous to demand the time of the day.

FALSTAFF Indeed, you come near me now Hal, for we that take purses go by the moon and the seven stars, and not 'by Phoebus, he, that wandering knight so fair'. And I prithee sweet wag, when thou art King as God save thy grace – majesty I should say, for grace thou wilt have none –

PRINCE HAL What, none?

FALSTAFF No, by my troth, not so much as will serve to be prologue to an egg and butter.

PRINCE HAL Well, how then? Come, roundly, roundly.

FALSTAFF Marry then, sweet wag, when thou art King let not us that are squires of the night's body be called thieves of the day's beauty. Let us be Diana's foresters, gentlemen of the shade, minions of the moon. And let men say we be men of good government, being governed as the sea is, by our noble and chaste mistress the moon, under whose countenance we steal.

PRINCE HAL Thou sayest well, and it holds well too, for 30 the fortune of us that are the moon's men doth ebb and flow like the sea, being governed as the sea is, by the moon. As for proof? Now, a purse of gold most resolutely snatched on Monday night, and most dissolutely spent on Tuesday morning, got with swearing 'Lay by!', and spent with crying 'Bring in!', now in as low an ebb as the foot of the ladder, and by and by in as high a flow as the ridge of the gallows.

FALSTAFF By the Lord thou sayest true lad – and is not my Hostess of the tavern a most sweet wench? 40

PRINCE HAL As the honey of Hybla, my old lad of the

castle. And is not a buff jerkin a most sweet robe of durance?

FALSTAFF How now, how now, mad wag? What, in thy quips and thy quiddities? What a plague have I to do with a buff jerkin?

PRINCE HAL Why, what a pox have I to do with my Hostess of the tavern?

FALSTAFF Well, thou hast called her to a reckoning many
50 a time and oft.

PRINCE HAL Did I ever call for thee to pay thy part?

FALSTAFF No, I'll give thee thy due, thou hast paid all there.

PRINCE HAL Yea, and elsewhere, so far as my coin would stretch, and where it would not I have used my credit.

FALSTAFF Yea, and so used it that were it not here apparent that thou art heir apparent – but I prithee sweet wag, shall there be gallows standing in England when thou art King? And resolution thus fubbed as it is with
60 the rusty curb of old Father Antic the law? Do not thou when thou art King hang a thief.

PRINCE HAL No, thou shalt.

FALSTAFF Shall I? O rare! By the Lord, I'll be a brave judge!

PRINCE HAL Thou judgest false already! I mean thou shalt have the hanging of the thieves, and so become a rare hangman.

FALSTAFF Well, Hal, well! And in some sort it jumps with my humour – as well as waiting in the court, I can
70 tell you.

PRINCE HAL For obtaining of suits? TRIAL

FALSTAFF Yea, for obtaining of suits, whereof the hangman hath no lean wardrobe. 'Sblood, I am as melancholy as a gib cat, or a lugged bear.

PRINCE HAL Or an old lion, or a lover's lute.

FALSTAFF Yea, or the drone of a Lincolnshire bagpipe.

PRINCE HAL What sayest thou to a hare, or the melancholy of Moorditch?

FALSTAFF Thou hast the most unsavoury similes, and art indeed the most comparative rascalliest sweet young 80 prince. But Hal, I prithee trouble me no more with vanity. I would to God thou and I knew where a commodity of good names were to be bought. An old lord of the Council rated me the other day in the street about you, sir, but I marked him not, and yet he talked very wisely, but I regarded him not, and yet he talked wisely – and in the street too.

PRINCE HAL Thou didst well, for wisdom cries out in the streets and no man regards it.

FALSTAFF O, thou hast damnable iteration, and art 90 indeed able to corrupt a saint. Thou hast done much harm upon me, Hal, God forgive thee for it. Before I knew thee Hal, I knew nothing, and now am I, if a man should speak truly, little better than one of the wicked. I must give over this life, and I will give it over. By the Lord, an I do not I am a villain. I'll be damned for never a king's son in Christendom.

PRINCE HAL Where shall we take a purse tomorrow, Jack?

FALSTAFF Zounds, where thou wilt lad, I'll make one; an 100 I do not, call me a villain and baffle me.

PRINCE HAL I see a good amendment of life in thee, from praying to purse-taking.

FALSTAFF Why Hal, 'tis my vocation, Hal. 'Tis no sin for a man to labour in his vocation.

Enter Poins

Poins! Now shall we know if Gadshill have set a match! O, if men were to be saved by merit, what hole in hell were hot enough for him? This is the most omnipotent villain that ever cried 'Stand!' to a true man.

110 PRINCE HAL Good morrow, Ned.

POINS Good morrow, sweet Hal. What says Monsieur Remorse? What says Sir John Sack – and Sugar? Jack! How agrees the devil and thee about thy soul, that thou soldest him on Good Friday last, for a cup of Madeira and a cold capon's leg?

PRINCE HAL Sir John stands to his word, the devil shall have his bargain, for he was never yet a breaker of proverbs. He will give the devil his due.

POINS Then art thou damned for keeping thy word with 120 the devil.

PRINCE HAL Else he had been damned for cozening the devil.

POINS But my lads, my lads, tomorrow morning, by four o'clock early at Gad's Hill, there are pilgrims going to Canterbury with rich offerings and traders riding to London with fat purses. I have vizards for you all – you have horses for yourselves. Gadshill lies tonight in Rochester. I have bespoke supper tomorrow night in Eastcheap. We may do it as secure as sleep. If you will 130 go, I will stuff your purses full of crowns. If you will not, tarry at home and be hanged.

FALSTAFF Hear ye, Yedward, if I tarry at home and go not, I'll hang you for going.

POINS You will, chops?

FALSTAFF Hal, wilt thou make one?

PRINCE HAL Who I? Rob? I a thief? Not I, by my faith.

FALSTAFF There's neither honesty, manhood, nor good fellowship in thee, nor thou camest not of the blood royal, if thou darest not stand for ten shillings.

140 PRINCE HAL Well then, once in my days I'll be a madcap.

FALSTAFF Why, that's well said.

PRINCE HAL Well, come what will, I'll tarry at home.

FALSTAFF By the Lord, I'll be a traitor then, when thou art King.

PRINCE HAL I care not.

POINS Sir John, I prithee leave the Prince and me alone. I will lay him down such reasons for this adventure that he shall go.

FALSTAFF Well, God give thee the spirit of persuasion, 150 and him the ears of profiting, that what thou speakest may move, and what he hears may be believed, that the true prince may – for recreation sake – prove a false thief, for the poor abuses of the time want countenance. Farewell, you shall find me in Eastcheap.

PRINCE HAL Farewell, the latter spring! Farewell, All-hallown summer! *Exit Falstaff*

POINS Now my good sweet honey lord, ride with us tomorrow. I have a jest to execute that I cannot manage alone. Falstaff, Bardolph, Peto, and Gadshill shall rob 160 those men that we have already waylaid – yourself and I will not be there. And when they have the booty, if you and I do not rob them – cut this head off from my shoulders.

PRINCE HAL How shall we part with them in setting forth?

POINS Why, we will set forth before or after them, and appoint them a place of meeting – wherein it is at our pleasure to fail – and then will they adventure upon the exploit themselves, which they shall have no sooner 170 achieved but we'll set upon them.

PRINCE HAL Yea, but 'tis like that they will know us by our horses, by our habits, and by every other appointment to be ourselves.

POINS Tut, our horses they shall not see, I'll tie them in the wood. Our vizards we will change after we leave them. And, sirrah, I have cases of buckram for the nonce, to immask our noted outward garments.   *Disguise*

PRINCE HAL Yea, but I doubt they will be too hard for
180   us.

POINS Well, for two of them, I know them to be as true-bred cowards as ever turned back, and for the third, if he fight longer than he sees reason, I'll forswear arms. The virtue of this jest will be the incomprehensible lies that this same fat rogue will tell us when we meet at supper. How thirty at least he fought with, what wards, what blows, what extremities he endured, and in the reproof of this lives the jest.

Poins dodgy plan

PRINCE HAL Well, I'll go with thee. Provide us all things
190   necessary and meet me tomorrow night in Eastcheap. There I'll sup. Farewell.

POINS Farewell, my lord.   *Exit*

PRINCE HAL
I know you all, and will awhile uphold
The unyoked humour of your idleness.   *Soliloquy*
Yet herein will I imitate the sun,   *friends*
Who doth permit the base contagious clouds   *metaphor*
To smother up his beauty from the world,
That when he please again to be himself,   *Sun → him*
Being wanted, he may be more wondered at   *king*
200 By breaking through the foul and ugly mists
Of vapours that did seem to strangle him.
If all the year were playing holidays,
To sport would be as tedious as to work;
But when they seldom come, they wished-for come,
And nothing pleaseth but rare accidents.
So when this loose behaviour I throw off,
And pay the debt I never promisèd,   *good*
By how much better than my word I am,
By so much shall I falsify men's hopes.

And like bright metal on a sullen ground,   210
My reformation, glittering o'er my fault,
Shall show more goodly, and attract more eyes
Than that which hath no foil to set it off.
I'll so offend, to make offence a skill,
Redeeming time when men think least I will.

Exit

Enter the King, Northumberland, Worcester, Hot-   I.3
spur, Sir Walter Blunt, with others   coming from scene 1

KING HENRY
My blood hath been too cold and temperate,   changing
Unapt to stir at these indignities,   mode of
And you have found me – for accordingly   keeping order
You tread upon my patience. But be sure
I will from henceforth rather be myself,
Mighty, and to be feared, than my condition,
Which hath been smooth as oil, soft as young down,
And therefore lost that title of respect
Which the proud soul ne'er pays but to the proud.

WORCESTER
Our house, my sovereign liege, little deserves   10
The scourge of greatness to be used on it,
And that same greatness too which our own hands
Have helped to make so portly. fat .

NORTHUMBERLAND   My lord –

KING HENRY
Worcester, get thee gone, for I do see   sent off
Danger and disobedience in thine eye.
O sir, your presence is too bold and peremptory,
And majesty might never yet endure
The moody frontier of a servant brow.
You have good leave to leave us. When we need

57

20 Your use and counsel we shall send for you.

Exit Worcester

(*To Northumberland*) You were about to speak.

NORTHUMBERLAND   Yea, my good lord.
Those prisoners in your highness' name demanded,
Which Harry Percy here at Holmedon took,
Were, as he says, not with such strength denied
As is delivered to your majesty.
Either envy therefore, or misprision,
Is guilty of this fault, and not my son.

HOTSPUR
My liege, I did deny no prisoners.
But I remember when the fight was done,
30 When I was dry with rage and extreme toil,
Breathless and faint, leaning upon my sword,
Came there a certain lord, neat and trimly dressed,
Fresh as a bridegroom, and his chin new reaped
Showed like a stubble-land at harvest-home.
He was perfumèd like a milliner,
And 'twixt his finger and his thumb he held
A pouncet-box, which ever and anon
He gave his nose, and took it away again –
Who therewith angry, when it next came there,
40 Took it in snuff. And still he smiled and talked.
And as the soldiers bore dead bodies by,
He called them untaught knaves, unmannerly,
To bring a slovenly unhandsome corpse
Betwixt the wind and his nobility.
With many holiday and lady terms
He questioned me, amongst the rest demanded
My prisoners in your majesty's behalf.
I then, all smarting with my wounds being cold,
To be so pestered with a popinjay,
50 Out of my grief and my impatience

Answered neglectingly, I know not what,
He should, or he should not, for he made me mad
To see him shine so brisk, and smell so sweet,
And talk so like a waiting-gentlewoman
Of guns, and drums, and wounds, God save the mark!
And telling me the sovereignest thing on earth
Was parmacity for an inward bruise,
And that it was great pity, so it was,
This villainous saltpetre should be digged
Out of the bowels of the harmless earth,   60
Which many a good tall fellow had destroyed
So cowardly, and but for these vile guns
He would himself have been a soldier.
This bald unjointed chat of his, my lord,
I answered indirectly, as I said,
And I beseech you, let not his report
Come current for an accusation
Betwixt my love and your high majesty.

BLUNT

The circumstance considered, good my lord,
Whate'er Lord Harry Percy then had said   70
To such a person, and in such a place,
At such a time, with all the rest retold,
May reasonably die, and never rise
To do him wrong, or any way impeach
What then he said, so he unsay it now.

KING HENRY

Why, yet he doth deny his prisoners,
But with proviso and exception,
That we at our own charge shall ransom straight
His brother-in-law, the foolish Mortimer,
Who, on my soul, hath wilfully betrayed   80
The lives of those that he did lead to fight
Against that great magician, damned Glendower,

59

Whose daughter, as we hear, that Earl of March
Hath lately married. Shall our coffers then
Be emptied to redeem a traitor home?
Shall we buy treason, and indent with fears
When they have lost and forfeited themselves?
No, on the barren mountains let him starve.
For I shall never hold that man my friend
90   Whose tongue shall ask me for one penny cost
To ransom home revolted Mortimer.

HOTSPUR
Revolted Mortimer!
He never did fall off, my sovereign liege,
But by the chance of war. To prove that true
Needs no more but one tongue for all those wounds,
Those mouthèd wounds, which valiantly he took,
When on the gentle Severn's sedgy bank,
In single opposition hand to hand,
He did confound the best part of an hour
100   In changing hardiment with great Glendower.
Three times they breathed, and three times did they
        drink
Upon agreement of swift Severn's flood,
Who then affrighted with their bloody looks
Ran fearfully among the trembling reeds,
And hid his crisp head in the hollow bank,
Bloodstainèd with these valiant combatants.
Never did bare and rotten policy
Colour her working with such deadly wounds,
Nor never could the noble Mortimer
110   Receive so many, and all willingly.
Then let not him be slandered with revolt.

KING HENRY
Thou dost belie him, Percy, thou dost belie him,
He never did encounter with Glendower.

I tell thee, he durst as well have met the devil alone
As Owen Glendower for an enemy.
Art thou not ashamed? But sirrah, henceforth
Let me not hear you speak of Mortimer.
Send me your prisoners with the speediest means –
Or you shall hear in such a kind from me
As will displease you. My Lord Northumberland: 120
We license your departure with your son.
Send us your prisoners, or you will hear of it.

Exit the King with Blunt and train

HOTSPUR
And if the devil come and roar for them
I will not send them. I will after straight
And tell him so, for I will ease my heart,
Albeit I make a hazard of my head.

NORTHUMBERLAND
What? Drunk with choler? Stay, and pause awhile,
Here comes your uncle.

Enter Worcester

HOTSPUR   Speak of Mortimer?
Zounds, I will speak of him, and let my soul
Want mercy if I do not join with him.   130
Yea, on his part I'll empty all these veins
And shed my dear blood, drop by drop in the dust,
But I will lift the down-trod Mortimer
As high in the air as this unthankful King,
As this ingrate and cankered Bolingbroke.

NORTHUMBERLAND
Brother, the King hath made your nephew mad.

WORCESTER
Who struck this heat up after I was gone?

HOTSPUR
He will forsooth have all my prisoners,
And when I urged the ransom once again

140 Of my wife's brother, then his cheek looked pale,
And on my face he turned an eye of death,
Trembling even at the name of Mortimer.

WORCESTER
I cannot blame him. Was not he proclaimed,
By Richard that dead is, the next of blood?

NORTHUMBERLAND
He was, I heard the proclamation.
And then it was, when the unhappy King –
Whose wrongs in us God pardon! – did set forth
Upon his Irish expedition;
From whence he, intercepted, did return
150 To be deposed, and shortly murderèd.

WORCESTER
And for whose death we in the world's wide mouth
Live scandalized and foully spoken of.

HOTSPUR
But soft, I pray you, did King Richard then
Proclaim my brother Edmund Mortimer
Heir to the crown?

NORTHUMBERLAND He did, myself did hear it.

HOTSPUR
Nay then, I cannot blame his cousin King
That wished him on the barren mountains starve.
But shall it be that you that set the crown
Upon the head of this forgetful man,
160 And for his sake wear the detested blot
Of murderous subornation – shall it be
That you a world of curses undergo,
Being the agents, or base second means,
The cords, the ladder, or the hangman rather?
O pardon me, that I descend so low,
To show the line and the predicament
Wherein you range under this subtle King!

Shall it for shame be spoken in these days,
Or fill up chronicles in time to come,
That men of your nobility and power   170
Did gage them both in an unjust behalf –
As both of you, God pardon it, have done –
To put down Richard, that sweet lovely rose,
And plant this thorn, this canker Bolingbroke?
And shall it in more shame be further spoken,
That you are fooled, discarded, and shook off
By him for whom these shames ye underwent?
No, yet time serves wherein you may redeem
Your banished honours, and restore yourselves
Into the good thoughts of the world again: 180
Revenge the jeering and disdained contempt
Of this proud King, who studies day and night
To answer all the debt he owes to you,
Even with the bloody payment of your deaths.
Therefore, I say –
WORCESTER   Peace, cousin, say no more.
And now I will unclasp a secret book,
And to your quick-conceiving discontents
I'll read you matter deep and dangerous,
As full of peril and adventurous spirit
As to o'er-walk a current roaring loud   190
On the unsteadfast footing of a spear.

HOTSPUR
If he fall in, good night, or sink, or swim!
Send danger from the east unto the west,
So honour cross it from the north to south,
And let them grapple. O, the blood more stirs
To rouse a lion than to start a hare!

NORTHUMBERLAND
Imagination of some great exploit
Drives him beyond the bounds of patience.

63

HOTSPUR

By heaven, methinks it were an easy leap
200 To pluck bright honour from the pale-faced moon,
Or dive into the bottom of the deep,
Where fathom-line could never touch the ground,
And pluck up drowned honour by the locks,
So he that doth redeem her thence might wear
Without corrival all her dignities.
But out upon this half-faced fellowship!

WORCESTER

He apprehends a world of figures here,   Imaginative
But not the form of what he should attend.   mp.
Good cousin, give me audience for a while.

HOTSPUR

I cry you mercy.

210 **WORCESTER**   Those same noble Scots
That are your prisoners –

HOTSPUR   I'll keep them all!
By God he shall not have a Scot of them,
No, if a scot would save his soul he shall not.
I'll keep them, by this hand!

WORCESTER   You start away,
And lend no ear unto my purposes.
Those prisoners you shall keep –

HOTSPUR   Nay, I will. That's flat!
He said he would not ransom Mortimer,
Forbade my tongue to speak of Mortimer,
But I will find him when he lies asleep,
220 And in his ear I'll holla 'Mortimer!'
Nay, I'll have a starling shall be taught to speak
Nothing but 'Mortimer', and give it him
To keep his anger still in motion.

WORCESTER

Hear you, cousin, a word.

HOTSPUR

  All studies here I solemnly defy,
  Save how to gall and pinch this Bolingbroke.
  And that same sword-and-buckler Prince of Wales –
  But that I think his father loves him not
  And would be glad he met with some mischance –
  I would have him poisoned with a pot of ale.   230

WORCESTER

  Farewell, kinsman. I'll talk to you
  When you are better tempered to attend.

NORTHUMBERLAND

  Why, what a wasp-stung and impatient fool
  Art thou to break into this woman's mood,
  Tying thine ear to no tongue but thine own!

HOTSPUR

  Why, look you, I am whipped and scourged with rods,
  Nettled, and stung with pismires, when I hear
  Of this vile politician Bolingbroke.
  In Richard's time – what do you call the place?
  A plague upon it, it is in Gloucestershire.   240
  'Twas where the madcap Duke his uncle kept –
  His uncle York – where I first bowed my knee
  Unto this king of smiles, this Bolingbroke –
  'Sblood, when you and he came back from Ravens-
      purgh –

NORTHUMBERLAND

  At Berkeley Castle.

HOTSPUR

  You say true.
  Why, what a candy deal of courtesy
  This fawning greyhound then did proffer me!
  'Look when his infant fortune came to age',
  And 'gentle Harry Percy', and 'kind cousin'.   250
  O, the devil take such cozeners – God forgive me!

Good uncle, tell your tale. I have done.

WORCESTER

Nay, if you have not, to it again,

We will stay your leisure.

HOTSPUR   I have done, i'faith.

WORCESTER

Then once more to your Scottish prisoners.

Deliver them up without their ransom straight,

And make the Douglas' son your only mean

For powers in Scotland, which, for divers reasons

Which I shall send you written, be assured

260   Will easily be granted. (*To Northumberland*) You my

           lord,

Your son in Scotland being thus employed,

Shall secretly into the bosom creep

Of that same noble prelate well-beloved,

The Archbishop.

HOTSPUR   Of York, is it not?

WORCESTER   True, who bears hard

His brother's death at Bristol, the Lord Scroop.

I speak not this in estimation,

As what I think might be, but what I know

Is ruminated, plotted, and set down,

And only stays but to behold the face

270   Of that occasion that shall bring it on.

HOTSPUR

I smell it! Upon my life it will do well!

NORTHUMBERLAND

Before the game is afoot thou still lettest slip.

HOTSPUR

Why, it cannot choose but be a noble plot;

And then the power of Scotland, and of York,

To join with Mortimer, ha?

WORCESTER   And so they shall.

HOTSPUR

In faith it is exceedingly well aimed.

WORCESTER

And 'tis no little reason bids us speed,
To save our heads by raising of a head.
For, bear ourselves as even as we can,
The King will always think him in our debt,   280
And think we think ourselves unsatisfied,
Till he hath found a time to pay us home.
And see already how he doth begin
To make us strangers to his looks of love.

HOTSPUR

He does, he does, we'll be revenged on him.

WORCESTER

Cousin, farewell. No further go in this
Than I by letters shall direct your course.
When time is ripe, which will be suddenly,
I'll steal to Glendower, and Lord Mortimer,
Where you, and Douglas, and our powers at once,   290
As I will fashion it, shall happily meet
To bear our fortunes in our own strong arms,
Which now we hold at much uncertainty.

NORTHUMBERLAND

Farewell, good brother. We shall thrive, I trust.

HOTSPUR

Uncle, adieu. O, let the hours be short,
Till fields, and blows, and groans applaud our sport!

Exeunt

*

Enter a Carrier with a lantern in his hand

FIRST CARRIER Heigh-ho! An it be not four by the day
I'll be hanged. Charles's Wain is over the new chimney,
and yet our horse not packed. What, Ostler!

OSTLER (*within*) Anon, anon.

FIRST CARRIER I prithee, Tom, beat Cut's saddle, put a
few flocks in the point; poor jade is wrung in the withers
out of all cess.

  Enter another Carrier

SECOND CARRIER Peas and beans are as dank here as a
dog, and that is the next way to give poor jades the bots.
10 This house is turned upside down since Robin Ostler
died.

FIRST CARRIER Poor fellow never joyed since the price of
oats rose, it was the death of him.

SECOND CARRIER I think this be the most villainous
house in all London road for fleas, I am stung like a
tench.

FIRST CARRIER Like a tench! By the mass, there is ne'er
a king Christian could be better bit than I have been
since the first cock.

20 SECOND CARRIER Why, they will allow us ne'er a
jordan, and then we leak in your chimney, and your
chamber-lye breeds fleas like a loach.

FIRST CARRIER What, Ostler! Come away, and be
hanged, come away!

SECOND CARRIER I have a gammon of bacon, and two
razes of ginger, to be delivered as far as Charing Cross.

FIRST CARRIER God's body! The turkeys in my pannier
are quite starved. What, Ostler! A plague on thee, hast
thou never an eye in thy head? Canst not hear? An
30 'twere not as good deed as drink to break the pate on
thee, I am a very villain. Come, and be hanged! Hast no
faith in thee?

68

Enter Gadshill

GADSHILL Good morrow, carriers, what's o'clock?

FIRST CARRIER I think it be two o'clock.

GADSHILL I prithee lend me thy lantern, to see my gelding in the stable.

FIRST CARRIER Nay, by God, soft! I know a trick worth two of that, i'faith.

GADSHILL I pray thee lend me thine.

SECOND CARRIER Ay, when? Canst tell? Lend me thy 40 lantern, quoth he! Marry I'll see thee hanged first.

GADSHILL Sirrah carrier, what time do you mean to come to London?

SECOND CARRIER Time enough to go to bed with a candle, I warrant thee! Come, neighbour Mugs, we'll call up the gentlemen, they will along with company, for they have great charge. *Exeunt Carriers*

GADSHILL What ho! Chamberlain!

Enter Chamberlain

CHAMBERLAIN 'At hand, quoth pick-purse.'

GADSHILL That's even as fair as 'At hand, quoth the 50 chamberlain', for thou variest no more from picking of purses than giving direction doth from labouring. Thou layest the plot how.

CHAMBERLAIN Good morrow, Master Gadshill. It holds current that I told you yesternight. There's a franklin in the Weald of Kent hath brought three hundred marks with him in gold – I heard him tell it to one of his company last night at supper, a kind of auditor, one that hath abundance of charge too, God knows what. They are up already, and call for eggs and butter. They will 60 away presently.

GADSHILL Sirrah, if they meet not with Saint Nicholas' clerks, I'll give thee this neck.

CHAMBERLAIN No, I'll none of it, I pray thee keep that

for the hangman, for I know thou worshippest Saint Nicholas, as truly as a man of falsehood may.

GADSHILL What talkest thou to me of the hangman? If I hang, I'll make a fat pair of gallows. For if I hang, old Sir John hangs with me, and thou knowest he is no starveling. Tut, there are other Troyans that thou dreamest not of, the which for sport sake are content to do the profession some grace, that would, if matters should be looked into, for their own credit sake make all whole. I am joined with no foot-landrakers, no long-staff sixpenny strikers, none of these mad mustachio purple-hued maltworms, but with nobility and tranquillity, Burgomasters and great O-yeas, such as can hold in, such as will strike sooner than speak, and speak sooner than drink, and drink sooner than pray. And yet, zounds, I lie, for they pray continually to their saint the commonwealth, or rather not pray to her, but prey on her, for they ride up and down on her, and make her their boots.

CHAMBERLAIN What, the commonwealth their boots? Will she hold out water in foul way?

GADSHILL She will, she will, justice hath liquored her. We steal as in a castle, cock-sure. We have the receipt of fern-seed, we walk invisible.

CHAMBERLAIN Nay, by my faith, I think you are more beholding to the night than to fern-seed for your walking invisible.

GADSHILL Give me thy hand, thou shalt have a share in our purchase, as I am a true man.

CHAMBERLAIN Nay, rather let me have it as you are a false thief.

GADSHILL Go to, *homo* is a common name to all men. Bid the ostler bring my gelding out of the stable. Farewell, you muddy knave.   *Exeunt*

POINS Come, shelter, shelter! I have removed Falstaff's
horse, and he frets like a gummed velvet.

PRINCE HAL Stand close!

   They hide
   Enter Falstaff

FALSTAFF Poins! Poins, and be hanged! Poins!

PRINCE HAL (*coming forward*) Peace, ye fat-kidneyed
rascal, what a brawling dost thou keep!

FALSTAFF Where's Poins, Hal?

PRINCE HAL He is walked up to the top of the hill. I'll
go seek him.

   He steps to one side

FALSTAFF I am accursed to rob in that thief's company. 10
The rascal hath removed my horse and tied him I know
not where. If I travel but four foot by the square further
afoot, I shall break my wind. Well, I doubt not but to
die a fair death for all this, if I scape hanging for killing
that rogue. I have forsworn his company hourly any
time this two-and-twenty years, and yet I am bewitched
with the rogue's company. If the rascal have not given
me medicines to make me love him, I'll be hanged. It
could not be else. I have drunk medicines. Poins! Hal!
A plague upon you both! Bardolph! Peto! I'll starve ere 20
I'll rob a foot further – an 'twere not as good a deed as
drink to turn true man, and to leave these rogues, I am
the veriest varlet that ever chewed with a tooth. Eight
yards of uneven ground is threescore-and-ten miles
afoot with me, and the stony-hearted villains know it
well enough. A plague upon it when thieves cannot be
true one to another!

   They whistle

Whew! A plague upon you all. Give me my horse you
rogues, give me my horse and be hanged!

30 PRINCE HAL (*coming forward*) Peace, ye fat-guts, lie down, lay thine ear close to the ground and list if thou canst hear the tread of travellers.

FALSTAFF Have you any levers to lift me up again, being down? 'Sblood, I'll not bear my own flesh so far afoot again for all the coin in thy father's exchequer. What a plague mean ye to colt me thus?

PRINCE HAL Thou liest, thou art not colted, thou art uncolted.

FALSTAFF I prithee good Prince Hal, help me to my
40 horse, good king's son.

PRINCE HAL Out, ye rogue, shall I be your ostler?

FALSTAFF Hang thyself in thine own heir-apparent garters! If I be taken, I'll peach for this. An I have not ballads made on you all, and sung to filthy tunes, let a cup of sack be my poison. When a jest is so forward – and afoot too – I hate it!

Enter Gadshill, Bardolph, and Peto

GADSHILL Stand!

FALSTAFF So I do, against my will.

POINS O, 'tis our setter, I know his voice. Bardolph, what
50 news?

BARDOLPH Case ye, case ye, on with your vizards, there's money of the King's coming down the hill. 'Tis going to the King's exchequer.

FALSTAFF You lie, ye rogue, 'tis going to the King's tavern.

GADSHILL There's enough to make us all –

FALSTAFF To be hanged.

PRINCE HAL Sirs, you four shall front them in the narrow lane. Ned Poins and I will walk lower – if they scape
60 from your encounter, then they light on us.

PETO How many be there of them?

GADSHILL Some eight or ten.

FALSTAFF Zounds, will they not rob us?

PRINCE HAL What, a coward, Sir John Paunch?

FALSTAFF Indeed, I am not John of Gaunt your grandfather, but yet no coward, Hal.

PRINCE HAL Well, we leave that to the proof.

POINS Sirrah Jack, thy horse stands behind the hedge. When thou needest him, there thou shalt find him. Farewell, and stand fast! 70

FALSTAFF Now cannot I strike him, if I should be hanged.

PRINCE HAL (*aside to Poins*) Ned, where are our disguises?

POINS Here, hard by, stand close. *Exeunt Prince and Poins*

FALSTAFF Now, my masters, happy man be his dole, say I. Every man to his business.

Enter the Travellers

FIRST TRAVELLER Come, neighbour, the boy shall lead our horses down the hill. We'll walk afoot awhile and ease our legs.

THIEVES Stand! 80

SECOND TRAVELLER Jesus bless us!

FALSTAFF Strike, down with them, cut the villains' throats! Ah, whoreson caterpillars, bacon-fed knaves, they hate us youth! Down with them, fleece them!

FIRST TRAVELLER O, we are undone, both we and ours for ever!

FALSTAFF Hang ye, gorbellied knaves, are ye undone? No, ye fat chuffs, I would your store were here! On, bacons, on! What, ye knaves, young men must live! You are grandjurors, are ye? We'll jure ye, faith. 90

Here they rob them and bind them

Exeunt

Enter the Prince and Poins, disguised

PRINCE HAL The thieves have bound the true men. Now, could thou and I rob the thieves, and go merrily to

73

London, it would be argument for a week, laughter for a
month, and a good jest for ever.

POINS Stand close, I hear them coming.

They hide
Enter the thieves again

FALSTAFF Come my masters, let us share, and then to
horse before day. An the Prince and Poins be not two
arrant cowards there's no equity stirring. There's no
more valour in that Poins than in a wild duck.

As they are sharing the Prince and Poins set upon
them

100 PRINCE HAL Your money!

POINS Villains!

They all run away, and Falstaff after a blow or two
runs away too, leaving the booty behind them

PRINCE HAL

Got with much ease. Now merrily to horse.
The thieves are all scattered and possessed with fear
So strongly that they dare not meet each other.
Each takes his fellow for an officer!
Away, good Ned! Falstaff sweats to death,
And lards the lean earth as he walks along.
Were it not for laughing I should pity him.

POINS How the fat rogue roared!   *Exeunt*

II.3   *Enter Hotspur alone, reading a letter*

HOTSPUR *But for mine own part, my lord, I could be well*
contented to be there, in respect of the love I bear your
house.

He could be contented! Why is he not then? In respect
of the love he bears our house? He shows in this he
loves his own barn better than he loves our house. Let
me see some more.

The purpose you undertake is dangerous,
Why, that's certain. 'Tis dangerous to take a cold, to
sleep, to drink. But I tell you, my lord fool, out of this 10
nettle, danger, we pluck this flower, safety.
*The purpose you undertake is dangerous, the friends you
have named uncertain, the time itself unsorted, and your
whole plot too light, for the counterpoise of so great an
opposition.*
Say you so, say you so? I say unto you again, you are a
shallow cowardly hind, and you lie. What a lack-brain is
this! By the Lord, our plot is a good plot, as ever was
laid, our friends true and constant. A good plot, good
friends, and full of expectation. An excellent plot, very 20
good friends. What a frosty-spirited rogue is this! Why,
my Lord of York commends the plot, and the general
course of the action. Zounds, an I were now by this
rascal I could brain him with his lady's fan. Is there not
my father, my uncle, and myself? Lord Edmund
Mortimer, my Lord of York, and Owen Glendower? Is
there not besides the Douglas? Have I not all their
letters to meet me in arms by the ninth of the next
month, and are they not some of them set forward
already? What a pagan rascal is this, an infidel! Ha! 30
You shall see now in very sincerity of fear and cold heart
will he to the King, and lay open all our proceedings!
O, I could divide myself, and go to buffets, for moving
such a dish of skim milk with so honourable an action!
Hang him, let him tell the King, we are prepared. I will
set forward tonight.
        Enter his lady
How now, Kate? I must leave you within these two
hours.

LADY PERCY
O my good lord, why are you thus alone?

75

40　For what offence have I this fortnight been
　　A banished woman from my Harry's bed?
　　Tell me, sweet lord, what is it that takes from thee
　　Thy stomach, pleasure, and thy golden sleep?
　　Why dost thou bend thine eyes upon the earth,
　　And start so often when thou sittest alone?
　　Why hast thou lost the fresh blood in thy cheeks,
　　And given my treasures and my rights of thee
　　To thick-eyed musing, and curst melancholy?
　　In thy faint slumbers I by thee have watched
50　And heard thee murmur tales of iron wars,
　　Speak terms of manage to thy bounding steed,
　　Cry 'Courage! To the field!' And thou hast talked
　　Of sallies, and retires, of trenches, tents,
　　Of palisadoes, frontiers, parapets,
　　Of basilisks, of cannon, culverin,
　　Of prisoners' ransom, and of soldiers slain,
　　And all the currents of a heady fight.
　　Thy spirit within thee hath been so at war,
　　And thus hath so bestirred thee in thy sleep,
60　That beads of sweat have stood upon thy brow
　　Like bubbles in a late-disturbèd stream,
　　And in thy face strange motions have appeared,
　　Such as we see when men restrain their breath
　　On some great sudden hest. O, what portents are these?
　　Some heavy business hath my lord in hand,
　　And I must know it, else he loves me not.

HOTSPUR
　　What ho!

　　　　Enter a Servant

　　　　　　Is Gilliams with the packet gone?
SERVANT He is, my lord, an hour ago.
HOTSPUR Hath Butler brought those horses from the
70　sheriff?

76

SERVANT One horse, my lord, he brought even now.
HOTSPUR What horse? A roan, a crop-ear is it not?
SERVANT
It is, my lord.
HOTSPUR   That roan shall be my throne.
Well, I will back him straight. O Esperance!
Bid Butler lead him forth into the park.

Exit Servant

LADY PERCY But hear you, my lord.
HOTSPUR What sayest thou, my lady?
LADY PERCY What is it carries you away?
HOTSPUR Why, my horse, my love, my horse.
LADY PERCY
Out, you mad-headed ape!   80
A weasel hath not such a deal of spleen
As you are tossed with. In faith,
I'll know your business, Harry, that I will.
I fear my brother Mortimer doth stir
About his title, and hath sent for you
To line his enterprise. But if you go –
HOTSPUR
So far afoot I shall be weary, love.
LADY PERCY
Come, come, you paraquito, answer me
Directly unto this question that I ask.
In faith, I'll break thy little finger, Harry,   90
An if thou wilt not tell me all things true.
HOTSPUR
Away,
Away, you trifler! Love! I love thee not,
I care not for thee, Kate? This is no world
To play with mammets, and to tilt with lips.
We must have bloody noses, and cracked crowns,
And pass them current too. God's me! My horse!

What sayst thou, Kate? What wouldst thou have with
    me?

LADY PERCY

Do you not love me? Do you not indeed?
100 Well, do not then, for since you love me not
I will not love myself. Do you not love me?
Nay, tell me if you speak in jest or no?

HOTSPUR

Come, wilt thou see me ride?
And when I am a-horseback I will swear
I love thee infinitely. But hark you, Kate,
I must not have you henceforth question me
Whither I go, nor reason whereabout.
Whither I must, I must. And, to conclude,
This evening must I leave you, gentle Kate.
110 I know you wise, but yet no farther wise
Than Harry Percy's wife. Constant you are,
But yet a woman. And for secrecy,
No lady closer, for I well believe
Thou wilt not utter – what thou dost not know.
And so far will I trust thee, gentle Kate.

LADY PERCY

How? So far?

HOTSPUR

Not an inch further. But hark you, Kate,
Whither I go, thither shall you go too.
Today will I set forth, tomorrow you.
120 Will this content you, Kate?

LADY PERCY   It must, of force.   *Exeunt*

II.4   *Enter Prince and Poins*

PRINCE HAL Ned, prithee come out of that fat room, and
lend me thy hand to laugh a little.

POINS Where hast been, Hal?

PRINCE HAL With three or four loggerheads, amongst
three or fourscore hogsheads. I have sounded the very
bass string of humility. Sirrah, I am sworn brother to a
leash of drawers, and can call them all by their Christian
names, as Tom, Dick, and Francis. They take it already
upon their salvation that though I be but Prince of
Wales yet I am the king of courtesy, and tell me flatly I 10
am no proud Jack like Falstaff, but a Corinthian, a lad of
mettle, a good boy – by the Lord, so they call me! – and
when I am King of England I shall command all the
good lads in Eastcheap. They call drinking deep
'dyeing scarlet', and when you breathe in your watering
they cry 'Hem!' and bid you 'Play it off!' To conclude,
I am so good a proficient in one quarter of an hour that I
can drink with any tinker in his own language during my
life. I tell thee, Ned, thou hast lost much honour that
thou wert not with me in this action. But, sweet Ned – 20
to sweeten which name of Ned I give thee this pennyworth of sugar, clapped even now into my hand by an
underskinker, one that never spake other English in his
life than 'Eight shillings and sixpence', and 'You are
welcome', with this shrill addition, 'Anon, anon, sir!
Score a pint of bastard in the Half-moon!', or so. But
Ned, to drive away the time till Falstaff come – I
prithee do thou stand in some by-room while I question
my puny drawer to what end he gave me the sugar. And
do thou never leave calling 'Francis!', that his tale to me 30
may be nothing but 'Anon'. Step aside, and I'll show
thee a precedent. *Exit Poins*

POINS (*within*) Francis!

PRINCE HAL Thou art perfect.

POINS (*within*) Francis!

Enter Francis, a Drawer

79

FRANCIS Anon, anon, sir. Look down into the Pomgarnet, Ralph!

PRINCE HAL Come hither, Francis.

FRANCIS My lord?

40 PRINCE HAL How long hast thou to serve, Francis?

FRANCIS Forsooth, five years, and as much as to –

POINS (*within*) Francis!

FRANCIS Anon, anon, sir.

PRINCE HAL Five year! By'r lady, a long lease for the clinking of pewter. But Francis, darest thou be so valiant as to play the coward with thy indenture, and show it a fair pair of heels, and run from it?

FRANCIS O Lord, sir, I'll be sworn upon all the books in England, I could find in my heart –

50 POINS (*within*) Francis!

FRANCIS Anon, sir.

PRINCE HAL How old art thou, Francis?

FRANCIS Let me see, about Michaelmas next I shall be –

POINS (*within*) Francis!

FRANCIS Anon, sir – pray stay a little, my lord.

PRINCE HAL Nay but hark you, Francis, for the sugar thou gavest me, 'twas a pennyworth, was it not?

FRANCIS O Lord, I would it had been two!

PRINCE HAL I will give thee for it a thousand pound –
60 ask me when thou wilt, and thou shalt have it.

POINS (*within*) Francis!

FRANCIS Anon, anon.

PRINCE HAL Anon, Francis? No, Francis, but tomorrow, Francis. Or Francis, a-Thursday. Or indeed Francis, when thou wilt. But Francis!

FRANCIS My lord?

PRINCE HAL Wilt thou rob this leathern-jerkin, crystal-button, not-pated, agate-ring, puke-stocking, caddis-garter, smooth-tongue Spanish pouch?

FRANCIS O Lord, sir, who do you mean? 70

PRINCE HAL Why then your brown bastard is your only drink. For look you, Francis, your white canvas doublet will sully. In Barbary, sir, it cannot come to so much.

FRANCIS What, sir?

POINS (*within*) Francis!

PRINCE HAL Away, you rogue, dost thou not hear them call?

> *Here they both call him; the Drawer stands amazed,*
> *not knowing which way to go*
> *Enter Vintner*

VINTNER What, standest thou still and hearest such a calling? Look to the guests within. *Exit Francis*
My lord, old Sir John with half-a-dozen more are at the 80 door. Shall I let them in?

PRINCE HAL Let them alone awhile, and then open the door. *Exit Vintner*
Poins!

> *Enter Poins*

POINS Anon, anon, sir.

PRINCE HAL Sirrah, Falstaff and the rest of the thieves are at the door. Shall we be merry?

POINS As merry as crickets, my lad. But hark ye, what cunning match have you made with this jest of the drawer? Come, what's the issue? 90

PRINCE HAL I am now of all humours that have showed themselves humours since the old days of goodman Adam to the pupil age of this present twelve o'clock at midnight.

> *Enter Francis*

What's o'clock, Francis?

FRANCIS Anon, anon, sir. *Exit*

PRINCE HAL That ever this fellow should have fewer words than a parrot, and yet the son of a woman! His

industry is up-stairs and down-stairs, his eloquence the
100 parcel of a reckoning. I am not yet of Percy's mind, the
Hotspur of the north, he that kills me some six or seven
dozen of Scots at a breakfast, washes his hands, and says
to his wife, 'Fie upon this quiet life, I want work.' 'O
my sweet Harry,' says she, 'how many hast thou killed
today?' 'Give my roan horse a drench,' says he, and
answers, 'Some fourteen,' an hour after, 'a trifle, a
trifle'. I prithee call in Falstaff. I'll play Percy, and that
damned brawn shall play Dame Mortimer his wife.
'Rivo!' says the drunkard. Call in Ribs, call in Tallow!

> *Enter Falstaff, Gadshill, Bardolph, and Peto;
> followed by Francis, with wine*

110 POINS Welcome, Jack, where hast thou been?

FALSTAFF A plague of all cowards, I say, and a vengeance
too, marry and amen! Give me a cup of sack, boy. Ere I
lead this life long, I'll sew nether-stocks, and mend
them and foot them too. A plague of all cowards! Give
me a cup of sack, rogue. Is there no virtue extant?

> *He drinks*

PRINCE HAL Didst thou never see Titan kiss a dish of
butter – pitiful-hearted Titan! – that melted at the sweet
tale of the sun's? If thou didst, then behold that
compound.

120 FALSTAFF You rogue, here's lime in this sack too. There
is nothing but roguery to be found in villainous man, yet
a coward is worse than a cup of sack with lime in it. A
villainous coward! Go thy ways, old Jack, die when thou
wilt. If manhood, good manhood, be not forgot upon
the face of the earth, then am I a shotten herring. There
lives not three good men unhanged in England, and one
of them is fat, and grows old. God help the while, a bad
world I say. I would I were a weaver: I could sing
psalms – or anything. A plague of all cowards, I say still.

PRINCE HAL How now, woolsack, what mutter you? 130

FALSTAFF A king's son! If I do not beat thee out of thy kingdom with a dagger of lath, and drive all thy subjects afore thee like a flock of wild geese, I'll never wear hair on my face more. You, Prince of Wales!

PRINCE HAL Why, you whoreson round man, what's the matter?

FALSTAFF Are not you a coward? Answer me to that – and Poins there?

POINS Zounds, ye fat paunch, an ye call me coward by the Lord I'll stab thee. 140

FALSTAFF I call thee coward? I'll see thee damned ere I call thee coward, but I would give a thousand pound I could run as fast as thou canst. You are straight enough in the shoulders, you care not who sees your back. Call you that backing of your friends? A plague upon such backing, give me them that will face me! Give me a cup of sack! I am a rogue if I drunk today.

PRINCE HAL O villain! Thy lips are scarce wiped since thou drunkest last.

FALSTAFF All is one for that. *(He drinks)* A plague of all 150 cowards, still say I.

PRINCE HAL What's the matter?

FALSTAFF What's the matter? There be four of us here have taken a thousand pound this day morning.

PRINCE HAL Where is it, Jack, where is it?

FALSTAFF Where is it? Taken from us it is. A hundred upon poor four of us.

PRINCE HAL What, a hundred, man?

FALSTAFF I am a rogue if I were not at half-sword with a dozen of them two hours together. I have scaped by 160 miracle. I am eight times thrust through the doublet, four through the hose, my buckler cut through and through, my sword hacked like a handsaw – *ecce signum*! I never dealt better since I was a man. All would not do. A plague of all cowards! Let them speak. If they speak more or less than truth, they are villains and the sons of darkness.

PRINCE HAL Speak, sirs, how was it?

GADSHILL We four set upon some dozen –

170 FALSTAFF Sixteen at least, my lord.

GADSHILL And bound them.

PETO No, no, they were not bound.

FALSTAFF You rogue, they were bound, every man of them, or I am a Jew else: an Ebrew Jew.

GADSHILL As we were sharing, some six or seven fresh men set upon us –

FALSTAFF And unbound the rest, and then come in the other.

PRINCE HAL What, fought you with them all?

180 FALSTAFF All? I know not what you call all, but if I fought not with fifty of them I am a bunch of radish. If there were not two or three and fifty upon poor old Jack, then am I no two-legg'd creature.

PRINCE HAL Pray God you have not murdered some of them.

FALSTAFF Nay, that's past praying for, I have peppered two of them. Two I am sure I have paid, two rogues in buckram suits. I tell thee what, Hal, if I tell thee a lie, spit in my face, call me horse. Thou knowest my old

190 ward – here I lay, and thus I bore my point. Four rogues in buckram let drive at me –

PRINCE HAL What, four? Thou saidst but two even now.

FALSTAFF Four, Hal, I told thee four.

POINS Ay, ay, he said four.

FALSTAFF These four came all afront, and mainly thrust at me. I made me no more ado, but took all their seven points in my target, thus!

PRINCE HAL Seven? Why, there were but four even now.

FALSTAFF In buckram?   200

POINS Ay, four, in buckram suits.

FALSTAFF Seven, by these hilts, or I am a villain else.

PRINCE HAL Prithee let him alone, we shall have more anon.

FALSTAFF Dost thou hear me, Hal?

PRINCE HAL Ay, and mark thee too, Jack.

FALSTAFF Do so, for it is worth the listening to. These nine in buckram that I told thee of –

PRINCE HAL So, two more already.

FALSTAFF Their points being broken –   210

POINS Down fell their hose.

FALSTAFF – began to give me ground. But I followed me close, came in, foot and hand, and, with a thought, seven of the eleven I paid.

PRINCE HAL O monstrous! Eleven buckram men grown out of two!

FALSTAFF But as the devil would have it, three misbegotten knaves in Kendal green came at my back and let drive at me, for it was so dark, Hal, that thou couldst not see thy hand.   220

PRINCE HAL These lies are like their father that begets them, gross as a mountain, open, palpable. Why, thou clay-brained guts, thou knotty-pated fool, thou whoreson obscene greasy tallow-catch –

FALSTAFF What, art thou mad? Art thou mad? Is not the truth the truth?

PRINCE HAL Why, how couldst thou know these men in Kendal green when it was so dark thou couldst not see thy hand? Come, tell us your reason. What sayest thou to this?   230

POINS Come, your reason, Jack, your reason!

FALSTAFF What, upon compulsion? Zounds, an I were
at the strappado, or all the racks in the world, I would
not tell you on compulsion. Give you a reason on compulsion? If reasons were as plentiful as blackberries, I
would give no man a reason upon compulsion, I.

PRINCE HAL I'll be no longer guilty of this sin. This
sanguine coward, this bed-presser, this horse-back-
breaker, this huge hill of flesh –

240 FALSTAFF 'Sblood, you starveling, you elf-skin, you dried
neat's-tongue, you bull's-pizzle, you stock-fish! O for
breath to utter what is like thee! You tailor's-yard, you
sheath, you bow-case, you vile standing tuck!

PRINCE HAL Well, breathe awhile, and then to it again,
and when thou hast tired thyself in base comparisons
hear me speak but this.

POINS Mark, Jack!

PRINCE HAL We two saw you four set on four, and bound
them and were masters of their wealth – mark now how a
250 plain tale shall put you down. Then did we two set on
you four, and, with a word, out-faced you from your
prize, and have it, yea, and can show it you here in the
house. And Falstaff, you carried your guts away as
nimbly, with as quick dexterity, and roared for mercy,
and still run and roared, as ever I heard bull-calf. What
a slave art thou to hack thy sword as thou hast done, and
then say it was in fight! What trick, what device, what
starting-hole canst thou now find out, to hide thee from
this open and apparent shame?

260 POINS Come, let's hear Jack, what trick hast thou now?

FALSTAFF By the Lord, I knew ye as well as he that made
ye. Why, hear you, my masters, was it for me to kill the
heir apparent? Should I turn upon the true prince?
Why, thou knowest I am as valiant as Hercules. But
beware instinct. The lion will not touch the true prince.

86

Instinct is a great matter. I was now a coward on instinct. I shall think the better of myself, and thee, during my life – I for a valiant lion, and thou for a true prince. But by the Lord lads, I am glad you have the money! Hostess, clap to the doors! Watch tonight, pray 270 tomorrow! Gallants, lads, boys, hearts of gold, all the titles of good fellowship come to you! What, shall we be merry? Shall we have a play extempore?

PRINCE HAL Content, and the argument shall be thy running away.

FALSTAFF Ah, no more of that Hal, an thou lovest me.

Enter Hostess

HOSTESS O Jesu, my lord the Prince!

PRINCE HAL How now, my lady the Hostess, what sayest thou to me?

HOSTESS Marry my lord, there is a nobleman of the court 280 at door would speak with you. He says he comes from your father.

PRINCE HAL Give him as much as will make him a royal man and send him back again to my mother.

FALSTAFF What manner of man is he?

HOSTESS An old man.

FALSTAFF What doth gravity out of his bed at midnight? Shall I give him his answer?

PRINCE HAL Prithee do, Jack.

FALSTAFF Faith, and I'll send him packing.   *Exit* 290

PRINCE HAL Now, sirs, by'r lady, you fought fair, so did you, Peto, so did you, Bardolph. You are lions too, you ran away upon instinct, you will not touch the true prince, no, fie!

BARDOLPH Faith, I ran when I saw others run.

PRINCE HAL Faith, tell me now in earnest, how came Falstaff's sword so hacked?

PETO Why, he hacked it with his dagger, and said he

would swear truth out of England but he would make
you believe it was done in fight, and persuaded us to do
the like.

BARDOLPH Yea, and to tickle our noses with spear-grass,
to make them bleed, and then to beslubber our garments
with it, and swear it was the blood of true men. I did
that I did not this seven year before: I blushed to hear
his monstrous devices.

PRINCE HAL O villain, thou stolest a cup of sack eighteen
years ago, and wert taken with the manner, and ever
since thou hast blushed extempore. Thou hadst fire and
sword on thy side, and yet thou rannest away. What
instinct hadst thou for it?

BARDOLPH My lord, do you see these meteors? Do you
behold these exhalations?

PRINCE HAL I do.

BARDOLPH What think you they portend?

PRINCE HAL Hot livers, and cold purses.

BARDOLPH Choler, my lord, if rightly taken.

PRINCE HAL No, if rightly taken, halter.

Enter Falstaff

Here comes lean Jack, here comes bare-bone. How now
my sweet creature of bombast, how long is't ago, Jack,
since thou sawest thine own knee?

FALSTAFF My own knee? When I was about thy years,
Hal, I was not an eagle's talon in the waist – I could have
crept into any alderman's thumb-ring. A plague of
sighing and grief, it blows a man up like a bladder.
There's villainous news abroad. Here was Sir John
Bracy from your father. You must to the court in the
morning. That same mad fellow of the north, Percy,
and he of Wales that gave Amamon the bastinado, and
made Lucifer cuckold, and swore the devil his true

liegeman upon the cross of a Welsh hook – what a plague call you him?

POINS O, Glendower.

FALSTAFF Owen, Owen, the same. And his son-in-law Mortimer, and old Northumberland, and that sprightly Scot of Scots, Douglas, that runs a-horseback up a hill perpendicular –

PRINCE HAL He that rides at high speed, and with his pistol kills a sparrow flying.

FALSTAFF You have hit it. 340

PRINCE HAL So did he never the sparrow.

FALSTAFF Well, that rascal hath good mettle in him, he will not run.

PRINCE HAL Why, what a rascal art thou then, to praise him so for running!

FALSTAFF A-horseback, ye cuckoo, but afoot he will not budge a foot.

PRINCE HAL Yes, Jack, upon instinct.

FALSTAFF I grant ye, upon instinct. Well, he is there too, and one Mordake, and a thousand blue-caps more. 350 Worcester is stolen away tonight. Thy father's beard is turned white with the news. You may buy land now as cheap as stinking mackerel.

PRINCE HAL Why then, it is like if there come a hot June, and this civil buffeting hold, we shall buy maidenheads as they buy hob-nails, by the hundreds.

FALSTAFF By the mass, lad, thou sayest true, it is like we shall have good trading that way. But tell me, Hal, art not thou horrible afeard? Thou being heir apparent, could the world pick thee out three such enemies again, 360 as that fiend Douglas, that spirit Percy, and that devil Glendower? Art thou not horribly afraid? Doth not thy blood thrill at it?

PRINCE HAL Not a whit, i'faith, I lack some of thy
instinct.

FALSTAFF Well, thou wilt be horribly chid tomorrow
when thou comest to thy father. If thou love me,
practise an answer.

PRINCE HAL Do thou stand for my father and examine
370 me upon the particulars of my life.

FALSTAFF Shall I? Content! This chair shall be my state,
this dagger my sceptre, and this cushion my crown.

PRINCE HAL Thy state is taken for a joint-stool, thy
golden sceptre for a leaden dagger, and thy precious rich
crown for a pitiful bald crown.

FALSTAFF Well, an the fire of grace be not quite out of
thee, now shalt thou be moved. Give me a cup of sack to
make my eyes look red, that it may be thought I have
wept, for I must speak in passion, and I will do it in
380 King Cambyses' vein.

PRINCE HAL Well, here is my leg.

FALSTAFF And here is my speech. Stand aside, nobility.

HOSTESS O Jesu, this is excellent sport, i'faith.

FALSTAFF

Weep not, sweet Queen, for trickling tears are vain.

HOSTESS O the Father, how he holds his countenance!

FALSTAFF

For God's sake, lords, convey my tristful Queen,
For tears do stop the floodgates of her eyes.

HOSTESS O Jesu, he doth it as like one of these harlotry
players as ever I see!

390 FALSTAFF Peace, good pint-pot, peace, good tickle-
brain.

(*as* KING)

Harry, I do not only marvel where thou spendest thy time,
but also how thou art accompanied. For though the camomile, the more it is trodden on the faster it grows, yet youth,

the more it is wasted the sooner it wears. That thou art my
son I have partly thy mother's word, partly my own opinion,
but chiefly a villainous trick of thine eye, and a foolish hanging of thy nether lip, that doth warrant me. If then thou be
son to me – here lies the point – why, being son to me, art
thou so pointed at? Shall the blessed sun of heaven prove a 400
micher, and eat blackberries? A question not to be asked.
Shall the son of England prove a thief, and take purses? A
question to be asked. There is a thing, Harry, which thou
hast often heard of, and it is known to many in our land by
the name of pitch. This pitch – as ancient writers do report –
doth defile, so doth the company thou keepest. For, Harry,
now I do not speak to thee in drink, but in tears; not in
pleasure, but in passion; not in words only, but in woes also.
And yet there is a virtuous man whom I have often noted in
thy company, but I know not his name. 410

PRINCE HAL (as himself)
What manner of man, an it like your Majesty?

FALSTAFF (as KING)
A goodly portly man, i'faith, and a corpulent; of a cheerful
look, a pleasing eye, and a most noble carriage; and, as I
think, his age some fifty, or by'r lady inclining to threescore.
And now I remember me, his name is Falstaff. If that man
should be lewdly given, he deceiveth me, for, Harry, I see
virtue in his looks. If then the tree may be known by the
fruit, as the fruit by the tree, then peremptorily I speak it,
there is virtue in that Falstaff. Him keep with, the rest
banish. And tell me now, thou naughty varlet, tell me where 420
hast thou been this month?

PRINCE HAL Dost thou speak like a king? Do thou stand
for me, and I'll play my father.

FALSTAFF Depose me? If thou dost it half so gravely, so
majestically, both in word and matter, hang me up by the
heals for a rabbit-sucker, or a poulter's hare.

PRINCE HAL Well, here I am set.

FALSTAFF And here I stand. Judge, my masters.

PRINCE HAL (*as* KING)
Now, Harry, whence come you?

FALSTAFF (*as* HAL)
430 My noble lord, from Eastcheap.

PRINCE HAL (*as* KING)
The complaints I hear of thee are grievous.

FALSTAFF (*as* HAL)
'Sblood, my lord, they are false!
Nay, I'll tickle ye for a young prince, i'faith.

PRINCE HAL (*as* KING)
Swearest thou, ungracious boy? Henceforth ne'er look on me.
Thou art violently carried away from grace. There is a devil
haunts thee in the likeness of an old fat man, a tun of man is
thy companion. Why dost thou converse with that trunk of
humours, that bolting-hutch of beastliness, that swollen
parcel of dropsies, that huge bombard of sack, that stuffed
440 cloak-bag of guts, that roasted Manningtree ox with the
pudding in his belly, that reverend Vice, that grey Iniquity,
that Father Ruffian, that Vanity in years? Wherein is he
good, but to taste sack and drink it? Wherein neat and
cleanly, but to carve a capon and eat it? Wherein cunning,
but in craft? Wherein crafty, but in villainy? Wherein
villainous, but in all things? Wherein worthy, but in nothing?

FALSTAFF (*as* HAL)
I would your grace would take me with you. Whom means
your grace?

PRINCE HAL (*as* KING)
That villainous abominable misleader of youth, Falstaff,
450 that old white-bearded Satan.

FALSTAFF (*as* HAL)
My lord, the man I know.

PRINCE HAL (*as* KING)

   I know thou dost.

FALSTAFF (*as* HAL)

   But to say I know more harm in him than in myself were to
say more than I know. That he is old, the more the pity, his
white hairs do witness it, but that he is, saving your reverence, a whoremaster, that I utterly deny. If sack and sugar
be a fault, God help the wicked! If to be old and merry be a
sin, then many an old host that I know is damned. If to be
fat be to be hated, then Pharaoh's lean kine are to be loved.
No, my good lord! Banish Peto, banish Bardolph, banish 460
Poins – but for sweet Jack Falstaff, kind Jack Falstaff, true
Jack Falstaff, valiant Jack Falstaff – and therefore more
valiant, being as he is old Jack Falstaff – banish not him thy
Harry's company, banish not him thy Harry's company.
Banish plump Jack, and banish all the world.

PRINCE HAL (*as* KING)

   I do, I will.

     A knocking heard

          Exeunt Hostess, Francis and Bardolph
     Enter Bardolph, running

BARDOLPH O my lord, my lord, the sheriff with a most
monstrous watch is at the door.

FALSTAFF Out, ye rogue! Play out the play! I have much
to say in the behalf of that Falstaff. 470

     Enter the Hostess

HOSTESS O Jesu, my lord, my lord!

PRINCE HAL Heigh, heigh, the devil rides upon a fiddlestick. What's the matter?

HOSTESS The sheriff and all the watch are at the door.
They are come to search the house. Shall I let them in?

FALSTAFF Dost thou hear, Hal? Never call a true piece of
gold a counterfeit. Thou art essentially made without
seeming so.

PRINCE HAL And thou a natural coward without instinct.

FALSTAFF I deny your major. If you will deny the sheriff, so; if not, let him enter. If I become not a cart as well as another man, a plague on my bringing up! I hope I shall as soon be strangled with a halter as another.

PRINCE HAL Go hide thee behind the arras. The rest, walk up above. Now, my masters, for a true face, and good conscience.

FALSTAFF Both which I have had, but their date is out, and therefore I'll hide me.

Exeunt all but the Prince and Peto

PRINCE HAL Call in the Sheriff.

Enter Sheriff and the Carrier

Now, master Sheriff, what is your will with me?

SHERIFF
First, pardon me, my lord. A hue and cry
Hath followed certain men unto this house.

PRINCE HAL
What men?

SHERIFF
One of them is well known my gracious lord,
A gross fat man.

CARRIER   As fat as butter.

PRINCE HAL
The man I do assure you is not here,
For I myself at this time have employed him.
And Sheriff, I will engage my word to thee,
That I will by tomorrow dinner-time
Send him to answer thee, or any man,
For anything he shall be charged withal.
And so let me entreat you leave the house.

SHERIFF
I will, my lord. There are two gentlemen

94

Have in this robbery lost three hundred marks.

PRINCE HAL

It may be so. If he have robbed these men
He shall be answerable. And so, farewell.

SHERIFF

Good night, my noble lord.

PRINCE HAL

I think it is good morrow, is it not?

SHERIFF

Indeed, my lord, I think it be two o'clock.   510

Exit with Carrier

PRINCE HAL This oily rascal is known as well as Paul's.
Go call him forth.

PETO Falstaff! Fast asleep behind the arras, and snorting
like a horse.

PRINCE HAL Hark how hard he fetches breath. Search
his pockets.

Peto searcheth his pockets, and findeth certain papers
What hast thou found?

PETO Nothing but papers, my lord.

PRINCE HAL Let's see what they be, read them.

PETO *Item a capon* 2s. 2d.   520
Item sauce . . . . . 4d.
Item sack two gallons . . . 5s. 8d.
Item anchovies and sack after supper 2s. 6d.
Item bread . . . . . ob.

PRINCE HAL O monstrous! But one halfpennyworth of
bread to this intolerable deal of sack? What there is else
keep close, we'll read it at more advantage. There let him
sleep till day. I'll to the court in the morning. We must
all to the wars, and thy place shall be honourable. I'll
procure this fat rogue a charge of foot, and I know his   530
death will be a march of twelve score. The money shall

95

be paid back again with advantage. Be with me betimes
in the morning, and so, good morrow, Peto.

PETO Good morrow, good my lord. *Exeunt*

III.1   *Enter Hotspur, Worcester, Lord Mortimer, Owen
Glendower*

MORTIMER
These promises are fair, the parties sure,
And our induction full of prosperous hope.

HOTSPUR
Lord Mortimer, and cousin Glendower, will you sit
          down?
And uncle Worcester. A plague upon it!
I have forgot the map.

GLENDOWER   No, here it is.
Sit, cousin Percy, sit – good cousin Hotspur –
For by that name as oft as Lancaster doth speak of you
His cheek looks pale, and with a rising sigh
He wisheth you in heaven.

HOTSPUR   And you in hell,
10   As oft as he hears Owen Glendower spoke of.

GLENDOWER
I cannot blame him. At my nativity
The front of heaven was full of fiery shapes,
Of burning cressets, and at my birth
The frame and huge foundation of the earth
Shaked like a coward.

HOTSPUR   Why, so it would have done
At the same season if your mother's cat
Had but kittened, though yourself had never been born.

GLENDOWER
I say the earth did shake when I was born.

Handwritten margin note: Hotspur says Glendower a boor is a bore

96

HOTSPUR

    And I say the earth was not of my mind,
    If you suppose as fearing you it shook.   20

GLENDOWER

    The heavens were all on fire, the earth did tremble –

HOTSPUR

    O, then the earth shook to see the heavens on fire,
    And not in fear of your nativity.
    Diseasèd nature oftentimes breaks forth
    In strange eruptions, oft the teeming earth
    Is with a kind of colic pinched and vexed
    By the imprisoning of unruly wind
    Within her womb, which for enlargement striving
    Shakes the old beldam earth, and topples down
    Steeples and moss-grown towers. At your birth   30
    Our grandam earth, having this distemperature,
    In passion shook.

GLENDOWER   Cousin, of many men
    I do not bear these crossings. Give me leave
    To tell you once again that at my birth
    The front of heaven was full of fiery shapes,
    The goats ran from the mountains, and the herds
    Were strangely clamorous to the frighted fields.
    These signs have marked me extraordinary,
    And all the courses of my life do show
    I am not in the roll of common men.   40
    Where is he living, clipped in with the sea
    That chides the banks of England, Scotland, Wales,
    Which calls me pupil or hath read to me?
    And bring him out that is but woman's son
    Can trace me in the tedious ways of art,
    And hold me pace in deep experiments.

HOTSPUR

    I think there's no man speaks better Welsh.

I'll to dinner.

MORTIMER

Peace, cousin Percy, you will make him mad.

GLENDOWER

50   I can call spirits from the vasty deep.

HOTSPUR

Why, so can I, or so can any man:
But will they come when you do call for them?

GLENDOWER

Why, I can teach you, cousin, to command the devil.

HOTSPUR

And I can teach thee, coz, to shame the devil
By telling truth. Tell truth, and shame the devil.
If thou have power to raise him, bring him hither,
And I'll be sworn I have power to shame him hence.
O, while you live, tell truth, and shame the devil!

MORTIMER

Come, come, no more of this unprofitable chat.

GLENDOWER

60   Three times hath Henry Bolingbroke made head
Against my power, thrice from the banks of Wye
And sandy-bottomed Severn have I sent him
Bootless home, and weather-beaten back.

HOTSPUR

Home without boots, and in foul weather too!
How scapes he agues, in the devil's name?

GLENDOWER

Come, here is the map, shall we divide our right
According to our threefold order taken?

MORTIMER

The Archdeacon hath divided it
Into three limits very equally.

70   England, from Trent and Severn hitherto,

By south and east is to my part assigned.
All westward, Wales beyond the Severn shore,
And all the fertile land within that bound,
To Owen Glendower. And, dear coz, to you
The remnant northward lying off from Trent.
And our indentures tripartite are drawn,
Which being sealed interchangeably –
A business that this night may execute –
Tomorrow, cousin Percy, you and I
And my good Lord of Worcester will set forth   80
To meet your father and the Scottish power,
As is appointed us, at Shrewsbury.
My father Glendower is not ready yet,
Nor shall we need his help these fourteen days.
(*To Glendower*) Within that space you may have drawn
                together
Your tenants, friends, and neighbouring gentlemen.

GLENDOWER

A shorter time shall send me to you, lords,
And in my conduct shall your ladies come,
From whom you now must steal and take no leave,
For there will be a world of water shed   90
Upon the parting of your wives and you.

HOTSPUR

Methinks my moiety, north from Burton here,
In quantity equals not one of yours.
See how this river comes me cranking in,
And cuts me from the best of all my land
A huge half-moon, a monstrous cantle out.
I'll have the current in this place dammed up,
And here the smug and silver Trent shall run
In a new channel fair and evenly.
It shall not wind with such a deep indent,   100

To rob me of so rich a bottom here.

GLENDOWER

Not wind? It shall, it must – you see it doth.

MORTIMER

Yea,
But mark how he bears his course, and runs me up
With like advantage on the other side,
Gelding the opposèd continent as much
As on the other side it takes from you.

WORCESTER

Yea, but a little charge will trench him here,
And on this north side win this cape of land,
110 And then he runs straight and even.

HOTSPUR

I'll have it so, a little charge will do it.

GLENDOWER

I'll not have it altered.

HOTSPUR   Will not you?

GLENDOWER

No, nor you shall not.

HOTSPUR   Who shall say me nay?

GLENDOWER

Why, that will I.

HOTSPUR

Let me not understand you then, speak it in Welsh.

GLENDOWER

I can speak English, lord, as well as you,
For I was trained up in the English court,
Where being but young I framèd to the harp
Many an English ditty lovely well,
120 And gave the tongue a helpful ornament –
A virtue that was never seen in you.

HOTSPUR

Marry and I am glad of it with all my heart!

I had rather be a kitten and cry 'mew'
Than one of these same metre ballad-mongers.
I had rather hear a brazen canstick turned,
Or a dry wheel grate on the axle-tree,
And that would set my teeth nothing on edge,
Nothing so much as mincing poetry.
'Tis like the forced gait of a shuffling nag.

GLENDOWER

Come, you shall have Trent turned. 130

HOTSPUR

I do not care, I'll give thrice so much land
To any well-deserving friend.
But in the way of bargain, mark ye me,
I'll cavil on the ninth part of a hair.
Are the indentures drawn? Shall we be gone?

GLENDOWER

The moon shines fair, you may away by night.
I'll haste the writer, and withal
Break with your wives of your departure hence.
I am afraid my daughter will run mad,
So much she doteth on her Mortimer. *Exit* 140

MORTIMER

Fie, cousin Percy, how you cross my father!

HOTSPUR

I cannot choose. Sometime he angers me
With telling me of the moldwarp and the ant,
Of the dreamer Merlin and his prophecies,
And of a dragon and a finless fish,
A clip-winged griffin and a moulten raven,
A couching lion and a ramping cat,
And such a deal of skimble-skamble stuff
As puts me from my faith. I tell you what –
He held me last night at least nine hours 150
In reckoning up the several devils' names

That were his lackeys. I cried 'Hum', and 'Well, go to!'
But marked him not a word. O, he is as tedious
As a tired horse, a railing wife,
Worse than a smoky house. I had rather live
With cheese and garlic in a windmill, far,
Than feed on cates and have him talk to me
In any summer house in Christendom.

MORTIMER

In faith, he is a worthy gentleman,
160 Exceedingly well read, and profited
In strange concealments, valiant as a lion,
And wondrous affable, and as bountiful
As mines of India. Shall I tell you, cousin?
He holds your temper in a high respect
And curbs himself even of his natural scope
When you come 'cross his humour, faith he does.
I warrant you that man is not alive
Might so have tempted him as you have done
Without the taste of danger and reproof.
170 But do not use it oft, let me entreat you.

WORCESTER

In faith, my lord, you are too wilful-blame,
And since your coming hither have done enough
To put him quite besides his patience.
You must needs learn, lord, to amend this fault.
Though sometimes it show greatness, courage, blood –
And that's the dearest grace it renders you –
Yet oftentimes it doth present harsh rage,
Defect of manners, want of government,
Pride, haughtiness, opinion, and disdain,
180 The least of which haunting a nobleman
Loseth men's hearts and leaves behind a stain
Upon the beauty of all parts besides,
Beguiling them of commendation.

HOTSPUR

    Well, I am schooled – good manners be your speed!

    Here come our wives, and let us take our leave.

    Enter Glendower with the ladies

MORTIMER

    This is the deadly spite that angers me,

    My wife can speak no English, I no Welsh.

GLENDOWER

    My daughter weeps, she'll not part with you,

    She'll be a soldier too, she'll to the wars.

MORTIMER

    Good father, tell her that she and my aunt Percy   190

    Shall follow in your conduct speedily.

    Glendower speaks to her in Welsh, and she answers him
    in the same

GLENDOWER She is desperate here, a peevish, self-willed

    harlotry, one that no persuasion can do good upon.

    The lady speaks in Welsh

MORTIMER

    I understand thy looks, that pretty Welsh

    Which thou pourest down from these swelling heavens

    I am too perfect in, and but for shame

    In such a parley should I answer thee.

    The lady speaks again in Welsh

    I understand thy kisses, and thou mine,

    And that's a feeling disputation,

    But I will never be a truant, love,   200

    Till I have learnt thy language, for thy tongue

    Makes Welsh as sweet as ditties highly penned,

    Sung by a fair queen in a summer's bower

    With ravishing division to her lute.

GLENDOWER

    Nay, if you melt, then will she run mad.

    The lady speaks again in Welsh

MORTIMER

    O, I am ignorance itself in this!

GLENDOWER

    She bids you on the wanton rushes lay you down,
    And rest your gentle head upon her lap,
    And she will sing the song that pleaseth you,
210   And on your eyelids crown the god of sleep,
    Charming your blood with pleasing heaviness,
    Making such difference 'twixt wake and sleep
    As is the difference betwixt day and night,
    The hour before the heavenly-harnessed team
    Begins his golden progress in the east.

MORTIMER

    With all my heart I'll sit and hear her sing,
    By that time will our book I think be drawn.

GLENDOWER

    Do so, and those musicians that shall play to you
    Hang in the air a thousand leagues from hence,
220   And straight they shall be here. Sit, and attend.

HOTSPUR

    Come, Kate, thou art perfect in lying down.
    Come, quick, quick, that I may lay my head in thy lap.

LADY PERCY Go, ye giddy goose.

        The music plays

HOTSPUR

    Now I perceive the devil understands Welsh,
    And 'tis no marvel he is so humorous,
    By'r lady, he is a good musician.

LADY PERCY

    Then should you be nothing but musical,
    For you are altogether governed by humours.
    Lie still, ye thief, and hear the lady sing in Welsh.

230 HOTSPUR I had rather hear Lady my brach howl in Irish.

LADY PERCY Wouldst thou have thy head broken?

HOTSPUR No.

LADY PERCY Then be still.

HOTSPUR Neither, 'tis a woman's fault.

LADY PERCY Now, God help thee!

HOTSPUR To the Welsh lady's bed.

LADY PERCY What's that?

HOTSPUR Peace, she sings.

Here the lady sings a Welsh song

Come, Kate, I'll have your song too.

LADY PERCY Not mine, in good sooth.   240

HOTSPUR Not yours, in good sooth! Heart, you swear like
a comfit-maker's wife – 'Not you, in good sooth!', and
'As true as I live!', and 'As God shall mend me!', and
'As sure as day!' –
And givest such sarcenet surety for thy oaths
As if thou never walkest further than Finsbury.
Swear me, Kate, like a lady as thou art,
A good mouth-filling oath, and leave 'In sooth',
And such protest of pepper-gingerbread,
To velvet-guards, and Sunday citizens.   250
Come, sing.

LADY PERCY I will not sing.

HOTSPUR 'Tis the next way to turn tailor, or be redbreast
teacher. An the indentures be drawn I'll away within
these two hours. And so, come in when ye will.   *Exit*

GLENDOWER
Come, come, Lord Mortimer, you are as slow
As hot Lord Percy is on fire to go.
By this our book is drawn – we'll but seal,
And then to horse immediately.

MORTIMER   With all my heart.

Exeunt

Enter the King, Prince of Wales, and others

KING HENRY

Lords, give us leave. The Prince of Wales and I
Must have some private conference – but be near at
        hand,
For we shall presently have need of you. *Exeunt Lords*
I know not whether God will have it so
For some displeasing service I have done,
That in his secret doom out of my blood
He'll breed revengement and a scourge for me.
But thou dost in thy passages of life
Make me believe that thou art only marked
10 For the hot vengeance and the rod of heaven,
To punish my mistreadings. Tell me else,
Could such inordinate and low desires,
Such poor, such bare, such lewd, such mean attempts,
Such barren pleasures, rude society,
As thou art matched withal, and grafted to,
Accompany the greatness of thy blood
And hold their level with thy princely heart?

PRINCE HAL

So please your majesty, I would I could
Quit all offences with as clear excuse
20 As well as I am doubtless I can purge
Myself of many I am charged withal.
Yet such extenuation let me beg
As, in reproof of many tales devised,
Which oft the ear of greatness needs must hear,
By smiling pickthanks, and base newsmongers,
I may for some things true, wherein my youth
Hath faulty wandered and irregular,
Find pardon on my true submission.

KING HENRY

God pardon thee! Yet let me wonder, Harry,

At thy affections, which do hold a wing   30
Quite from the flight of all thy ancestors.
Thy place in Council thou hast rudely lost,
Which by thy younger brother is supplied,
And art almost an alien to the hearts
Of all the court and princes of my blood.
The hope and expectation of thy time
Is ruined, and the soul of every man
Prophetically do forethink thy fall.
Had I so lavish of my presence been,
So common-hackneyed in the eyes of men,   40
So stale and cheap to vulgar company,
Opinion, that did help me to the crown,
Had still kept loyal to possession,
And left me in reputeless banishment,
A fellow of no mark nor likelihood.
By being seldom seen, I could not stir
But like a comet I was wondered at,
That men would tell their children, 'This is he!'
Others would say, 'Where, which is Bolingbroke?'
And then I stole all courtesy from heaven,   50
And dressed myself in such humility
That I did pluck allegiance from men's hearts,
Loud shouts and salutations from their mouths,
Even in the presence of the crownèd King.
Thus did I keep my person fresh and new,
My presence, like a robe pontifical,
Ne'er seen but wondered at, and so my state,
Seldom, but sumptuous, showed like a feast,
And won by rareness such solemnity.
The skipping King, he ambled up and down,   60
With shallow jesters, and rash bavin wits,
Soon kindled and soon burnt, carded his state,
Mingled his royalty with capering fools,

King uses
popular
in wrong
sense

Had his great name profanèd with their scorns,
And gave his countenance against his name
To laugh at gibing boys, and stand the push
Of every beardless vain comparative,
Grew a companion to the common streets,
Enfeoffed himself to popularity,
70 That, being daily swallowed by men's eyes,
They surfeited with honey, and began
To loathe the taste of sweetness, whereof a little
More than a little is by much too much.
So, when he had occasion to be seen,
He was but as the cuckoo is in June,
Heard, not regarded; seen, but with such eyes
As, sick and blunted with community,
Afford no extraordinary gaze,
Such as is bent on sun-like majesty

Says he
timed his
own offer
Richard

80 When it shines seldom in admiring eyes,
But rather drowsed and hung their eyelids down,
Slept in his face, and rendered such aspect
As cloudy men use to their adversaries,
Being with his presence glutted, gorged, and full.
And in that very line, Harry, standest thou,
For thou hast lost thy princely privilege
With vile participation. Not an eye

Crys

But is a-weary of thy common sight,
Save mine, which hath desired to see thee more,
90 Which now doth that I would not have it do,
Make blind itself with foolish tenderness.

PRINCE HAL
I shall hereafter, my thrice-gracious lord,
Be more myself.
KING HENRY   For all the world
As thou art to this hour was Richard then

When I from France set foot at Ravenspurgh,
And even as I was then is Percy now.
Now by my sceptre, and my soul to boot,
He hath more worthy interest to the state
Than thou the shadow of succession.
For of no right, nor colour like to right,   100
He doth fill fields with harness in the realm,
Turns head against the lion's armèd jaws,
And being no more in debt to years than thou
Leads ancient lords and reverend bishops on
To bloody battles, and to bruising arms.
What never-dying honour hath he got
Against renownèd Douglas! Whose high deeds,
Whose hot incursions and great name in arms,
Holds from all soldiers chief majority
And military title capital   110
Through all the kingdoms that acknowledge Christ.
Thrice hath this Hotspur, Mars in swaddling clothes,
This infant warrior, in his enterprises
Discomfited great Douglas, taken him once,
Enlargèd him, and made a friend of him,
To fill the mouth of deep defiance up,
And shake the peace and safety of our throne.
And what say you to this? Percy, Northumberland,
The Archbishop's Grace of York, Douglas, Mortimer,
Capitulate against us and are up.   120
But wherefore do I tell these news to thee?
Why, Harry, do I tell thee of my foes,
Which art my nearest and dearest enemy?
Thou that art like enough, through vassal fear,
Base inclination, and the start of spleen,
To fight against me under Percy's pay,
To dog his heels, and curtsy at his frowns,

To show how much thou art degenerate.

PRINCE HAL

Do not think so, you shall not find it so;

130   And God forgive them that so much have swayed

Your majesty's good thoughts away from me!

I will redeem all this on Percy's head,

And in the closing of some glorious day

Be bold to tell you that I am your son,

When I will wear a garment all of blood,

And stain my favours in a bloody mask,

Which, washed away, shall scour my shame with it.

And that shall be the day, whene'er it lights,

That this same child of honour and renown,

140   This gallant Hotspur, this all-praisèd knight,

And your unthought-of Harry chance to meet.

For every honour sitting on his helm,

Would they were multitudes, and on my head

My shames redoubled. For the time will come

That I shall make this northern youth exchange

His glorious deeds for my indignities.

Percy is but my <u>factor</u>, good my lord,

To engross up glorious deeds on my behalf,

And I will call him to so strict account

150   That he shall render every glory up,

Yea, even the slightest worship of his time,

Or I will tear the reckoning from his heart.

This in the name of God I promise here,

The which if He be pleased I shall perform,

I do beseech your majesty may salve

The long-grown wounds of my intemperance.

If not, the end of life cancels all bonds,

And I will die a hundred thousand deaths

Ere break the smallest parcel of this vow.

Handwritten annotations:

- Blames suppliers of rumor
- Not justified as we have seen him in action
- Saying he will beat this young man
- Saying in beating him he will secure renown and take all the honors
- Take all titles from battlefield
- agent
- sounds sincere
- responding to father's letters?
- Hal does not make a complete confession. Appears he has reformed.
- Treason doesn't fully change

KING HENRY

    A hundred thousand rebels die in this.   160

    Thou shalt have charge and sovereign trust herein.

    Enter Blunt

    How now, good Blunt? Thy looks are full of speed.

BLUNT

    So hath the business that I come to speak of.

    Lord Mortimer of Scotland hath sent word

    That Douglas and the English rebels met

    The eleventh of this month at Shrewsbury.

    A mighty and a fearful head they are,

    If promises be kept on every hand,

    As ever offered foul play in a state.

KING HENRY

    The Earl of Westmorland set forth today,   170

    With him my son, Lord John of Lancaster,

    For this advertisement is five days old.

    On Wednesday next, Harry, you shall set forward.

    On Thursday we ourselves will march.

    Our meeting is Bridgnorth, and, Harry, you

    Shall march through Gloucestershire, by which account,

    Our business valued, some twelve days hence

    Our general forces at Bridgnorth shall meet.

    Our hands are full of business, let's away,

    Advantage feeds him fat while men delay.   180

                            Exeunt

    Enter Falstaff and Bardolph   III.3

FALSTAFF Bardolph, am I not fallen away vilely since this [*Gadhill where he was made a fool of*]
last action? Do I not bate? Do I not dwindle? Why, my
skin hangs about me like an old lady's loose gown. I am
withered like an old apple-john. Well, I'll repent, and

[*Claiming to repent*]   111

that suddenly, while I am in some liking. I shall be out
of heart shortly, and then I shall have no strength to
repent. An I have not forgotten what the inside of a
church is made of, I am a peppercorn, a brewer's horse.
The inside of a church! Company, villainous company,
hath been the spoil of me.

BARDOLPH Sir John, you are so fretful you cannot live
long.

FALSTAFF Why, there is it. Come, sing me a bawdy song,
make me merry. I was as virtuously given as a gentleman need to be. Virtuous enough. Swore little. Diced
not above seven times a week. Went to a bawdy-house
not above once in a quarter – of an hour. Paid money
that I borrowed – three or four times. Lived well, and in
good compass: and now I live out of all order, out of all
compass.

BARDOLPH Why, you are so fat, Sir John, that you must
needs be out of all compass, out of all reasonable compass, Sir John.

FALSTAFF Do thou amend thy face, and I'll amend my
life. Thou art our admiral, thou bearest the lantern in
the poop, but 'tis in the nose of thee. Thou art the
Knight of the Burning Lamp.

BARDOLPH Why, Sir John, my face does you no harm.

FALSTAFF No, I'll be sworn, I make as good use of it as
many a man doth of a death's-head, or a *memento mori*.
I never see thy face but I think upon hell-fire, and Dives
that lived in purple: for there he is in his robes, burning,
burning. If thou wert any way given to virtue, I would
swear by thy face. My oath should be 'By this fire, that's
God's angel!' But thou art altogether given over, and
wert indeed, but for the light in thy face, the son of
utter darkness. When thou rannest up Gad's Hill in the
night to catch my horse, if I did not think thou hadst

been an *ignis fatuus*, or a ball of wildfire, there's no
purchase in money. O, thou art a perpetual triumph, an 40
everlasting bonfire-light! Thou hast saved me a thousand
marks in links and torches, walking with thee in the
night betwixt tavern and tavern. But the sack that thou
hast drunk me would have bought me lights as good
cheap at the dearest chandler's in Europe. I have
maintained that salamander of yours with fire any time
this two-and-thirty years, God reward me for it!

BARDOLPH 'Sblood, I would my face were in your belly!

FALSTAFF God-a-mercy! So should I be sure to be heart-
burnt.   50

> *Enter Hostess*

How now, dame Partlet the hen, have you enquired yet
who picked my pocket?

HOSTESS Why, Sir John, what do you think, Sir John, do
you think I keep thieves in my house? I have searched, I
have enquired, so has my husband, man by man, boy by
boy, servant by servant – the tithe of a hair was never
lost in my house before.

FALSTAFF Ye lie, hostess. Bardolph was shaved and lost
many a hair, and I'll be sworn my pocket was picked.
Go to, you are a woman, go!   60

HOSTESS Who, I? No, I defy thee! God's light, I was
never called so in mine own house before.

FALSTAFF Go to, I know you well enough.

HOSTESS No, Sir John, you do not know me, Sir John, I
know you, Sir John, you owe me money, Sir John, and
now you pick a quarrel to beguile me of it. I bought you
a dozen of shirts to your back.

FALSTAFF Dowlas, filthy dowlas. I have given them away
to bakers' wives. They have made bolters of them.

HOSTESS Now as I am a true woman, holland of eight 70
shillings an ell! You owe money here besides, Sir John,

for your diet, and by-drinkings, and money lent you,
four-and-twenty pound.

FALSTAFF He had his part of it, let him pay.

HOSTESS He? Alas, he is poor, he hath nothing.

FALSTAFF How? Poor? Look upon his face. What call
you rich? Let them coin his nose, let them coin his
cheeks, I'll not pay a denier. What, will you make a
younker of me? Shall I not take mine ease in mine inn
80 but I shall have my pocket picked? I have lost a seal-
ring of my grandfather's worth forty mark.

HOSTESS O Jesu, I have heard the Prince tell him I know
not how oft, that that ring was copper.

FALSTAFF How? The Prince is a Jack, a sneak-up.
'Sblood, an he were here I would cudgel him like a dog
if he would say so.

*Enter the Prince marching, with Peto, and Falstaff
meets him, playing upon his truncheon like a fife*

How now, lad? Is the wind in that door, i'faith, must
we all march?

BARDOLPH Yea, two and two, Newgate fashion.

90 HOSTESS My lord, I pray you hear me.

PRINCE HAL What sayest thou, Mistress Quickly? How
doth thy husband? I love him well, he is an honest man.

HOSTESS Good my lord, hear me.

FALSTAFF Prithee let her alone, and list to me.

PRINCE HAL What sayest thou, Jack?

FALSTAFF The other night I fell asleep here, behind the
arras, and had my pocket picked. This house is turned
bawdy-house, they pick pockets.

PRINCE HAL What didst thou lose, Jack?

100 FALSTAFF Wilt thou believe me, Hal, three or four bonds
of forty pound apiece, and a seal-ring of my grandfather's.

PRINCE HAL A trifle, some eightpenny matter.

HOSTESS So I told him, my lord, and I said I heard your grace say so. And, my lord, he speaks most vilely of you, like a foul-mouthed man as he is, and said he would cudgel you.

PRINCE HAL What! He did not?

HOSTESS There's neither faith, truth, nor womanhood in me else.   110

FALSTAFF There's no more faith in thee than in a stewed prune, nor no more truth in thee than in a drawn fox – and for womanhood, Maid Marian may be the deputy's wife of the ward to thee. Go, you thing, go!

HOSTESS Say, what thing, what thing?

FALSTAFF What thing? Why, a thing to thank God on.

HOSTESS I am no thing to thank God on, I would thou shouldst know it, I am an honest man's wife, and setting thy knighthood aside, thou art a knave to call me so.

FALSTAFF Setting thy womanhood aside, thou art a beast 120 to say otherwise.

HOSTESS Say, what beast, thou knave, thou?

FALSTAFF What beast? Why – an otter.

PRINCE HAL An otter, Sir John? Why an otter?

FALSTAFF Why? She's neither fish nor flesh, a man knows not where to have her.

HOSTESS Thou art an unjust man in saying so, thou or any man knows where to have me, thou knave, thou.

PRINCE HAL Thou sayest true, Hostess, and he slanders thee most grossly.   130

HOSTESS So he doth you, my lord, and said this other day you owed him a thousand pound.

PRINCE HAL Sirrah, do I owe you a thousand pound?

FALSTAFF A thousand pound, Hal? A million, thy love is worth a million, thou owest me thy love.

HOSTESS Nay my lord, he called you Jack, and said he would cudgel you.

FALSTAFF Did I, Bardolph?

BARDOLPH Indeed, Sir John, you said so.

140 FALSTAFF Yea, if he said my ring was copper.

PRINCE HAL I say 'tis copper, darest thou be as good as thy word now?

FALSTAFF Why Hal, thou knowest as thou art but man I dare, but as thou art prince, I fear thee as I fear the roaring of the lion's whelp.

PRINCE HAL And why not as the lion?

FALSTAFF The King himself is to be feared as the lion. Dost thou think I'll fear thee as I fear thy father? Nay, an I do, I pray God my girdle break.

150 PRINCE HAL O, if it should, how would thy guts fall about thy knees! But sirrah, there's no room for faith, truth, nor honesty in this bosom of thine. It is all filled up with guts and midriff. Charge an honest woman with picking thy pocket? Why, thou whoreson impudent embossed rascal, if there were anything in thy pocket but tavern reckonings, memorandums of bawdy-houses, and one poor pennyworth of sugar-candy to make thee long-winded, if thy pocket were enriched with any other injuries but these, I am a villain. And yet 160 you will stand to it, you will not pocket up wrong! Art thou not ashamed?

FALSTAFF Dost thou hear, Hal? Thou knowest in the state of innocency Adam fell, and what should poor Jack Falstaff do in the days of villainy? Thou seest I have more flesh than another man, and therefore more frailty. You confess then, you picked my pocket?

PRINCE HAL It appears so by the story.

FALSTAFF Hostess, I forgive thee, go make ready breakfast, love thy husband, look to thy servants, 170 cherish thy guests, thou shalt find me tractable to any

honest reason, thou seest I am pacified still – nay
prithee be gone.   *Exit Hostess*
Now, Hal, to the news at court: for the robbery, lad,
how is that answered?

PRINCE HAL O my sweet beef, I must still be good angel
to thee – the money is paid back again.

FALSTAFF O, I do not like that paying back, 'tis a double
labour.

PRINCE HAL I am good friends with my father and may
do anything. ~~Drawn wool over eyes~~   180

FALSTAFF Rob me the exchequer the first thing thou
dost, and do it with unwashed hands too.

BARDOLPH Do, my lord.

PRINCE HAL I have procured thee, Jack, a charge of foot.

FALSTAFF I would it had been of horse. Where shall I
find one that can steal well? O for a fine thief of the age
of two-and-twenty or thereabouts! I am heinously un-
provided. Well, God be thanked for these rebels, they
offend none but the virtuous. I laud them, I praise them.

PRINCE HAL Bardolph!   190

BARDOLPH My lord?

PRINCE HAL

Go bear this letter to Lord John of Lancaster,
To my brother John, this to my Lord of Westmorland.
                               Exit Bardolph
Go, Peto, to horse, to horse, for thou and I
Have thirty miles to ride yet ere dinner-time.
                               Exit Peto
Jack, meet me tomorrow in the Temple hall
At two o'clock in the afternoon.
There shalt thou know thy charge, and there receive
Money and order for their furniture.
The land is burning, Percy stands on high,   200

And either we or they must lower lie.   *Exit*

FALSTAFF
Rare words! Brave world! Hostess, my breakfast, come!
O, I could wish this tavern were my drum.   *Exit*

✳

IV.1   *Enter Hotspur, Worcester, and Douglas*

HOTSPUR
Well said, my noble Scot! If speaking truth
In this fine age were not thought flattery,
Such attribution should the Douglas have
As not a soldier of this season's stamp
Should go as general current through the world.
By God, I cannot flatter, I do defy
The tongues of soothers, but a braver place
In my heart's love hath no man than yourself.
Nay, task me to my word, approve me, lord.

DOUGLAS
10   Thou art the king of honour.
No man so potent breathes upon the ground
But I will beard him.

HOTSPUR   Do so, and 'tis well.
    Enter one with letters
What letters hast thou there? – I can but thank you.

MESSENGER
These letters come from your father.

HOTSPUR
Letters from him? Why comes he not himself?

MESSENGER
He cannot come, my lord, he is grievous sick.

HOTSPUR
Zounds, how has he the leisure to be sick

In such a justling time? Who leads his power?
Under whose government come they along?

MESSENGER

His letters bear his mind, not I, my lord.   20

WORCESTER

I prithee tell me, doth he keep his bed?

MESSENGER

He did, my lord, four days ere I set forth,
And at the time of my departure thence
He was much feared by his physicians.

WORCESTER

I would the state of time had first been whole
Ere he by sickness had been visited.
His health was never better worth than now.

HOTSPUR

Sick now? Droop now? This sickness doth infect
The very life-blood of our enterprise.
'Tis catching hither, even to our camp.   30
He writes me here that inward sickness –
And that his friends by deputation could not
So soon be drawn, nor did he think it meet
To lay so dangerous and dear a trust
On any soul removed but on his own.
Yet doth he give us bold advertisement
That with our small conjunction we should on,
To see how fortune is disposed to us.
For, as he writes, there is no quailing now,
Because the King is certainly possessed   40
Of all our purposes. What say you to it?

WORCESTER

Your father's sickness is a maim to us.

HOTSPUR

A perilous gash, a very limb lopped off –
And yet, in faith, it is not! His present want

Seems more than we shall find it. Were it good
To set the exact wealth of all our states
All at one cast? To set so rich a main
On the nice hazard of one doubtful hour?
It were not good, for therein should we read
50 The very bottom and the soul of hope,
The very list, the very utmost bound
Of all our fortunes.

DOUGLAS

Faith, and so we should, where now remains
A sweet reversion – we may boldly spend
Upon the hope of what is to come in.
A comfort of retirement lives in this.

HOTSPUR

A rendezvous, a home to fly unto,
If that the devil and mischance look big
Upon the maidenhead of our affairs.

WORCESTER

60 But yet I would your father had been here.
The quality and hair of our attempt
Brooks no division. It will be thought,
By some that know not why he is away,
That wisdom, loyalty, and mere dislike
Of our proceedings kept the Earl from hence.
And think how such an apprehension
May turn the tide of fearful faction,
And breed a kind of question in our cause.
For well you know we of the offering side
70 Must keep aloof from strict arbitrement,
And stop all sight-holes, every loop from whence
The eye of reason may pry in upon us.
This absence of your father's draws a curtain
That shows the ignorant a kind of fear
Before not dreamt of.

HOTSPUR   You strain too far.
  I rather of his absence make this use.
  It lends a lustre and more great opinion,
  A larger dare to our great enterprise,
  Than if the Earl were here. For men must think
  If we without his help can make a head   80
  To push against a kingdom, with his help
  We shall o'erturn it topsy-turvy down.
  Yet all goes well, yet all our joints are whole.

DOUGLAS
  As heart can think. There is not such a word
  Spoke of in Scotland as this term of fear.

    Enter Sir Richard Vernon

HOTSPUR
  My cousin Vernon! Welcome, by my soul!

VERNON
  Pray God my news be worth a welcome, lord.
  The Earl of Westmorland seven thousand strong
  Is marching hitherwards, with him Prince John.

HOTSPUR
  No harm, what more?

VERNON   And further, I have learned,   90
  The King himself in person is set forth,
  Or hitherwards intended speedily,
  With strong and mighty preparation.

HOTSPUR
  He shall be welcome too. Where is his son,
  The nimble-footed madcap Prince of Wales,
  And his comrades that daffed the world aside
  And bid it pass?

VERNON   All furnished, all in arms,
  All plumed like estridges that with the wind
  Bated, like eagles having lately bathed,
  Glittering in golden coats like images,   100

As full of spirit as the month of May,
And gorgeous as the sun at midsummer,
Wanton as youthful goats, wild as young bulls.
I saw young Harry with his beaver on,
His cuishes on his thighs, gallantly armed,
Rise from the ground like feathered Mercury,
And vaulted with such ease into his seat
As if an angel dropped down from the clouds
To turn and wind a fiery Pegasus,
110   And witch the world with noble horsemanship.

HOTSPUR
No more, no more! Worse than the sun in March,
This praise doth nourish agues. Let them come!
They come like sacrifices in their trim,
And to the fire-eyed maid of smoky war
All hot and bleeding will we offer them.
The mailèd Mars shall on his altar sit
Up to the ears in blood. I am on fire
To hear this rich reprisal is so nigh,
And yet not ours! Come, let me taste my horse,
120   Who is to bear me like a thunderbolt
Against the bosom of the Prince of Wales.
Harry to Harry shall, hot horse to horse,
Meet and ne'er part till one drop down a corpse.
O that Glendower were come!

VERNON   There is more news.
I learned in Worcester as I rode along
He cannot draw his power this fourteen days.

DOUGLAS
That's the worst tidings that I hear of yet.

WORCESTER
Ay, by my faith, that bears a frosty sound.

HOTSPUR
What may the King's whole battle reach unto?

VERNON
  To thirty thousand.
HOTSPUR   Forty let it be.   130
  My father and Glendower being both away,
  The powers of us may serve so great a day.
  Come, let us take a muster speedily.
  Doomsday is near. Die all, die merrily.

DOUGLAS
  Talk not of dying, I am out of fear
  Of death or death's hand for this one half year.

                                          Exeunt

        Enter Falstaff and Bardolph   IV.2
FALSTAFF Bardolph, get thee before to Coventry. Fill me
  a bottle of sack. Our soldiers shall march through. We'll
  to Sutton Coldfield tonight.
BARDOLPH Will you give me money, captain?
FALSTAFF Lay out, lay out.
BARDOLPH This bottle makes an angel.
FALSTAFF And if it do, take it for thy labour – and if it
  make twenty, take them all, I'll answer the coinage. Bid
  my lieutenant Peto meet me at town's end.
BARDOLPH I will, captain. Farewell.   *Exit* 10
FALSTAFF If I be not ashamed of my soldiers, I am a
  soused gurnet. I have misused the King's press damn-
  ably. I have got in exchange of a hundred and fifty
  soldiers three hundred and odd pounds. I press me
  none but good householders, yeomen's sons, enquire
  me out contracted bachelors, such as had been asked
  twice on the banns, such a commodity of warm slaves as
  had as lief hear the devil as a drum, such as fear the
  report of a caliver worse than a struck fowl or a hurt wild
  duck. I pressed me none but such toasts-and-butter, 20

with hearts in their bellies no bigger than pins' heads,
and they have bought out their services. And now my
whole charge consists of ancients, corporals, lieutenants,
gentlemen of companies – slaves as ragged as Lazarus in
the painted cloth, where the glutton's dogs licked his
sores. And such as indeed were never soldiers, but discarded unjust serving-men, younger sons to younger
brothers, revolted tapsters, and ostlers trade-fallen, the
cankers of a calm world and a long peace, ten times more
dishonourable-ragged than an old fazed ancient. And
such have I to fill up the rooms of them as have bought
out their services, that you would think that I had a
hundred and fifty tattered prodigals lately come from
swine-keeping, from eating draff and husks. A mad
fellow met me on the way, and told me I had unloaded
all the gibbets and pressed the dead bodies. No eye hath
seen such scarecrows. I'll not march through Coventry
with them, that's flat. Nay, and the villains march wide
betwixt the legs as if they had gyves on, for indeed I had
the most of them out of prison. There's not a shirt and a
half in all my company, and the half shirt is two napkins
tacked together and thrown over the shoulders like a
herald's coat without sleeves. And the shirt to say the
truth stolen from my host at Saint Albans, or the red-
nose innkeeper of Daventry. But that's all one, they'll
find linen enough on every hedge.

Enter the Prince and the Lord of Westmorland

PRINCE HAL How now, blown Jack? How now, quilt?

FALSTAFF What, Hal! How now, mad wag? What a devil
dost thou in Warwickshire? My good Lord of Westmorland, I cry you mercy, I thought your honour had
already been at Shrewsbury.

WESTMORLAND Faith, Sir John, 'tis more than time that
I were there, and you too, but my powers are there

already. The King I can tell you looks for us all, we must
away all night.

FALSTAFF Tut, never fear me, I am as vigilant as a cat to
steal cream.

PRINCE HAL I think, to steal cream indeed, for thy theft
hath already made thee butter. But tell me, Jack, whose
fellows are these that come after?   60

FALSTAFF Mine, Hal, mine.

PRINCE HAL I did never see such pitiful rascals.

FALSTAFF Tut, tut, good enough to toss, food for powder, food for powder, they'll fill a pit as well as better.
Tush, man, mortal men, mortal men.

WESTMORLAND Ay, but Sir John, methinks they are
exceeding poor and bare, too beggarly.

FALSTAFF Faith, for their poverty I know not where they
had that. And for their bareness I am sure they never
learned that of me.   70

PRINCE HAL No, I'll be sworn, unless you call three
fingers in the ribs bare. But sirrah, make haste. Percy is
already in the field.   *Exit*

FALSTAFF What, is the King encamped?

WESTMORLAND He is, Sir John, I fear we shall stay too
long.   *Exit*

FALSTAFF Well,
To the latter end of a fray, and the beginning of a feast
Fits a dull fighter and a keen guest.   *Exit*

Enter Hotspur, Worcester, Douglas, Vernon   IV.3

HOTSPUR
We'll fight with him tonight.

WORCESTER   It may not be.

DOUGLAS
You give him then advantage.

125

VERNON   Not a whit.

HOTSPUR

Why say you so, looks he not for supply?

VERNON

So do we.

HOTSPUR   His is certain, ours is doubtful.

WORCESTER

Good cousin, be advised, stir not tonight.

VERNON

Do not, my lord.

DOUGLAS   You do not counsel well.

You speak it out of fear and cold heart.

VERNON

Do me no slander, Douglas. By my life,
And I dare well maintain it with my life,
If well-respected honour bid me on,
I hold as little counsel with weak fear
As you, my lord, or any Scot that this day lives.
Let it be seen tomorrow in the battle
Which of us fears.

DOUGLAS   Yea, or tonight.

VERNON   Content.

HOTSPUR

Tonight, say I.

VERNON

Come, come, it may not be. I wonder much,
Being men of such great leading as you are,
That you foresee not what impediments
Drag back our expedition. Certain horse
Of my cousin Vernon's are not yet come up,
Your uncle Worcester's horse came but today,
And now their pride and mettle is asleep,
Their courage with hard labour tame and dull,
That not a horse is half the half himself.

HOTSPUR

So are the horses of the enemy
In general journey-bated and brought low.
The better part of ours are full of rest.

WORCESTER

The number of the King exceedeth ours.
For God's sake, cousin, stay till all come in.
The trumpet sounds a parley
Enter Sir Walter Blunt

BLUNT

I come with gracious offers from the King,   30
If you vouchsafe me hearing and respect.

HOTSPUR

Welcome, Sir Walter Blunt: and would to God
You were of our determination!
Some of us love you well, and even those some
Envy your great deservings and good name,
Because you are not of our quality,
But stand against us like an enemy.

BLUNT

And God defend but still I should stand so,
So long as out of limit and true rule
You stand against anointed majesty.   40
But to my charge. The King hath sent to know
The nature of your griefs, and whereupon
You conjure from the breast of civil peace
Such bold hostility, teaching his duteous land
Audacious cruelty. If that the King
Have any way your good deserts forgot,
Which he confesseth to be manifold,
He bids you name your griefs, and with all speed
You shall have your desires with interest
And pardon absolute for yourself, and these   50
Herein misled by your suggestion.

HOTSPUR

The King is kind, and well we know the King
Knows at what time to promise, when to pay.
My father, and my uncle, and myself
Did give him that same royalty he wears,
And when he was not six-and-twenty strong,
Sick in the world's regard, wretched and low,
A poor unminded outlaw sneaking home,
My father gave him welcome to the shore.
60 And when he heard him swear and vow to God
He came but to be Duke of Lancaster,
To sue his livery, and beg his peace
With tears of innocency and terms of zeal,
My father, in kind heart and pity moved,
Swore him assistance, and performed it too.
Now when the lords and barons of the realm
Perceived Northumberland did lean to him,
The more and less came in with cap and knee,
Met him in boroughs, cities, villages,
70 Attended him on bridges, stood in lanes,
Laid gifts before him, proffered him their oaths,
Gave him their heirs as pages, followed him
Even at the heels in golden multitudes.
He presently, as greatness knows itself,
Steps me a little higher than his vow
Made to my father while his blood was poor
Upon the naked shore at Ravenspurgh;
And now forsooth takes on him to reform
Some certain edicts and some strait decrees
80 That lie too heavy on the commonwealth,
Cries out upon abuses, seems to weep
Over his country's wrongs – and by this face,
This seeming brow of justice, did he win
The hearts of all that he did angle for.

Proceeded further – cut me off the heads
Of all the favourites that the absent King
In deputation left behind him here,
When he was personal in the Irish war.

BLUNT

Tut, I came not to hear this.

HOTSPUR   Then to the point.

In short time after he deposed the King,   90
Soon after that deprived him of his life,
And in the neck of that tasked the whole state.
To make that worse, suffered his kinsman March –
Who is, if every owner were well placed,
Indeed his King – to be engaged in Wales,
There without ransom to lie forfeited.
Disgraced me in my happy victories,
Sought to entrap me by intelligence,
Rated mine uncle from the Council-board,
In rage dismissed my father from the court,   100
Broke oath on oath, committed wrong on wrong,
And in conclusion drove us to seek out
This head of safety, and withal to pry
Into his title, the which we find
Too indirect for long continuance.

BLUNT

Shall I return this answer to the King?

HOTSPUR

Not so, Sir Walter. We'll withdraw awhile.
Go to the King, and let there be impawned
Some surety for a safe return again,
And in the morning early shall mine uncle   110
Bring him our purposes – and so, farewell.

BLUNT

I would you would accept of grace and love.

IV.3–4

HOTSPUR
And may be so we shall.

BLUNT   Pray God you do.   *Exeunt*

IV.4   *Enter the Archbishop of York and Sir Michael*

ARCHBISHOP
Hie, good Sir Michael, bear this sealèd brief
With wingèd haste to the Lord Marshal,
This to my cousin Scroop, and all the rest
To whom they are directed. If you knew
How much they do import you would make haste.

SIR MICHAEL
My good lord,
I guess their tenor.

ARCHBISHOP   Like enough you do.
Tomorrow, good Sir Michael, is a day
Wherein the fortune of ten thousand men
10 Must bide the touch. For, sir, at Shrewsbury,
As I am truly given to understand,
The King with mighty and quick-raisèd power
Meets with Lord Harry, and I fear, Sir Michael,
What with the sickness of Northumberland,
Whose power was in the first proportion,
And what with Owen Glendower's absence thence,
Who with them was a rated sinew too,
And comes not in, o'er-ruled by prophecies,
I fear the power of Percy is too weak
20 To wage an instant trial with the King.

SIR MICHAEL
Why, my good lord, you need not fear,
There is Douglas, and Lord Mortimer.

ARCHBISHOP
No, Mortimer is not there.

SIR MICHAEL

But there is Mordake, Vernon, Lord Harry Percy,
And there is my Lord of Worcester, and a head
Of gallant warriors, noble gentlemen.

ARCHBISHOP

And so there is. But yet the King hath drawn
The special head of all the land together.
The Prince of Wales, Lord John of Lancaster,
The nóble Westmorland, and warlike Blunt,   30
And many more corrivals and dear men
Of estimation and command in arms.

SIR MICHAEL

Doubt not, my lord, they shall be well opposed.

ARCHBISHOP

I hope no less, yet needful 'tis to fear,
And to prevent the worst, Sir Michael, speed.
For if Lord Percy thrive not, ere the King
Dismiss his power he means to visit us,
For he hath heard of our confederacy,
And 'tis but wisdom to make strong against him.
Therefore make haste – I must go write again   40
To other friends. And so, farewell, Sir Michael.

Exeunt

*

Enter the King, Prince of Wales, Lord John V.1
of Lancaster, Sir Walter Blunt, Falstaff

KING HENRY

How bloodily the sun begins to peer
Above yon bulky hill! The day looks pale
At his distemperature.

PRINCE HAL   The southern wind

131

Doth play the trumpet to his purposes,
And by his hollow whistling in the leaves
Foretells a tempest and a blustering day.

KING HENRY

Then with the losers let it sympathize,
For nothing can seem foul to those that win.

The trumpet sounds
Enter Worcester and Vernon

How now, my Lord of Worcester! 'Tis not well

10 That you and I should meet upon such terms
As now we meet. You have deceived our trust,
And made us doff our easy robes of peace
To crush our old limbs in ungentle steel.
This is not well, my lord, this is not well.
What say you to it? Will you again unknit
The churlish knot of all-abhorrèd war,
And move in that obedient orb again
Where you did give a fair and natural light,
And be no more an exhaled meteor,

20 A prodigy of fear, and a portent
Of broachèd mischief to the unborn times?

WORCESTER

Hear me, my liege.
For mine own part I could be well content
To entertain the lag end of my life
With quiet hours. For I protest
I have not sought the day of this dislike.

KING HENRY

You have not sought it? How comes it, then?

FALSTAFF Rebellion lay in his way, and he found it.

PRINCE HAL Peace, chewet, peace!

WORCESTER

30 It pleased your majesty to turn your looks
Of favour from myself, and all our house,

132

And yet I must remember you, my lord,
We were the first and dearest of your friends.
For you my staff of office did I break
In Richard's time, and posted day and night
To meet you on the way, and kiss your hand,
When yet you were in place and in account
Nothing so strong and fortunate as I.
It was myself, my brother, and his son,
That brought you home, and boldly did outdare   40
The dangers of the time. You swore to us,
And you did swear that oath at Doncaster,
That you did nothing purpose 'gainst the state,
Nor claim no further than your new-fallen right,
The seat of Gaunt, dukedom of Lancaster.
To this we swore our aid. But in short space
It rained down fortune showering on your head,
And such a flood of greatness fell on you,
What with our help, what with the absent King,
What with the injuries of a wanton time,   50
The seeming sufferances that you had borne,
And the contrarious winds that held the King
So long in his unlucky Irish wars
That all in England did repute him dead.
And from this swarm of fair advantages
You took occasion to be quickly wooed
To gripe the general sway into your hand,
Forget your oath to us at Doncaster,
And being fed by us, you used us so
As that ungentle gull the cuckoo's bird   60
Useth the sparrow – did oppress our nest,
Grew by our feeding to so great a bulk
That even our love durst not come near your sight
For fear of swallowing. But with nimble wing
We were enforced for safety sake to fly

V.1

Out of your sight, and raise this present head,
Whereby we stand opposèd by such means
As you yourself have forged against yourself,
By unkind usage, dangerous countenance,
70 And violation of all faith and troth
Sworn to us in your younger enterprise.

KING HENRY

These things indeed you have articulate,
Proclaimed at market crosses, read in churches,
To face the garment of rebellion
With some fine colour that may please the eye
Of fickle changelings and poor discontents,
Which gape and rub the elbow at the news
Of hurlyburly innovation.
And never yet did insurrection want
80 Such water-colours to impaint his cause,
Nor moody beggars starving for a time
Of pell-mell havoc and confusion.

PRINCE HAL

In both your armies there is many a soul
Shall pay full dearly for this encounter
If once they join in trial. Tell your nephew,
The Prince of Wales doth join with all the world
In praise of Henry Percy. By my hopes,
This present enterprise set off his head,
I do not think a braver gentleman,
More active-valiant or more valiant-young,
More daring or more bold, is now alive
To grace this latter age with noble deeds.
For my part, I may speak it to my shame,
I have a truant been to chivalry,
And so I hear he doth account me too.
Yet this before my father's majesty –
I am content that he shall take the odds

134

Of his great name and estimation,
And will, to save the blood on either side, *Direct challenge*
Try fortune with him in a single fight. 100

KING HENRY

And, Prince of Wales, so dare we venture thee, *Saying no*
Albeit considerations infinite
Do make against it. No, good Worcester, no,
We love our people well, even those we love
That are misled upon your cousin's part,
And will they take the offer of our grace,
Both he, and they, and you, yea, every man
Shall be my friend again, and I'll be his.
So tell your cousin, and bring me word
What he will do. But if he will not yield, 110
Rebuke and dread correction wait on us,
And they shall do their office. So, be gone.
We will not now be troubled with reply.
We offer fair, take it advisedly.

Exeunt Worcester and Vernon

PRINCE HAL

It will not be accepted, on my life.
The Douglas and the Hotspur both together
Are confident against the world in arms.

KING HENRY

Hence, therefore, every leader to his charge, *Could mean regardless.*
For on their answer will we set on them, *or say no they will*
And God befriend us as our cause is just! 120 *accept it - they will deceive*

Exeunt all but the Prince and Falstaff

FALSTAFF Hal, if thou see me down in the battle and
bestride me, so. 'Tis a point of friendship.

PRINCE HAL Nothing but a Colossus can do thee that
friendship. Say thy prayers, and farewell.

FALSTAFF I would 'twere bed-time, Hal, and all well. *Doesn't*

PRINCE HAL Why, thou owest God a death. *Exit* *to get a jolt*

135

FALSTAFF 'Tis not due yet – I would be loath to pay him
before his day. What need I be so forward with him that
calls not on me? Well, 'tis no matter, honour pricks
130 me on. Yea, but how if honour prick me off when I
come on, how then? Can honour set to a leg? No. Or
an arm? No. Or take away the grief of a wound? No.
Honour hath no skill in surgery then? No. What is
honour? A word. What is in that word honour? What is
that honour? Air. A trim reckoning! Who hath it? He
that died a'Wednesday. Doth he feel it? No. Doth he
hear it? No. 'Tis insensible, then? Yea, to the dead.
But will it not live with the living? No. Why? Detraction will not suffer it. Therefore I'll none of it. Honour
140 is a mere scutcheon – and so ends my catechism. *Exit*

V.2   *Enter Worcester and Sir Richard Vernon*

WORCESTER
    O no, my nephew must not know, Sir Richard,
    The liberal and kind offer of the King.

VERNON
    'Twere best he did.

WORCESTER   Then are we all undone.
    It is not possible, it cannot be,
    The King should keep his word in loving us.
    He will suspect us still, and find a time
    To punish this offence in other faults.
    Supposition all our lives shall be stuck full of eyes,
    For treason is but trusted like the fox,
10 Who, never so tame, so cherished and locked up,
    Will have a wild trick of his ancestors.
    Look how we can or sad or merrily,
    Interpretation will misquote our looks,
    And we shall feed like oxen at a stall,

The better cherished still the nearer death.
My nephew's trespass may be well forgot,
It hath the excuse of youth and heat of blood,
And an adopted name of privilege –
A hare-brained Hotspur, governed by a spleen.
All his offences live upon my head   20
And on his father's. We did train him on,
And, his corruption being taken from us,
We as the spring of all shall pay for all.
Therefore, good cousin, let not Harry know
In any case the offer of the King.

VERNON
Deliver what you will; I'll say 'tis so.
Here comes your cousin.
     Enter Hotspur and Douglas

HOTSPUR   My uncle is returned;
Deliver up my Lord of Westmorland.
Uncle, what news?

WORCESTER
The King will bid you battle presently.   30

DOUGLAS
Defy him by the Lord of Westmorland.

HOTSPUR
Lord Douglas, go you and tell him so.

DOUGLAS
Marry, and shall, and very willingly.   *Exit*

WORCESTER
There is no seeming mercy in the King.

HOTSPUR
Did you beg any? God forbid!

WORCESTER
I told him gently of our grievances,
Of his oath-breaking – which he mended thus,
By now forswearing that he is forsworn.

He calls us rebels, traitors, and will scourge
40   With haughty arms this hateful name in us.
    Enter Douglas

DOUGLAS

Arm, gentlemen, to arms! For I have thrown
A brave defiance in King Henry's teeth,
And Westmorland that was engaged did bear it,
Which cannot choose but bring him quickly on.

WORCESTER

The Prince of Wales stepped forth before the King,
And, nephew, challenged you to single fight.

HOTSPUR

O, would the quarrel lay upon our heads,
And that no man might draw short breath today
But I and Harry Monmouth! Tell me, tell me,
50   How showed his tasking? Seemed it in contempt?

VERNON

No, by my soul, I never in my life
Did hear a challenge urged more modestly,
Unless a brother should a brother dare
To gentle exercise and proof of arms.
He gave you all the duties of a man,
Trimmed up your praises with a princely tongue,
Spoke your deserving like a chronicle,
Making you ever better than his praise
By still dispraising praise valued with you,
60   And, which became him like a prince indeed,
He made a blushing cital of himself,
And chid his truant youth with such a grace
As if he mastered there a double spirit
Of teaching and of learning instantly.
There did he pause. But let me tell the world –
If he outlive the envy of this day,
England did never owe so sweet a hope

So much misconstrued in his wantonness.

HOTSPUR
Cousin, I think thou art enamourèd
On his follies! Never did I hear   70
Of any prince so wild a liberty.
But be he as he will, yet once ere night
I will embrace him with a soldier's arm,
That he shall shrink under my courtesy.
Arm, arm with speed! And fellows, soldiers, friends,
Better consider what you have to do
Than I that have not well the gift of tongue
Can lift your blood up with persuasion.
          Enter a Messenger

FIRST MESSENGER My lord, here are letters for you.

HOTSPUR I cannot read them now.   80
O gentlemen, the time of life is short!
To spend that shortness basely were too long
If life did ride upon a dial's point,
Still ending at the arrival of an hour.
And if we live, we live to tread on kings,
If die, brave death when princes die with us!
Now, for our consciences, the arms are fair
When the intent of bearing them is just.
          Enter another Messenger

SECOND MESSENGER
My lord, prepare, the King comes on apace.

HOTSPUR
I thank him that he cuts me from my tale,   90
For I profess not talking. Only this –
Let each man do his best. And here draw I
A sword whose temper I intend to stain
With the best blood that I can meet withal
In the adventure of this perilous day.
Now, Esperance! Percy! and set on!

Sound all the lofty instruments of war,
And by that music let us all embrace,
For, heaven to earth, some of us never shall
100 A second time do such a courtesy.

Here they embrace, the trumpets sound

Exeunt

V.3   *The King enters with his power. Alarum to the battle.*
Then enter Douglas, and Sir Walter Blunt, disguised
as the King

BLUNT
What is thy name that in the battle thus
Thou crossest me? What honour dost thou seek
Upon my head?

DOUGLAS   Know then my name is Douglas,
And I do haunt thee in the battle thus
Because some tell me that thou art a king.

BLUNT
They tell thee true.

DOUGLAS
The Lord of Stafford dear today hath bought
Thy likeness, for instead of thee, King Harry,
This sword hath ended him: so shall it thee
10 Unless thou yield thee as my prisoner.

BLUNT
I was not born a yielder, thou proud Scot,
And thou shalt find a king that will revenge
Lord Stafford's death.

They fight; Douglas kills Blunt
Then enter Hotspur

HOTSPUR
O Douglas, hadst thou fought at Holmedon thus
I never had triumphed upon a Scot.

DOUGLAS

  All's done, all's won. Here breathless lies the King.

HOTSPUR Where?

DOUGLAS Here.

HOTSPUR

  This, Douglas? No, I know this face full well.

  A gallant knight he was, his name was Blunt,   20

  Semblably furnished like the King himself.

DOUGLAS

  A fool go with thy soul, whither it goes!

  A borrowed title hast thou bought too dear.

  Why didst thou tell me that thou wert a king?

HOTSPUR

  The King hath many marching in his coats.

DOUGLAS

  Now, by my sword, I will kill all his coats!

  I'll murder all his wardrobe, piece by piece,

  Until I meet the King.

HOTSPUR   Up and away!

  Our soldiers stand full fairly for the day.   *Exeunt*

    Alarum. Enter Falstaff alone

FALSTAFF Though I could scape shot-free at London, I 30
fear the shot here, here's no scoring but upon the pate.
Soft! Who are you? Sir Walter Blunt – there's honour
for you! Here's no vanity! I am as hot as molten lead,
and as heavy too. God keep lead out of me, I need no
more weight than mine own bowels. I have led my
ragamuffins where they are peppered. There's not three
of my hundred-and-fifty left alive – and they are for the
town's end, to beg during life. But who comes here?

    Enter the Prince

PRINCE HAL

  What, standest thou idle here? Lend me thy sword.

  Many a nobleman lies stark and stiff   40

Under the hoofs of vaunting enemies,
Whose deaths are yet unrevenged. I prithee
Lend me thy sword.

FALSTAFF O Hal, I prithee give me leave to breathe
awhile. Turk Gregory never did such deeds in arms as I
have done this day. I have paid Percy, I have made him
sure.

PRINCE HAL
He is indeed, and living to kill thee.
I prithee lend me thy sword.

50 FALSTAFF Nay, before God, Hal, if Percy be alive thou
gets not my sword, but take my pistol if thou wilt.

PRINCE HAL Give it me. What, is it in the case?

FALSTAFF Ay, Hal, 'tis hot, 'tis hot. There's that will
sack a city.

The Prince draws it out, and finds it to be a bottle of sack

PRINCE HAL
What, is it a time to jest and dally now?
He throws the bottle at him   *Exit*

FALSTAFF Well, if Percy be alive, I'll pierce him. If he do
come in my way, so. If he do not, if I come in his
willingly, let him make a carbonado of me. I like not
such grinning honour as Sir Walter hath. Give me life,
60 which if I can save, so. If not, honour comes unlooked
for, and there's an end.   *Exit*

V.4   *Alarum. Excursions. Enter the King, the Prince, Lord
               John of Lancaster, Earl of Westmorland*

KING HENRY
I prithee, Harry, withdraw thyself, thou bleedest too
much.

Lord John of Lancaster, go you with him.

LANCASTER

Not I, my lord, unless I did bleed too.

PRINCE HAL

I beseech your majesty, make up,
Lest your retirement do amaze your friends.

KING HENRY

I will do so. My Lord of Westmorland,
Lead him to his tent.

WESTMORLAND

Come, my lord, I'll lead you to your tent.

PRINCE HAL

Lead me, my lord? I do not need your help,
And God forbid a shallow scratch should drive   10
The Prince of Wales from such a field as this,
Where stained nobility lies trodden on,
And rebels' arms triumph in massacres!

LANCASTER

We breathe too long: come, cousin Westmorland,
Our duty this way lies: for God's sake, come.

          Exeunt Lancaster and Westmorland

PRINCE HAL

By God, thou hast deceived me, Lancaster,
I did not think thee lord of such a spirit:
Before, I loved thee as a brother, John,
But now I do respect thee as my soul.

KING HENRY

I saw him hold Lord Percy at the point   20
With lustier maintenance than I did look for
Of such an ungrown warrior.

PRINCE HAL   O, this boy

Lends mettle to us all!   *Exit*

    Enter Douglas

DOUGLAS

Another king! They grow like Hydra's heads.
I am the Douglas, fatal to all those
That wear those colours on them. What art thou
That counterfeitest the person of a king?

KING HENRY

The King himself, who, Douglas, grieves at heart
So many of his shadows thou hast met,
And not the very King. I have two boys
Seek Percy and thyself about the field,
But seeing thou fallest on me so luckily
I will assay thee, and defend thyself.

DOUGLAS

I fear thou art another counterfeit,
And yet, in faith, thou bearest thee like a king –
But mine I am sure thou art, whoe'er thou be,
And thus I win thee.
They fight, the King being in danger; enter
Prince of Wales

PRINCE HAL

Hold up thy head, vile Scot, or thou art like
Never to hold it up again! The spirits
Of valiant Shirley, Stafford, Blunt are in my arms.
It is the Prince of Wales that threatens thee,
Who never promiseth but he means to pay.
They fight; Douglas flees
Cheerly, my lord, how fares your grace?
Sir Nicholas Gawsey hath for succour sent,
And so hath Clifton – I'll to Clifton straight.

KING HENRY

Stay and breathe a while.
Thou hast redeemed thy lost opinion,
And showed thou makest some tender of my life

In this fair rescue thou hast brought to me.

PRINCE HAL

O God, they did me too much injury　　　　　　　　50
That ever said I hearkened for your death.
If it were so, I might have let alone
The insulting hand of Douglas over you,
Which would have been as speedy in your end
As all the poisonous potions in the world,
And saved the treacherous labour of your son.

KING HENRY

Make up to Clifton, I'll to Sir Nicholas Gawsey. *Exit*
　　Enter Hotspur

HOTSPUR

If I mistake not, thou art Harry Monmouth.

PRINCE HAL

Thou speakest as if I would deny my name.

HOTSPUR

My name is Harry Percy.

PRINCE HAL　　　　　　　　Why then I see　　　　　　60
A very valiant rebel of the name.
I am the Prince of Wales, and think not, Percy,
To share with me in glory any more.
Two stars keep not their motion in one sphere,
Nor can one England brook a double reign
Of Harry Percy and the Prince of Wales.

HOTSPUR

Nor shall it, Harry, for the hour is come
To end the one of us; and would to God
Thy name in arms were now as great as mine.

PRINCE HAL

I'll make it greater ere I part from thee,　　　　　70
And all the budding honours on thy crest
I'll crop to make a garland for my head.

145

V.4

HOTSPUR

I can no longer brook thy vanities.

They fight
Enter Falstaff

FALSTAFF Well said, Hal! To it, Hal! Nay, you shall find
no boy's play here, I can tell you.

*Enter Douglas; he fighteth with Falstaff, who falls
down as if he were dead*

Exit Douglas

The Prince mortally wounds Hotspur

HOTSPUR

O Harry, thou hast robbed me of my youth!
I better brook the loss of brittle life
Than those proud titles thou hast won of me.
They wound my thoughts worse than thy sword my
flesh.

80 But thoughts, the slaves of life, and life, time's fool,
And time, that takes survey of all the world,
Must have a stop. O, I could prophesy,
But that the earthy and cold hand of death
Lies on my tongue. No, Percy, thou art dust,
And food for –

He dies

PRINCE HAL

For worms, brave Percy. Fare thee well, great heart!
Ill-weaved ambition, how much art thou shrunk.
When that this body did contain a spirit,
A kingdom for it was too small a bound.

90 But now two paces of the vilest earth
Is room enough. This earth that bears thee dead
Bears not alive so stout a gentleman.
If thou wert sensible of courtesy
I should not make so dear a show of zeal,
But let my favours hide thy mangled face,

146

And even in thy behalf I'll thank myself
For doing these fair rites of tenderness.
Adieu, and take thy praise with thee to heaven!
Thy ignominy sleep with thee in the grave,
But not remembered in thy epitaph.   100

He spieth Falstaff on the ground
What, old acquaintance, could not all this flesh
Keep in a little life? Poor Jack, farewell!
I could have better spared a better man.
O, I should have a heavy miss of thee
If I were much in love with vanity.
Death hath not struck so fat a deer today,
Though many dearer, in this bloody fray.
Embowelled will I see thee by and by,
Till then in blood by noble Percy lie.   *Exit*

Falstaff riseth up
FALSTAFF Embowelled? If thou embowel me today, I'll   110
give you leave to powder me and eat me too tomorrow.
'Sblood, 'twas time to counterfeit, or that hot termagant
Scot had paid me, scot and lot too. Counterfeit? I lie,
I am no counterfeit. To die is to be a counterfeit, for he
is but the counterfeit of a man who hath not the life of
a man. But to counterfeit dying, when a man thereby
liveth, is to be no counterfeit, but the true and perfect
image of life indeed. The better part of valour is dis-
cretion, in the which better part I have saved my life.
Zounds, I am afraid of this gunpowder Percy, though he   120
be dead. How if he should counterfeit too and rise? By
my faith, I am afraid he would prove the better counterfeit. Therefore I'll make him sure, yea, and I'll swear I
killed him. Why may not he rise as well as I? Nothing
confutes me but eyes, and nobody sees me. Therefore,
sirrah (*stabbing him*), with a new wound in your thigh,
come you along with me.

He takes up Hotspur on his back
Enter Prince and John of Lancaster

PRINCE HAL
  Come, brother John, full bravely hast thou fleshed
  Thy maiden sword.

LANCASTER   But soft, whom have we here?
130 Did you not tell me this fat man was dead?

PRINCE HAL
  I did, I saw him dead,
  Breathless and bleeding on the ground. Art thou alive?
  Or is it fantasy that plays upon our eyesight?
  I prithee speak, we will not trust our eyes
  Without our ears. Thou art not what thou seemest.

FALSTAFF No, that's certain, I am not a double-man. But
  if I be not Jack Falstaff, then am I a Jack. There is
  Percy!

        He throws the body down

  If your father will do me any honour, sò. If not, let him
140 kill the next Percy himself. I look to be either earl or
  duke, I can assure you.

PRINCE HAL Why, Percy I killed myself, and saw thee
  dead.

FALSTAFF Didst thou? Lord, Lord, how this world is
  given to lying! I grant you I was down, and out of
  breath, and so was he, but we rose both at an instant,
  and fought a long hour by Shrewsbury clock. If I may
  be believed, so. If not, let them that should reward
  valour bear the sin upon their own heads. I'll take it
150 upon my death, I gave him this wound in the thigh. If
  the man were alive, and would deny it, zounds, I would
  make him eat a piece of my sword.

LANCASTER This is the strangest tale that ever I heard.

PRINCE HAL This is the strangest fellow, brother John.
  Come, bring your luggage nobly on your back.

(*Aside to Falstaff*) For my part, if a lie may do thee
    grace,
I'll gild it with the happiest terms I have.
    A retreat is sounded
The trumpet sounds retreat, the day is ours.
Come, brother, let us to the highest of the field,
To see what friends are living, who are dead.   160
             Exeunt Prince of Wales and Lancaster

FALSTAFF I'll follow, as they say, for reward. He that
rewards me, God reward him! If I do grow great, I'll
grow less, for I'll purge, and leave sack, and live
cleanly as a nobleman should do.
                    Exit, bearing off the body

    The trumpets sound. Enter the King, Prince of Wales, V.5
    Lord John of Lancaster, Earl of Westmorland, with
    Worcester and Vernon prisoners

KING HENRY
Thus ever did rebellion find rebuke.
Ill-spirited Worcester, did not we send grace,
Pardon, and terms of love to all of you?
And wouldst thou turn our offers contrary?
Misuse the tenor of thy kinsman's trust?
Three knights upon our party slain today,
A noble earl, and many a creature else
Had been alive this hour
If like a Christian thou hadst truly borne
Betwixt our armies true intelligence.   10

WORCESTER
What I have done my safety urged me to,
And I embrace this fortune patiently,
Since not to be avoided it falls on me.

KING HENRY

Bear Worcester to the death, and Vernon too.
Other offenders we will pause upon.

Exeunt Worcester and Vernon

How goes the field?

PRINCE HAL

The noble Scot, Lord Douglas, when he saw
The fortune of the day quite turned from him,
The noble Percy slain, and all his men
20 Upon the foot of fear, fled with the rest,
And falling from a hill he was so bruised
That the pursuers took him. At my tent
The Douglas is – and I beseech your grace
I may dispose of him.

KING HENRY   With all my heart.

PRINCE HAL

Then, brother John of Lancaster, to you
This honourable bounty shall belong.
Go to the Douglas and deliver him
Up to his pleasure, ransomless and free.
His valours shown upon our crests today
30 Have taught us how to cherish such high deeds,
Even in the bosom of our adversaries.

LANCASTER

I thank your grace for this high courtesy,
Which I shall give away immediately.

KING HENRY

Then this remains, that we divide our power.
You, son John, and my cousin Westmorland,
Towards York shall bend you with your dearest speed
To meet Northumberland and the prelate Scroop,
Who, as we hear, are busily in arms.
Myself and you, son Harry, will towards Wales,
40 To fight with Glendower and the Earl of March.

Rebellion in this land shall lose his sway,
Meeting the check of such another day,
And since this business so fair is done,
Let us not leave till all our own be won.   *Exeunt*

COMMENTARY

REFERENCES to plays by Shakespeare not yet available in the New Penguin Shakespeare are to Peter Alexander's edition of the *Complete Works*, London 1951.

I.1   Shakespeare does not give locations for any of the scenes in *1 Henry IV* and the first Quarto (Q1) is not even divided into scenes and Acts. Such divisions, and insistence on places of action, impose a formal and rigid structure which the play does not have. The transition from scene to scene in Elizabethan drama was rapid and informal and many modern productions have, with advantage, adopted a similar method of presenting plays of this period. What we need to know about location in *1 Henry IV* is told us in the play itself, either by direct statement – thus we know the robbery takes place at Gad's Hill and that the character Gadshill 'lies tonight in Rochester' (I.2.127–8), indicating the location of II.1 – or, less precisely, by the style of the language. Thus we can gather as much as we need to know about the situation of the action from the play itself. It has been customary in the past, particularly in the eighteenth century, for editors to obtain possible locations from external sources. Thus III.1 has sometimes been placed in the Archdeacon's House in Bangor, North Wales, because the historian Holinshed records that the 'tripartite indenture' was sealed there by the principal rebels. Such particularity is perhaps more distracting than helpful.

1   *we* (the nation and the King himself)

2   *frighted peace to pant*. Peace, like an animal terrified in the chase, needs to recover strength. The play concerning the deposition of Henry's predecessor, *Richard II*, concluded with the outbreak of civil strife and reports of the unruly behaviour of Henry's son, Prince Hal. These events are recalled in this opening scene.

3   *accents* words, discussion
       broils battles, warfare

4   *strands* shores, lands

5–6 *No more the thirsty entrance of this soil | Shall daub her lips with her own children's blood*. The fratricidal strife following the deposition of Richard is foretold by Carlisle in *Richard II*, IV.1.115–49, and by Richard himself, III.3.85–100. The King concludes his prophecy with a warning that seems from Henry's statement to have been fulfilled:

> *Ten thousand bloody crowns of mothers' sons*
> *Shall . . . bedew*
> *Her pastor's grass with faithful English blood.*

The idea of the earth as a thirsty mouth may have been suggested to Shakespeare by Genesis 4.11, where the earth is said to have 'opened her mouth to receive thy brother's blood from thy hand'. (The quotation, in a modernized spelling, is taken from the Bishops' Bible, 1568 – the version known to Shakespeare.)

6   *daub* paint, defile

7   *trenching* cutting, wounding

8   *flowerets*. It has been customary to indicate elisions by an apostrophe in texts of Shakespeare produced since the eighteenth century. Thus the 'flourets' of the first Quarto has been represented as 'flow'rets'. With the exception of 'e'er' and 'ne'er', which have established for themselves an existence of their own, at least in verse, this practice has not been followed in this edition. A major virtue of the English language is its infinite

variety of stress. It is possible to vary the number of
syllables in the iambic pentameter (a line not originally
designed for the English language) to give a wide range
of effects. This Shakespeare knew and any competent
actor can demonstrate. It has been thought more helpful to a modern reader to print the words fully and to
rely upon actors and actresses to give the amount
of stress and the degree of elision necessary to the
line as required by the context. (See also note on
V.2.32.)

9   *opposèd eyes* (the eyes of conflicting forces. These, after
being likened to meteors, are not thought of simply as
gazing at each other but actually meeting in the
'furious close of civil butchery'.)

10   *meteors of a troubled heaven.* Shakespeare frequently
relates human action to cosmic harmony and dis-
turbance. Meteors had for Elizabethans something of
the mystery and variable properties that some people
nowadays associate with unidentified flying objects of
other kinds. They might be associated with rain, hail,
snow, wind, thunder, or lightning, and they suggested
the involvement of other worlds in human affairs. (See
also the note on I.2.195.)

12   *intestine* internal

13   *close* engagement

19   *As far as to the sepulchre of Christ.* At the very end of
Richard II, Henry vows to 'make a voyage to the Holy
Land | To wash this blood off from my guilty hand' for
the part he played in Richard's murder. Shakespeare
here recalls that vow but in doing so brings the proposed crusade forward from the end of Henry's reign,
when plans were made for this expedition, to the early
months of his reign. This strengthens the sense of
continuation from the end of Richard's reign, and as
line 28 of this scene reveals, Shakespeare seemed
anxious to avoid there seeming to be too great a gap in
time between the two plays, presumably to be able to

stress the relationship, dramatic and historic, of cause and effect.

21 *impressèd* conscripted, bound (by his vow)

28 *twelve month old*. Two years had, in fact, elapsed between Richard's murder in February 1400 and the Battle of Holmedon.

29 *bootless* useless

30 *Therefor* for that purpose

31 *Of* from

33 *dear expedience* cherished and urgent expedition

34 *hot in question* urgently before us, actively debated

35 *limits of the charge set down* many duties and commands had been assigned

36 *all athwart* across (our purpose), thwartingly

37 *post* messenger

38 *Mortimer.* There were two Edmund Mortimers: one, Hotspur's brother-in-law; the other, that Edmund's nephew. These two men were confused by Shakespeare (and see also the notes to I.3.79, 83).

40 *irregular and wild Glendower.* The description hardly accords with the man who, he tells us, 'was trained up in the English court' and was capable of framing 'to the harp | Many an English ditty lovely well'!
    irregular (as in guerrilla warfare, and possibly also glancing at Glendower's conduct)

41 *rude* uncivilized

47 *broil* quarrel, strife

52 *Holy-rood day* Holy-cross day (14 September)

53 *Archibald.* Douglas's full title was Archibald, 4th Earl of Douglas.

55 *Holmedon.* That is, Humbleton, Northumberland, though the battle is also known as Homildon Hill. It took place nearly three months after Mortimer's defeat but Shakespeare brings the events together for dramatic effect. (Curiously the Scots were beaten at Nesbit on the day Mortimer lost to Glendower.)

57 *artillery.* This included catapults, slings, bows, and

arrows, although at II.3.55 basilisks, cannon, and culverin are mentioned.

58   *shape of likelihood* the way events were shaping

63   *Sir Walter Blunt*. The news was brought by Nicholas Merbury, who received a grant of £40 a year for this service. By assuming Blunt to be the messenger (no name is given by Holinshed), Shakespeare is able to draw attention to the King's dependence on Blunt, which will be of some importance in IV.3 and V.3. (See also the note to IV.3.30.)

66   *smooth* pleasant

68   *two-and-twenty* (three-and-twenty according to Holinshed)

69   *Balked in their own blood*. A balk is the ridge left between two furrows in ploughing. The bodies fell in blood-stained rows. Compare the use of 'trenching war channel her fields' at line 7.

71   *Mordake*. Murdoch Stewart was the eldest son of Robert, Duke of Albany, Regent of Scotland. Shakespeare's error stems from a misplaced comma in his source, Holinshed.

73   *Menteith* (not a separate individual but one of Mordake's titles)

75   *A gallant prize*. As we are told that Blunt left the battle at its climax – the 'pride of their contention' – it is a little odd that he should know the final outcome in such detail. It is also a little strange that the King should have spoken of the urgent preparations for an expedition to the Holy Land, though it is now evident he knew of trouble in the North. At first sight this might seem like duplicity but, though Hotspur had refused to give up his prisoners, the King could hardly have expected that this would lead to civil war. It is the tidings from Wales, which the King did not know, which cause him to break off the crusade (as is precisely stated in lines 47–8). This victory is, then, a gallant prize, securing rather than threatening the

safety of the country (that is, England, not Great Britain). By lines 99–101 Percy has become an excuse for delay.

82   *minion* darling

86–7   *exchanged* | *In cradle-clothes our children.* Shakespeare frequently makes radical changes in the ages of his characters. At this time, Hotspur was thirty-eight, Henry, three years younger, and Hal, only fifteen. What is of greater interest than these minor distortions of fact is the way in which Shakespeare uses age. He not only makes comparison frequently between youth and age, but will make some characters seem to age more rapidly than others. Richard II was only three months older than Henry IV, yet the former ages much more rapidly than the latter in *Richard II*, and Henry seems to age quickly in the year or two separating that play and *1 Henry IV*.

90   *coz* cousin (though often used loosely, as here).

91   *The prisoners.* Hotspur was entitled to retain all prisoners except those of the blood royal and it was, therefore, only Mordake who had to be surrendered.

97   *prune* preen (a term from falconry)

99   *I have sent for him to answer this.* According to Holinshed, Hotspur and his father came of their own accord to Windsor to outface the King. Shakespeare makes Henry seem to have the power to command their presence.

106   *out of anger can be utterèd* can be said in public in anger

I.2   Shakespeare does not state a location for this scene and it has at various times since the eighteenth century been placed in an apartment of the Prince's, in the palace, in a room in a tavern, before a tavern, and in the street. It has also been suggested that Hal should engage in some silent stage-business as he 'discovers' Falstaff asleep within the inner stage – a curtained-off recess. What is much more important than location is that Hal and Falstaff should be seen and heard together, without the intervention of their cronies, so that the audience can gauge the nature of Hal's association with Falstaff.

2   *fat-witted* thick-witted

3   *sack.* The precise nature of Falstaff's wine is a matter of dispute. It was probably a generic term for sweet white wines such as sherry and canary (which are confused in response to a cry for sack in a play by Thomas Heywood and William Rowley called *Fortune by Land and Sea*).

4-5   *thou hast forgotten to demand that truly which thou wouldst truly know.* Time for Falstaff is measured by sack and capons and as time is thus meaningless to him, he has not asked about what really concerns him.

6   *What a devil hast thou to do with the time of the day?* Night is Falstaff's time, not day.

9   *leaping-houses* brothels

10   *flame-coloured taffeta.* Prostitutes were traditionally dressed in red taffeta.

11   *superfluous* needlessly concerned (with quibble on the meaning 'self-indulgent')

14   *go by* 'travel by' and 'tell time by'
        the seven stars the Pleiades (and possibly an inn sign)

15   *'by Phoebus, he, that wandering knight so fair'* (possibly a line from a ballad of the time)

17   *grace.* Three meanings are suggested here: refinement; the favour of God – divine grace; majesty. It is given a fourth meaning when Falstaff says, in lines 20–1, that Hal will not have sufficient grace (before food) as would precede so simple a meal as 'an egg and butter'.

22   *roundly* plainly (and perhaps referring to Falstaff's girth)

23   *Marry.* This was a very mild oath derived from the name of Christ's mother, Mary; it was of such mildness that when oaths were expunged from the Folio

edition, *Marry* was unaffected. Its force is no more
than the exclamatory use of 'why'.

24   *squires of the night's body* nobleman's attendants (with
a quibble on *night* to give the meaning 'knight', and
body, 'bawdy')

25   *thieves of the day's beauty*. The general sense is clear
here, but the precise sense a little awkward. Those who
work, or rob, at night waste (rather than steal) the day.
Perhaps they may be said to rob the day of its beauty
and what it has to offer – its 'booty'.

    Diana's foresters. Diana was goddess of chastity, the
moon, and hunting. Falstaff's concern is not with
chastity, needless to say, but with hunting by moon-
light, robbery.

26   *gentlemen of the shade* (an ironic description like that
used for a pirate – a gentleman of fortune – derived
perhaps from an honourable title such as Gentlemen
of the Chamber or Gentlemen-at-Arms)

    minions favourites

27   *of good government* orderly, and serving a good ruler

29   *countenance* (with a quibble on 'face' and 'patronage')

    steal (both 'rob' and 'go stealthily')

30   *it holds well* the simile is apt

31   *the moon's men*. It has been suggested that as Queen
Elizabeth was frequently described as Diana, this
reference might be to her favourites – whose fortunes
certainly ebbed and flowed.

35   *'Lay by!'* (a robber's or highwayman's command)

36   *'Bring in!'* (a demand for food and drink)

36–7   *as low an ebb as the foot of the ladder*. For the robber,
the ebb and flow of fortune is likened to the low point
of his end, the foot of the ladder leading up to the
gallows, and the high point of his end, the 'ridge', or
crossbar, from which the hangman will launch him
into eternity.

41   *Hybla*. Hybla Major, near the modern town of Melilli
in Sicily, was famous for its honey in classical times.

41–2   *old lad of the castle*. This is surely a pun on Falstaff's original name, Oldcastle (see Introduction, page 29), and a famous brothel of the time called The Castle.

42–3   *is not a buff jerkin a most sweet robe of durance*. A *buff jerkin* was a close-fitting, leather jacket worn by soldiers; *durance* means long-wearing. Durance can also mean imprisonment and it is the idea that he might end up in prison that makes Falstaff react as he does. In relating the buff jerkin and durance to the Hostess and Hyblaean honey in this way, Hal is being ironically critical of Falstaff's attitudes. Subtly, here and elsewhere, Shakespeare distinguishes the natures of the two characters one from another, making it clear that the Prince is not wholly involved in the ways of the world he has temporarily adopted.

44   *wag* habitual joker. The word is repeated in line 58 and this leads in to Falstaff's request regarding hanging. There is possibly a suggestion here of 'waghalter' – one destined to hang.

45   *quiddities* quibbles

47   *what a pox*. The exclamation is given a particular point by its venereal association with the 'Hostess of the tavern'. The prince's exclamation echoes Falstaff's 'What a plague' in the preceding line.

49   *called her to a reckoning* 'asked for the bill', and also, 'demanded that she give an account of herself' (with sexual implications)

59   *resolution* enterprise
       fubbed fobbed off, cheated

60   *old Father Antic the law*. An Antic was, in Tudor drama, a clown, and thus Falstaff makes himself ridiculous by speaking of the law in terms which describe himself.

63   *brave* fine

65–6   *thou shalt have the hanging of the thieves*. Falstaff takes this to mean that he will be made hangman but Hal presumably also implies that Falstaff shall suffer the fate of all thieves in those days, hanging.

68   *jumps* agrees

69   *court* (1) king's court (as a courtier); (2) courts of justice

71   *suits* preferment at court

72   *suits* the condemned man's clothing (to which the executioner was entitled)

73   *no lean wardrobe* (because there are plenty of hangings)
      'Sblood God's blood (an oath)

74   *gib cat* castrated male cat
      lugged baited

76   *drone of a Lincolnshire bagpipe*. This is a very puzzling reference. It is possible that Shakespeare is referring to the sound of frogs or bitterns, but the word *drone* is particularly inexact for their croaking and booming. There was probably no such instrument as a Lincolnshire bagpipe, though bagpipes seem to have been played on festive occasions in Lincolnshire and Lancashire and we have references to this practice in Shakespeare's time (one by the man who probably played Touchstone, Feste and Lear's Fool – Robert Armin). The only known bagpipe associated with an English county is the Northumbrian bagpipe, but this seems to have been developed a little later. Further, it is hardly melancholy and does not have an obtrusive drone. And had Shakespeare heard of this bagpipe he would surely have related it to Hotspur. A final possibility is that Shakespeare had in mind the drone of a long-winded speaker. 'Bagpipe' is recorded as being used with this meaning in 1603 (compare 'windbag').

77   *hare*. The hare was traditionally melancholic, but *hare* here also meant 'whore'.

78   *Moorditch* (a filthy channel between Bishopsgate and Cripplegate, traditionally associated with melancholy – and with, probably, a suggestion of venereal disease)

80   *comparative* abusive (one who compares adversely – see also III.2.67)

82   *vanity* worldly things (see note on V.3.33)

82–87   *I would to God . . . and in the street too*. Shakespeare has Falstaff imitate a Puritan divine.

82–3   *commodity* supply (literally, a means of raising money)

84   *rated* scolded, rebuked

88–9   *for wisdom cries out in the streets and no man regards it.* Proverbs 1.20: 'Wisdom crieth without, and putteth forth her voice in the streets'; and verse 24: 'Because I have called, and ye refused, I have stretched out my hand, and no man regarded.'

90   *damnable iteration* (the devil's capacity to quote the Scriptures)

94   *the wicked* (again in imitation of the current Puritan jargon)

95   *I must give over this life*. Oldcastle (Falstaff's original name – see Introduction, page 29) was a Lollard (follower of John Wycliffe) and thus a heretic. It is possible that there is an allusion here to the original Oldcastle. It might have been humour of this kind, as much as the name itself, to which Oldcastle's descendants objected.

100   *Zounds* God's wounds (an oath)
        an if

101   *baffle*. A knight who perjured himself was baffled, that is, degraded by being hanged upside down. An effigy, or the knight's shield, might be used in place of the knight himself.

104–5   *'Tis no sin for a man to labour in his vocation*. This text, much favoured by Elizabethan divines, was one which secular writers took much delight in perverting.

106   *Gadshill*. In *The Famous Victories of Henry the Fifth* (see Introduction, pages 29–30) the thief is hailed by Derrick in the second scene as 'Gads Hill': 'Whoop hollo! Now Gads Hill, knowest thou me?' When he is tried in the fourth scene 'for setting upon a poor Carrier upon Gads Hill in Kent, and having beaten and wounded the said Carrier, and taken his goods from him', he is called Cutbert Cutter. Shakespeare

takes as a proper name the nickname used in the second scene.

106–7   *set a match* planned a robbery

107   *merit* personal quality or good works (more frequently the latter) which entitle one to reward from God. In *Love's Labour's Lost* the Princess maintains that her beauty 'will be saved by merit' (IV.1.201).

109   *a true* an honest

112   *Sack – and Sugar.* To further sweeten sack (see note to line 3) was regarded as a sign of advancing years.

118   *He will give the devil his due.* The devil's due will be Falstaff himself – and in this way Falstaff will break no proverb.

121   *cozening* cheating

124   *Gad's Hill.* This was a place notorious for robberies, two miles from Rochester in Kent. It is after this place, where he practised his vocation, that the character Gadshill is named.

126   *vizards* masks

129   *Eastcheap.* This is the scene for II.4. A tavern in Eastcheap is referred to in *The Famous Victories of Henry the Fifth* but it is never named by Shakespeare. The traditional name, the Boar's Head, is, however, suggested in *2 Henry IV* when Hal asks after Falstaff: *Doth the old boar feed in the old frank?*, and Bardolph replies: *At the old place, my lord, in Eastcheap* (II.2.141).

132   *Yedward* Edward

134   *chops* fat cheeks

139   *royal* (with a quibble on the meaning 'a coin worth ten shillings')
        stand for (1) be worth; (2) make a fight for

150–54 *God give thee the spirit of persuasion ... want countenance* (further imitation of Puritan pulpit oratory)

153   *for recreation sake* for amusement

154   *the poor abuses of the time want countenance.* Some *abuses of the time* were certainly given countenance by

Puritans at this time but they were not those which Falstaff, or Shakespeare, had in mind as needing attention. Philip Stubbes's *The Anatomy of Abuses* (1583) was a violent attack upon the stage. The players were, said Stubbes, 'painted sepulchres' and the plays they presented, did they not 'maintain bawdry, infinite foolery, and renew the remembrance of heathen idolatry?' and did they not 'induce whoredom and uncleanness?'

156   *the latter spring* youthful old age

156–7   *All-hallown summer* fine weather about All Saints' Day (1 November)

173   *habits* clothing

173–4   *appointment* accoutrement

177   *sirrah*. Here *sirrah* is used as a familiar form of 'sir'. It can be used to imply 'villain', as it is at I.3.116.
        cases of buckram 'rough cloth suits', or perhaps 'over-alls'. Buckram could be stiffened with glue and *case* suggests that this was so here.
        nonce occasion

178   *immask* hide (a word peculiar to Shakespeare)
        noted well-known

179   *hard* strong

184   *incomprehensible* infinite, beyond comprehension

186   *wards* postures of defence (a fencing term)

188   *reproof* disproof

190   *tomorrow night*. The meeting at Gad's Hill is to be the following morning; it is at the tavern in Eastcheap that they will all meet on the next evening.

193–
215   *I know you all . . . Redeeming time when men think least I will*. This speech is considered in detail in the Introduction, pages 18–20.

194   *unyoked humour* unbridled inclination

195   *the sun*. Like the eagle and the lion (see III.3.147), the sun was a traditional symbol of royalty. When Richard is forced to obey Henry IV when the latter is still Henry Bolingbroke, this image, as 'glistering Phaethon',

is brilliantly combined with the physical descent of the king from the battlements of the castle, where he stands, to the 'base' court:

> *Down, down I come like glistering Phaethon,*
> *Wanting the manage of unruly jades.*
> *In the base-court – base court, where kings grow base*
> *To come at traitors' calls, and do them grace.*
> *In the base court. Come down – down court, down King,*
> *For night-owls shriek where mounting larks should sing.*
> Richard II, III.3.178–83

It is noticeable that here Hal is only *imitating* the sun: he is not actually King yet.

201   *strangle* stifle

205   *accidents* incidental occasions

210   *sullen ground* dull background

215   *Redeeming time* making amends for wasted time (perhaps suggested by Ephesians 5.16, 'Redeeming the time, because the days are evil')

I.3   This scene is presumably the meeting of the Council ordered at I.1.102–3, and in this it accords with Shakespeare's source, Holinshed.

3   *found me* found me so

5   *be myself.* The precise nature of kingship is frequently discussed in drama of the Elizabethan and Jacobean period. A king had two selves: one was human, one royal (and perhaps divine). Separating these two selves is dramatized in *Richard II* (and was enacted before an even larger audience at the execution of Charles I). Henry is now resorting to his regal self, 'Mighty, and to be feared', abandoning his humane self, 'soft as young down'. The regal Richard is strikingly contrasted with the human being in the opening scenes of *Richard II*.

6   *condition* natural disposition

12–13   *that same greatness too which our own hands | Have helped to make so portly*. The Percies (of which the Earl of Worcester was one) had been largely instrumental in enabling Henry, as Bolingbroke, to regain his lands, and had then supported his usurpation of the throne. In all this, it is Northumberland who plays the major role in *Richard II*. Worcester does not appear (although he is mentioned) and Hotspur's part is small, though he recalls his first meeting with Henry later in this scene (lines 239–50).

13   *portly* stately

18   *moody frontier of a servant brow* angry defiance of a subject's frown

25   *delivered* reported

26   *envy* malice
        misprision misunderstanding

28–68   *My liege, I did deny no prisoners ... Betwixt my love and your high majesty*. The rhythm of Hotspur's speech is particularly varied. The first line has been made a flatter denial than the punctuation of Q1 might suggest. Q1 concludes the line with a comma but the nature of Hotspur's statement demands a stop here. The division of lines 31–3 is almost imitative of the breathlessness of which Hotspur speaks but this gives way to lines which run on into those that follow. Then, from line 48, the rhythm suggests Hotspur's short-temperedness. The three lines beginning with 'And' (54, 56, 58) give vent to the force of Hotspur's feelings; there is no pausing as he hastens on from indignity to absurdity. Hotspur's rhetoric is more fully examined in the Introduction, pages 22–7.

33   *new reaped* freshly barbered

34   *stubble-land at harvest-home*. His beard was closely clipped; not 'unkempt', of course.

37   *pouncet-box*. This was a word of Shakespeare's own for a small box with a perforated lid. It held snuff, made

possibly of powdered tobacco or, more probably, aromatic herbs.

40   *Took it in snuff* (1) was angry; (2) snuffed it up

45   *holiday* not everyday
        lady lady-like

46   *questioned me* conversed with me

49   *popinjay* parrot, prattler

50   *grief* pain

55   *God save the mark!* God avert evil! The meaning of *the mark* is uncertain; it may be the sign of the cross.

57   *parmacity* (a corruption of spermaceti – a fatty substance derived from the head of the sperm whale – by association with 'Parma city')

59   *saltpetre* (used in the manufacture of gunpowder)

61   *tall* valiant

65   *indirectly* without paying him full attention

67   *Come current* be accepted at its face value

74   *wrong* injury
        impeach discredit

76   *yet* (emphasized – 'despite all this')

79   *brother-in-law.* As noted at I.1.38, there were two Edmund Mortimers and these Holinshed and Shakespeare confused. Glendower's daughter was married to Sir Edmund Mortimer (1376–1409), brother of Roger Mortimer, already dead at this time, and Elizabeth, whom Hotspur married (though Shakespeare calls her Kate – and Holinshed Eleanor). See also the note below to line 83.

83   *that Earl of March.* This is the reading of the first two quartos. The later quartos and the Folio read 'the' but 'that' makes the relationship to Mortimer more obvious. As mentioned in the preceding note, Shakespeare was confused over the relationship of the Mortimers. The Earl of March, alive at the time of the play, was the son of Roger Mortimer (Hotspur's brother-in-law) but he had the same name, Edmund, as his uncle (another brother-in-law to Hotspur).

This Earl of March was *not* married to Glendower's daughter.

86   *indent* bargain
     fears 'things feared', and also, 'cowards'

91   *revolted* rebellious

96   *mouthèd wounds.* Compare I.1.5: 'the thirsty entrance of this soil' and the note thereon.

97   *sedgy* bordered with reeds and rushes

99   *confound* spend, consume

100 *changing hardiment* each displaying his valour to the other

105 *crisp* (1) curled; (2) rippled
     head (1) surface; (2) pressure of water (a head of water)

107 *bare* beggarly (and perhaps 'bare-faced)
     policy expediency

112 *belie* slander

116 *sirrah* (used scornfully; compare the usage at I.2.177)

119 *kind* manner

123 *if the devil come and roar for them.* This line has been likened to the 'roaring devil' of the old Morality plays, but it is no more than the extravagant reaction we might expect to what Hotspur doubtless considers to be the King's 'bald unjointed chat'.

124 *I will after straight* I'll immediately chase after him

130 *Want mercy* be damned

135 *cankered* rotten to the core
     Bolingbroke (Henry IV's name – as used in *Richard II*)

136 *Brother, the King hath made your nephew mad* (ironic understatement)

140 *brother* (see the notes to lines 83 and 154)

141 *an eye of death.* The meaning is not quite certain. It could mean 'an eye threatening death' but it more probably means 'an eye of mortal fear'.

144 *next of blood* heir to the throne

147 *in us* done by us

148 *Irish expedition.* Henry IV (when still Bolingbroke) returned to England from his banishment whilst

Richard was engaged in suppressing a rebellion in Ireland.

149–50 *From whence he, intercepted, did return | To be deposed, and shortly murderèd.* Northumberland's summary gives little indication of the part he played in Richard's deposition, particularly the treacherous interception of Richard in which he was involved. An Elizabethan audience hearing these words would not, however, be unmindful of the part he had played and the way that Shakespeare had dramatized him in *Richard II*. The audience's sympathies would not easily be aroused for the Percies, and this must particularly reflect upon the way in which Hotspur would be seen, even though his part in the deposition of Richard was so small.

151–2 *we in the world's wide mouth | Live scandalized.* Worcester seems to imply that public opinion misjudges the Percies. This is only true to the extent that Henry must share the blame, but Shakespeare, in this play, is subtly insulating Henry from his share in Richard's deposition (see especially his description of his and Richard's behaviour in III.2.50–73).

154 *Proclaim my brother.* The heirs proclaimed by Richard II were the Earls of March (Roger, then Edmund). By confusing the two Edmunds, Shakespeare took Glendower's prisoner to be Earl of March and rightful heir to the throne. (The true Earl of March was, in fact, loyal to Henry IV and Henry V.) See also note to line 83.

161 *murderous subornation* aiding and abetting murder

164 *The cords, the ladder, or the hangman rather?* The imagery used here first suggests of ascent (*cords, ladder*) and from this it is an easy leap to *hangman*.

165 *I descend so low.* Carrying on the hanging image, Hotspur 'drops' his tone.

166 *line* degree (and continuing the sense of 'cords' in line 164)

predicament (1) category; (2) the danger in which they find themselves

167 *range* are classified (according to 'line' – degree – and 'predicament' – category)

171 *gage them both* pledge both (the 'nobility and power' of the preceding line)

174 *canker* the wild- or dog-rose (contrasted with Richard, the 'sweet lovely [garden] rose', line 173); and also, both 'canker-worm' (which infects the rose) and 'ulcer'

181 *disdained* disdainful

187 *quick-conceiving discontents* discontented minds ready to catch the meaning

190–91 *As to o'er-walk a current roaring loud | On the unsteadfast footing of a spear.* A reference to a typical peril of medieval romances in which the knight crosses a perilous bridge.

192 *If he fall in, good night, or sink, or swim* (a knight falling from such a bridge is doomed, whether he sink or swim)

194 *So* provided that

196 *rouse . . . start* (from cover)

200 *bright honour.* The equation of Hotspur with honour is belied by the language in which he expresses himself. His extravagance and his use of clichés (particularly diving to an unfathomed depth) make him appear ridiculous. Similarly, his frequent return to the subject of his prisoners, and the way in which his uncle reacts to him (lines 231–2), and his father's impatience (lines 233–5), clearly reveal his immaturity. His undoubted valour sorts incongruously with his boyish petulance and we cannot take his adoration of honour at its face value.

203 *locks* hair (but honour with flowing locks is ridiculous)

205 *corrival* equal

206 *half-faced fellowship.* Hotspur is selfishly concerned with monopolizing honour – he has no wish to share

it. Unless he has it all (both sides of the coin) it will be incomplete so far as he is concerned.

207   *apprehends* snatches at
      figures figures of speech, and also, vain imaginings

208   *form* true meaning

213   *if a scot* if a small amount (a 'scot' was a small payment)

214   *You start away.* It is small animals that start – the hare, not the royal lion; the distinction has been made at line 196.

223   *still* continually

225   *studies* pursuits
      defy renounce

227   *sword-and-buckler.* A *buckler* was a small round shield. Hotspur's implication is that Hal's tastes are plebeian. In Shakespeare's day (though not in the time of Henry IV) the sword and buckler were no longer used by gentlemen, having been replaced by the rapier and dagger.

230   *pot of ale.* This is another reference to the lowliness of Hal's tastes; in theory at least, Elizabethan gentlemen drank wine.

234   *to break into this woman's mood.* This accusation is ironic in view of Hotspur's objection to the 'certain lord' who talked 'so like a waiting-gentlewoman' (line 54).

237   *pismires* ants

239–46   *In Richard's time ... You say true.* The colloquial urgency of Hotspur's search for the name of the place where he first met Bolingbroke breaks down the metre of the lines without their completely losing their shape. Hotspur's animation is skilfully, and attractively, conveyed.

241   *madcap Duke.* The historian Holinshed describes the Duke of York's love of pleasure rather than business, but this aspect is not dramatized by Shakespeare in *Richard II*. Hal says he will be a *madcap* at I.2.140–41 and he is called *madcap* at IV.1.95.

241   *kept* lived, kept up

244   *Ravenspurgh* (near Spurn Head, Yorkshire, where Bolingbroke landed; now covered by the sea)

247   *candy deal* sugary amount

248   *fawning greyhound.* Sweetmeats and treacherous dogs are frequently associated by Shakespeare – for example, in *Antony and Cleopatra*:

> *The hearts*
> *That spanielled me at heels, to whom I gave*
> *Their wishes, do discandy, melt their sweets*
> *On blossoming Caesar.*   IV.12.20–23

251   *cozeners* deceivers (with a quibble on 'coz', cousin)

254   *stay* await

257   *the Douglas' son* (the Earl of Fife, mistakenly said to be Douglas's son – see note to I.1.71)

259   *Which I shall send you written.* In this way Shakespeare avoids giving details tedious to relate and unnecessary to his major concerns.

262   *secretly into the bosom creep* win the confidence

264   *True.* Hotspur's interjection, 'Of York, is it not', and the breaking of the line into three parts, may suggest urgency, but the effect can also be comic. Worcester's *True* can reveal pained resignation.
      bears hard takes ill

265   *brother's death.* The William Scrope, Earl of Wiltshire, who was executed at Bristol by Bolingbroke in *Richard II* was a cousin of the Archbishop. The Earl's death is reported by his brother Sir Stephen Scroop at III.2.142 of that play. The error is Holinshed's. There is a reference to another member of the family in *1 Henry IV* at IV.4.3.

266   *estimation* conjecture

272   *thou still lettest slip.* Once again Northumberland rebukes his son for his childish impetuosity.

274   *power* army

278   *head* army

279   *even* carefully

282   *pay us home* 'pay us out', and perhaps also, 'send us to eternity'

288   *suddenly* at once

290   *at once* altogether

294   *thrive* be successful

296   *fields* battlefields. But if Act II runs straight on, it is not this applause that Hotspur's plea receives, but a mighty yawn from the First Carrier!

II.1   This scene is laid in Rochester, Kent, early in the morning. The language of the scene depicts remarkably vividly the uncomfortable, rough world of ordinary men and women. It presents the other side of the merry, irresponsible world of the Tavern in Eastcheap.

1   *by the day* in the morning

2   *Charles's Wain* (the Plough or Great Bear)

3   *horse* (plural here)

     packed loaded with goods (they are pack-horses)

5   *beat* (to soften)

     Cut (a work-horse)

5–6   *put a few flocks in the point* stuff wool into the saddle-bow (for comfort)

6   *jade* a worn-out horse

     wrung in the withers rubbed or bruised along the ridge between the shoulder-blades

7   *out of all cess* excessively

8   *Peas and beans* (horse-feed)

     dank damp (making an alliterative jingle with 'dog')

9   *next* quickest

     bots stomach worms

10   *house* inn

12–13   *since the price of oats rose.* There were too many poor harvests in the 1590s, resulting in higher prices, for this to be a specific topical allusion, although the price of oats was particularly high in 1596. It is such a passing reference as this that helps suggest another kind of low life than that shown in the Tavern in East-cheap.

15–16   *stung like a tench* (stung, as by its markings the tench appears to have been, or because it was thought to breed parasites)

17   *By the mass* (a mild oath, but not sufficiently so to save its being expunged from the Folio – see An Account of the Text)

17–18   *there is ne'er a king Christian could be better bit* there is no Christian king (who might be expected to have the best of things) who could receive more bites

19   *first cock.* By convention, the first cock-crow occurred at midnight; the second at 3 a.m.; and the third, an hour before dawn.

21   *jordan* chamber-pot
     leak urinate
     chimney fire-place

22   *chamber-lye* urine. The practice described must have been common for it was specifically condemned by a Tudor physician, Andrew Boorde, as early as 1542.
     loach. The loach, a small, fresh-water fish, was thought to breed parasites. The word was also a slang term for a simpleton and this meaning may also be implied.

23   *Come away* come along!

26   *razes* roots
     Charing Cross. Charing Cross was not at this time a district of London but a village lying between the city and Westminster.

27   *God's body* (another oath omitted from the Folio)

28–9   *What, Ostler! ... Canst not hear?* It was the ostler's responsibility to prepare the horses for travellers and to help them on their way. Evidently Robin the Ostler was very much better at this than his successor.

30   *as good deed as drink.* Falstaff uses this proverbial saying in the next scene (II.2.21–2). It is a little clearer as used in *Twelfth Night*:

SIR ANDREW *'Twere as good a deed as to drink when a man's a-hungry, to challenge him the field and then to break promise with him and make a fool of him.*

II.3.122-4

30-31   *the pate on thee* your head

31   *very* true

31-2   *Hast no faith in thee?* can't you be relied upon?

34   *two o'clock.* That it is four o'clock was established in the very first line of the scene. But this is no oversight on Shakespeare's part. From the first the Carriers are mistrustful of Gadshill. They are not prepared to give him the time of the day, never mind trust him with a lantern. This is an effective, and very economical, juxtaposition of the workaday world of the Carriers and that of Gadshill (and Falstaff).

37   *soft* gently, go easy

40   *Ay, when? Canst tell?* Oh yes, sure. But *when* do you think you'll get it? (The statement is tantamount to a refusal.)

44-5   *Time enough to go to bed with a candle.* The journey from Rochester to Charing Cross – about 30 miles – would be a long day's ride with a pack-horse, but the Carrier is being evasive, again, rather than informative.

46   *along with company* travel in a group (for safety's sake)

47   *great charge* much money (or baggage)

48   *Chamberlain* (servant in charge of guests' rooms)

49   *'At hand, quoth pick-purse'* 'Ready, said the pickpocket' (a popular catch-phrase of the time)

52   *giving direction* 'supervising (the servants' work)', and also, 'planning a robbery'
        labouring (the work of the servants, and also, that of the robbers)

52-3   *Thou layest the plot how.* The double meaning here is precisely the same as for 'giving direction' (line 52). Inn-servants at the time were frequently accused of providing robbers with information about those who stayed at their inns, giving details of what they had that was worth stealing, and whither they were bound and when.

54–5   *It holds current* it's still true

55   *that* what

    franklin rich freeholder

56   *Weald of Kent* (the land lying between the North and South Downs.) The spelling of Q1 is 'wilde of Kent' but the spelling of the origin of the word (Anglo-Saxon *weald*, a forest) is the same as the modern spelling and it has been adopted here; 'wilde' gives a false impression of the sense.

    three hundred marks (£200; a mark was an amount, not a coin – exactly as is a guinea nowadays)

58   *auditor* (an official of the Exchequer)

61   *presently* immediately

62–3   *Saint Nicholas' clerks*. This was a slang expression meaning 'highwaymen'. Saint Nicholas was the patron saint of, among others, children, scholars (clerks), and travellers, and the latter came to include robbers as well as those upon whom they preyed. The saint was depicted as holding three balls or purses of gold and it has been suggested that it was these that made him appear to be a patron appropriate to robbers. Various puns explaining the association have also been suggested. Nick can refer to Old Nick (the devil) or, as a verb, to cheating and defrauding. Nicholas also sounds like 'necklace' – the halter destined for robbers who were caught.

63   *I'll give thee this neck* you can hang me

68   *fat* full-bodied

70   *Troyans* roisterers, good companions (like the 'Corinthian' of II.4.11)

72   *the profession* (of highwayman)

74   *foot-landrakers* vagabond footpads

74–5   *long-staff* quarterstaff

75   *sixpenny strikers* footpads who would hold up a man for sixpence

75–6   *mad mustachio purple-hued maltworms* roaring, be-
       whiskered, purple-faced, drinkers (compare Falstaff's
       description of Bardolph, III.3.29–47)

77   *great O-yeas.* The word given for *O-yeas* in Q0 and Q1
       is 'Oneyres'; the later quartos and the Folio print
       'Oneyers'. Many attempts have been made to explain
       this word – to suggest either what it means as it stands
       or what it ought to be. The simplest interpretation has
       been 'one-ers' (used by Dickens and still heard
       colloquially); the most ingenious, that it comes from an
       obscure Exchequer term, 'to ony', meaning to mark
       the abbreviation *o. ni.* (*oneratur, nisi habeat sufficientem
       exonerationem*) against a sheriff's name to show he was
       responsible for certain moneys. Emendations suggested
       have included 'Seigniors', 'Moneyers', 'Wan-dyers',
       'one-eyers', 'owners', 'mynheers', 'meyers', and, for
       the whole expression, 'great ones; – yes'. Though the
       simple 'one-ers', seems possible, it is a thin expression
       in such a rich flow of language.

       It is argued in An Account of the Text that the men
       who set the type of Q1 were skilled craftsmen who
       followed their copy. 'Oneyres' must have seemed to
       them the word intended (which supports 'one-ers')
       but it does not guarantee that they understood the
       word they set. We can be fairly certain that 'Oneyres'
       closely represents what the word looked like in the
       manuscript and this excludes words of quite different
       outline like 'Moneyers'. The likely word must have
       been related to 'Burgomasters' in the same line (cf. the
       preceding 'nobility and tranquillity'), it must be cap-
       able of being used ironically, and ideally should fit the
       pattern of word-play that follows. It ought also to be a
       word Shakespeare might have used, although he did
       create words for a single occasion (so 'ony-ers' is pos-
       sible) and he was not always consistent in his word-
       play.

       The word that fits these stringent requirements is

O-yeas. It might well have been spelt by Shakespeare as it was sounded – 'Owyres'; 'w', of all letters in Elizabethan handwriting, is easily misread as two letters and quite easily as 'ne'. *O-yeas* imitates the 'Oyez!' of the Town Crier (for whom it stands), an office that goes well with that of Burgomaster (the 'o' of which it incidentally echoes). Shakespeare uses 'oyes' in *The Merry Wives of Windsor* (V.5.47, rhyming with 'toys') and *Troilus and Cressida* ('On whose bright crest Fame with her loud'st oyes | Cries, "This is he!"', IV.5.142–3) and the expression 'great O' (= capital O) is also Shakespearian (*cf. Twelfth Night*, II.5.87–8: 'and thus makes she her great P's'). The 'great O' is surely Falstaff (a 'capital' crier if ever there was one). The *great O* of Falstaff (his girth – *such as can hold in*) is as a cipher, signifying nothing (cf. *King Lear*, I.4.214). The puns on 'strike' and 'speak' are given just the right comic tone and point when related to Falstaff and there is an individuality about *O-yeas* which is lacking in 'one-ers'; and it would have had a more obvious, and more direct appeal, than the obscure *ony-ers*.

78   *hold in*. This is a multiple pun: (1) keep counsel; (2) stick together; (3) hold fast to the quarry (a hunting term); (4) be held within Falstaff's great girth.

   strike rob

   speak (second time) (1) swear; (2) rob

83   *boots* booty

85   *hold out water in foul way* remain waterproof (that is, protect you in difficulty)

86   *justice hath liquored her*. The general sense is clear and the pun on *liquored* is plain enough – 'greased' (as were boots in order to keep out water), 'bribed', and 'made drunk'. Gadshill means that he and his companions will be protected from the full rigour of the law – 'the commonwealth', line 84 – but *justice* ought to be equated with 'commonwealth' and

although, in the event, Hal intervenes, he is hardly *justice*.

87 *as in a castle* in complete security (with, perhaps, a reference in the unrevised version to Oldcastle)

 receipt recipe

88 *fern-seed*. Fern-seed was thought to be visible only on St John's Eve (Midsummer's Night). If gathered then it was thought to confer invisibility on whoever carried it.

93 *our purchase* what we obtain by robbery

93, 95 *true, false* (a repetition of the fairly simple kind of word-play used by the Chamberlain in line 66)

96 *'homo' is a common name to all men*. Gadshill is prepared to give his word simply as a man ('*homo*'), for, whether true or false, all are men. The definition is derived from a Latin grammar by William Lily and John Colet, *Grammatices Rudimenta*, known usually as *Lily's Latin Grammar* or *The Accidence*. It was the grammar that Shakespeare learned from and it is possible that it is referred to in *The Merry Wives of Windsor*; Sir Hugh Evans, at Mistress Page's request, asks William 'some questions in his accidence' (IV.1.18).

98 *muddy* dull-witted

II.2 (stage direction) *Enter Prince and Poins*. Q0 has here: *Enter Prince, Poines, and Peto, &c.* A separate entry is given for Falstaff (as here) after *Stand Close!* The *&c* would imply Bardolph, but if Peto and Bardolph were to enter here it would mean that these two were a party to Poins's plot for, presumably, they would hear him tell the Prince that Falstaff's horse had been removed (line 1, and Falstaff at lines 11–12) and they would have to be restrained from answering Falstaff when he called them at line 20. Whilst, doubtless, they would be willing parties to such a deception, it would rather spoil the private nature of the joke being practised on Falstaff. Furthermore, in II.4 they seem unaware of what the Prince and Poins have done and their ignorance is essential to the carrying out of the deception. It has sometimes been suggested that 'Bardolph' in line 49 is a speech prefix and that the speech given him beginning in line 51 ought to be Gadshill's. This is an attractive emendation from Qo, but the case for the change is not strong enough to justify alteration of the quarto. The stage direction at the beginning of the scene, as it is printed in Qo, ought, perhaps, to be taken as a general call for those involved in all the to-ing and fro-ing that this scene demands, much of which is not indicated in the original stage directions.

2   *frets like a gummed velvet.* Just as unpiled fabric could be treated with glue (as noted at I.2.177) so could velvet. As a result it was more inclined to wear quickly – to *fret* (here also meaning 'be vexed').

3   *Stand close!* hide!

12   *square* (a measuring instrument)

13   *break my wind* pant breathlessly (with an obscene quibble)

13–14   *to die a fair death for all this* to make a good end as a result of so much suffering

18   *medicines* love potions

20   *starve* die

21–22   *as good a deed as drink* (see note to II.1.30)

22   *true* honest

28   *Whew!* This may represent Falstaff's breathlessness, but there is comic business to be derived from his attempting vainly (because out of breath) to respond to the whistling of the Prince and Poins.

33   *Have you any levers to lift me up again.* Although Falstaff is unaware of the trick about to be played on him, his capacity to make a joke of his own size here suggests to the audience that he too is sharing in the joke. This has the effect of stressing the playfulness of

the action, robbing it of any pain (or inhibiting sympathy), so that an audience can enjoy the sport to the full.

34   *bear my own flesh* carry my own weight

      afoot on foot

36   *colt* trick

42-3 *Hang thyself in thine own heir-apparent garters!* The heir apparent was a Knight of the Garter and Falstaff has adapted this honour to the popular riposte: 'He may hang himself in his own garters.'

43   *peach* inform against you (thus saving himself)

44   *ballads.* The ballads to which Falstaff refers are those which were composed to mark special occasions (a victory, a murder, an execution) or to libel enemies. They were printed on broadsides (single sheets of paper) and sold in the street. Music was rarely printed with the ballad but an indication was given of a popular tune appropriate (in terms of its measure and rhythm if not its association) to the words of the new ballad. Such ballads were enormously popular and the practice flourished until late in the nineteenth century – until, that is, the rise of popular, cheap newspapers. Some ballads in the nineteenth century sold between two and three million copies. Figures for Shakespeare's time are not available, but from the number of references to such street ballads it is clear that they were comparably popular. A possible source of the pound of flesh story, used by Shakespeare in *The Merchant of Venice*, is 'The Ballad of the Cruelty of Gernutus', although the story appeared elsewhere. Cleopatra fears that 'scald rimers [will] | Ballad us out o'tune' (*Antony and Cleopatra*, V.2.214-15).

45   *is so forward* goes so far

49   *setter* informant

51   *Case ye* disguise yourselves

58   *front* confront

59   *lower* lower down

65   *John of Gaunt*. Falstaff is, of course, very fat; Hal, according to contemporary descriptions, was tall and thin, as the descriptions of him at II.4.240–43 indicate. In *Richard II*, II.1.74, Hal's grandfather, John of Gaunt, plays on his name – 'Old Gaunt indeed, and gaunt in being old' – and this is probably recalled here.

75   *happy man be his dole* may each man's lot be one of happiness (a proverbial expression)

76   *Every man to his business*. This is another proverbial expression, calling to mind Falstaff's assertion ''Tis no sin for a man to labour in his vocation' (I.2.104–5).

83   *caterpillars*. These parasites are twice referred to in *Richard II*. It is the 'caterpillars of the commonwealth' (II.3.166) who, according to the Gardener, swarm on England's 'wholesome herbs' (III.4.46). It has been pointed out that Falstaff's abuse is all applicable to himself.

       bacon-fed knaves. Andrew Boorde, the Tudor physician who condemned 'pissing in chimneys' (see notes to II.1.22), considered bacon to be good for carters and ploughmen, 'the which be ever labouring in the earth or dung'.

85   *undone* ruined

87   *gorbellied* pot-bellied

88   *chuffs* (a term of contempt for rich, and perhaps miserly, men)

       your store were here your property were in your bellies

89   *bacons* fat men (compare 'porkers')

90   *grandjurors* (men of substance who served on grand juries)

       We'll jure ye when we've finished with you, we shall have given you reason to serve on a jury. This literary device is still common. Another good example of its use by Shakespeare occurs in *Coriolanus*. Referring to the defeat of Aufidius by Coriolanus, Menenius says: 'I would not have been so fidiused for all the chests in Corioles' (II.1.125–6).

91   *true* honest

93   *argument* subject for discussion

97   *An* if

98   *there's no equity stirring* there's no justice in the world

102–8   *Got with much ease ... I should pity him.* This passage, like a number of others in the play, is printed as prose in Q1. Alexander Pope first arranged this passage as verse in the eighteenth century and most editors have followed his practice. It is not always possible to be sure that such relineation is correct – the passage at V.3.42–3 is usually regarded as prose though printed in verse in this edition – and this is particularly true of very short passages. The problem arises partly from the state of the original copy, where lines might be run one into another, giving rise to uncertainty in the printing-house, and partly because a passage of plain blank verse can read like prose, the rhythm of such verse not being unlike rather formal English speech. In the case of one dramatist of the period, Philip Massinger, it is not only possible to read much of his verse as if it were prose, but it has been shown to be possible to print certain known prose (the preliminaries to a play) as blank verse.

105   *an officer* a constable

106   *Away, good Ned! Falstaff sweats to death.* This line reads awkwardly as verse (see the note to lines 102–8), although one should not expect the metre to be rigidly exact. It has been pointed out, however, that the line would read normally if the name here were 'Oldcastle' for *Falstaff* (see Introduction, page 29).

107   *lards* drips fat in the form of sweat, bastes

II.3   Shakespeare gives no location for this scene, and Warkworth Castle in Northumberland has been proposed. Various authors have been suggested as the

letter-writer, the likeliest being George Dunbar, third
Earl of March (the Scottish, not the Marches of Wales
with which Mortimer is associated). Dunbar, though a
Scot, fought against his own people at Holmedon, and
then informed on the Percies and fought for Henry IV
at Shrewsbury against Hotspur and Douglas (see lines
31–2). He changed sides again some years later,
becoming reconciled with Douglas, and returned to
Scotland. What matters in the play, of course, is
Hotspur's reaction to the letter, not its author. An
eighteenth-century critic remarked that 'did not Sir
John need breathing-space' this scene 'might well be
spared'.

3   *house* family
6   *barn* (contemptuously for the writer's residence)
13   *unsorted* unsuitable
14   *for the counterpoise of* to weigh against
17   *hind* peasant
22   *Lord of York* (the Archbishop of York)
30   *pagan* lacking faith
33   *I could divide myself, and go to buffets* I could split
        myself into two parts and fall to blows with myself
37   *Kate.* Hotspur's wife was called Elizabeth, and
        Holinshed mistakenly called her Eleanor (the name of
        the loyal Edmund Mortimer's sister – see note to
        I.3.83). The change of name is presumably deliberate
        and Kate certainly seems to have been a favourite name
        of Shakespeare's.
39–66   *O my good lord . . . else he loves me not.* This speech, and
        the discussion that follows, have often been compared
        with the scene between Brutus and Portia in *Julius
        Caesar* (II.1.233–309). The similarity of situation, and
        Shakespeare's capacity to handle his material dif-
        ferently, have been noted. What is so characteristic
        of this scene is the juxtaposition of playful banter and
        Lady Percy's deep concern. These qualities are
        beautifully brought together in lines 88–103.

43   *stomach* appetite

45   *when thou sittest alone* (a sign of melancholy)

47   *given* given away

48   *thick-eyed* dull-sighted

    curst ill-tempered

51   *manage* manège, horsemanship

53   *retires* retreats

54   *palisadoes* (a defensive point constructed from iron-tipped stakes)

    frontiers outworks (of a fortified position)

55   *basilisks.* This was the largest size of cannon, named after a fabulous snake hatched by a reptile from a cock's egg (hence its alternative name, 'cockatrice'); its breath, or a look from it, were said to be fatal. The cannon's shot weighed about 200 lb.

    cannon (here a cannon of medium size)

    culverin. This was the smallest size of cannon, named after the French word for an adder. A number of cannons of the Elizabethan period that have come down to us have reptiles sculptured on them and it is possible that this is the source of their names.

57   *currents* eddies, movements

    heady impetuous, headstrong

62   *motions* (1) emotions; (2) workings (of the features)

64   *hest* behest, command

65   *heavy* weighty

74   *Esperance. Esperance* alone, or as '*Esperance ma comforte*', was the Percy motto. It means 'Hope is my reliance'. *Esperance* is used by Hotspur as a battle-cry at V.2.96.

78   *carries you away* (1) takes you away; (2) excites, 'transports' you

81   *A weasel hath not such a deal of spleen.* The *weasel* was thought to be particularly quarrelsome and the *spleen* was thought to be the organ of the body which excited sudden emotion or action and thus irritability and ill-humour.

82   *tossed* tossed about

84   *my brother Mortimer.* For this relationship, see the notes to I.3.79, 83, and 154.

85   *his title* (Mortimer's supposed claim to the throne – see I.3.143–4 and the notes to I.3.83 and 154)

86   *line* strengthen (as with a lining to a garment)

88   *paraquito* parrot

90   *break thy little finger* (a lovers' endearment)

91   *An if* if

93–4 *I love thee not, | I care not for thee, Kate?* The question mark has been added in this edition. Hotspur is more troubled here, about his enterprise, and about his wife, than his childishness in I.3 suggests. Lady Percy's vivid account of his nightmares and his melancholy suggests a character rather different from that described by Hal in the next scene: 'he that kills me some six or seven dozen of Scots at a breakfast, washes his hands, and says to his wife, "Fie upon this quiet life, I want work"' (II.4.101–103). Shakespeare's depiction of this side of Hotspur, so close to Hal's comment, is for a good dramatic purpose. Thus, this is no bold statement of fact to be denied a moment later (as at lines 102–3). It is the kind of self-questioning that suggests that Hotspur is beginning to be aware of the implications of rebellion. The way in which Kate and Hotspur exchange banter here implies that neither can quite face what they feel will be the outcome of this revolt. This momentary sign of maturity in Hotspur needs to be set against what often seems to be an unthinking brashness in him.

95   *mammets* dolls

      tilt with lips kiss (*tilt* has the implication of 'tourney')

97   *pass them current.* Cracked crowns (five-shilling pieces) were not legal tender ('current coinage').

      God's me! God save me. This was an oath which escaped the purging carried out when the Folio was printed – see An Account of the Text.

107   *whereabout* on what business

114   *Thou wilt not utter – what thou dost not know* (an ancient witticism that goes back to the Elder Seneca and was popular in Shakespeare's time)

118   *Whither I go, thither shall you go too.* This echoes closely Ruth's famous promise to Naomi ('whither thou goest, I will go also', Ruth 1.16). It is indicative of a much more serious Hotspur than was revealed in I.3, and it must modify our view of him when he is described by Hal in II.4. Kate, incidentally, has the answer to her question.

120   *of force* of necessity

II.4   This is the meeting planned at I.2.128-9 and traditionally the scene is set at the Boar's Head, Eastcheap (but see the note to I.2.129).

1   *fat* 'vat', or, 'stuffy' (though a pun seems unlikely)

4   *loggerheads* blockheads

4-5   *amongst three or fourscore hogsheads.* Favoured customers might be invited to drink in the cellar amidst the casks.

7   *leash* trio

11   *Jack* ill-mannered fellow

       Corinthian drinking companion (as 'Troyans', II.1.70)

15   '*dyeing scarlet*'. The obvious meaning here is that regular drinking results in a red complexion – Bardolph is 'the Knight of the Burning Lamp' (III.3.26-7). There may also be a reference to the Elizabethan use of urine as lye in textile processing, to assist in washing wool, for example, and particularly to assist in fixing the colour, to prevent undue running.

       breathe in your watering. Recently this passage has been interpreted to mean 'pause in the middle of drinking', at which there was a cry of 'Hem!', signifying that the throat should be cleared, and the drink polished off ('Play it off!', line 16). Eighteenth-century editors

offered an interpretation which Boswell castigated as
'filthy', but which is surely nearer the truth. It is difficult to believe that *watering* could be applied to the
drinking of sack. Although there are plenty of references to the iniquity of those who need to take breath
when they drink, none of these uses 'water' as a
synonym for beer or wine. *Watering* is surely 'urinating'
(carrying on the implication of 'dyeing scarlet', same
line) and such breathing that evokes the responses
'Hem!' and 'Play it off!' is 'breaking wind'.

18   *drink with any tinker in his own language.* Tinkers had
     the reputation of being great drinkers and they had
     their own slang.

20   *action* encounter

21–2 *pennyworth of sugar.* Dekker, in *The Gull's Horn-book*
      (1609), refers to the practice of sweetening wine 'in
      two pitiful papers of sugar'. Sugar for this purpose
      was sold by tapsters.

23   *underskinker* under wine-waiter (to *skink* is to draw wine)

25   *Anon, anon, sir!* coming, sir!

26   *Score* chalk up
     bastard (sweet Spanish wine)
     Half-moon (a fancy name for an inn-room)

29   *puny* inexperienced (a term applied to Oxford freshmen
     and new students at the Inns of Court, at one time)

32   *a precedent* an example (worth imitating). Q1 has
     'present' here but this was changed in F to 'President'
     (the Elizabethan spelling for 'precedent'). This has
     been thought by some editors to suggest that another
     manuscript written by Shakespeare (or copied from
     such a manuscript) was available and was used in the
     course of printing F. This change could, however,
     have been fairly readily made without the aid of
     another manuscript and the word is used here because
     it is a sound guess, not because it is supposed to have
     any special authority. (See also An Account of the
     Text.)

36   *Pomgarnet* Pomegranate (another fancy name for an inn-room)

40   *to serve* (as an apprentice)

41   *five years* (the full term was seven years; Francis will be fourteen to sixteen years of age)

46   *indenture* articles of apprenticeship

48   *books* Bibles

49   *I could find in my heart –*. John Dover Wilson has pointed out that the humour of this exchange lies in Francis's hopes of an appointment in the Prince's household – but the frequent interruptions dash these hopes. The interlude also delays Falstaff's entrance and builds up tension in the audience, eager to know what he will say and how he will behave.

67   *rob* (the Vintner by breaking his indenture)

67–9 *leather-jerkin ... Spanish pouch.* This catalogue describes the Vintner's dress, presumably, but it is reeled off in such a way as to confuse poor Francis, and his wits are further muddled by Hal's next speech.

68   *not-pated* crop-headed. 'Not' is not the common adverb of negation but a word meaning 'crop-headed' even without the addition of 'pated'. Although now a dialect word, 'not' still can be used for a 'hornless sheep'.

      agate-ring (wearing a seal ring with a carved agate mounted thereon)

      puke-stocking (dark-coloured woollen stockings)

68–9 *caddis-garter* (coloured tape used for garters by those who could not afford, or would not pay the price of, silk)

69   *Spanish pouch* (Spanish-leather wallet)

71–3 *Why then your brown bastard ... it cannot come to so much.* This is nonsense uttered in order to mystify Francis even further. The wretched apprentice hardly seems game worthy of Hal.

71   *brown bastard* (a particularly sweet Spanish wine)

72–3 *your white canvas doublet will sully.* The implication is, perhaps, stick to your apprenticeship and, in the modern colloquial expression, 'keep your nose clean'.

73 *In Barbary, sir, it cannot come to so much.* If Francis runs away, even to such a far-off place as Barbary, it (his white doublet) will not count for much. It was from Barbary (North Africa) that sugar was imported into England.

88–90 *what cunning match ... what's the issue?* Poins, whose trick with Falstaff is more ingenious and more fruitful of humour than Hal's with Francis, might well ask, *what's the issue?* One result has been to put Hal in an excellent humour. Hal's relish at his joke is not unlike Hotspur's enjoyment of his turn of words at III.1.54–8. One rather doubts if Poins will find it a 'precedent' (line 32) so much worth the repetition.

91–94 *I am now of all humours ... at midnight* I am now in the mood to enjoy any jest, any fancy, that man has enjoyed since time began

95 *What's o'clock, Francis?* Hal has just said 'this present twelve o'clock at midnight' (the repetition being designed to ensure that the audience is aware of the time) and thus his request to Francis is simply a prolongation of his 'precedent' – his joke with Francis.

100 *parcel of a reckoning* items making up a bill
I am not yet of Percy's mind. It has been suggested that it is the feverish activity of Francis that calls Hotspur to Hal's mind, or that Hal contrasts his delight in 'all humours' (line 91) with what he takes to be the single humour of Percy – bloodshed – which he proceeds to satirize. *I am not yet of Percy's mind* has more than one meaning. Hal means he is not as is Hotspur (as Hal's father wishes his son were); that he has not reached the stage of delighting in bloodshed that Hotspur has; and also, unwittingly, 'I am not fully aware of all that is in Hotspur's mind' – as can be seen by comparing Hal's satire with the perturbation dramatized in II.3. (See note to II.3.93–4.)

101– *he that kills me . . . 'a trifle, a trifle'*. Although it does
107   not quite accord with the Hotspur we have just seen,
      Hal's satire is superb. It has just the right degree of
      exaggeration, just the right touches of incongruity such
      as the killing of six or seven dozen Scots before break-
      fast, and the excellent take-off of Hotspur's trick of
      delaying an answer (compare how II.3.93 reverts to
      Lady Percy's words at line 66; and also at IV.1.13).
      Although we do not have the play of Hotspur and Lady
      Percy which Hal suggests at lines 108–9, this brief
      satire is not at all a bad substitute.

109   *Rivo!* So far, *Rivo* has not been satisfactorily explained.
      It presumably means 'More wine!' A recent sugges-
      tion that it is derived from the Italian 'riviva', meaning
      'Another toast!', is attractive.

113   *nether-stocks* stockings

116   *Titan* (the sun – Falstaff's red cheeks sunk into his cup
      of sack)

117   *pitiful-hearted Titan.* The repetition of *Titan* has
      troubled many editors and it has been suggested that
      the compositor should have set 'butter' for *Titan*.
      Although butter melts easily in the sun, *pitiful-hearted*
      makes a much less satisfactory epithet for 'butter' than
      it does for *Titan*.

120   *lime* (added to wine to improve its sparkle)

125   *a shotten herring* (as thin as) a herring that has shot its
      roe (yet another food image associated with Falstaff)

127   *God help the while* God help these times

128–9 *I would I were a weaver: I could sing psalms.* Weavers
      had a reputation for singing at their work and, as many
      were Puritans, they sang psalms. In *Twelfth Night* Sir
      Toby asks, 'Shall we rouse the night-owl in a catch that
      will draw three souls out of one weaver?' (II.3.55–7).

131–2 *beat thee out of thy kingdom with a dagger of lath.* A
      feature of the old Morality plays was the Vice, who,
      equipped with a dagger of lath, or wooden sword,
      belaboured the devil or fought his associates. Falstaff's

likening himself to the Vice is particularly interesting. It suggests the awareness of a character within a play of the part he is playing. An Elizabethan audience would be aware that the end for the Vice was to be beaten away and, occasionally, executed. It is not possible to know whether Shakespeare had this in mind for Falstaff when he wrote *1 Henry IV* (but see I.2.193–215); Falstaff is certainly turned away in the second part of the play, however (and in *Henry V* Bardolph will be hanged).

139   *an* if

145   *backing* supporting

154   *a thousand pound*. At II.1.56 and II.4.505 the amount is stated to be 300 marks – £200. This is probably just Falstaff's exaggeration, but, in his defence, it could be said that at II.1.58–9 the Chamberlain says the auditor is one 'that hath abundance of charge too'.

159   *half-sword* shortened swords (as used at close quarters)

162–3   *buckler . . . sword* (see note to I.3.227)

163–4   *ecce signum* behold the evidence (a popular tag of the time)

165   *of* on

167   *sons of darkness*. This may have been suggested by 1 Thessalonians 5.5: 'Ye are all the children of light... we are not of the night, neither of darkness'.

168   PRINCE HAL. This speech is given to Gadshill in Q1 and the speeches at lines 169, 171, and 175 to *Ross*. (presumably the Russell who has been expunged from the play and replaced by Peto, as discussed in An Account of the Text). It has been suggested that when it became necessary to remove *Ross.*, the prefix for Gadshill was written in once, adjacent to that for the Prince, and that in this way Gadshill was given the Prince's line (and he ought to be forward in asking this question here) while the lines below remained attributed to Russell. (See An Account of the Text.)

174   *an Ebrew Jew* a Jew of Jews, a very Jew

187   *paid* settled, killed

189   *horse* (taken to be stupid, like the ass or donkey)

190   *ward* posture of defence

192   *even* just

195   *afront* abreast

       mainly with might and main

196   *I made me* (an archaic dative construction; 'me' is not now required)

197   *target* shield (larger than the buckler with which Falstaff was equipped)

202   *these hilts.* The hilt was in three parts, so the word could be used in the plural.

210-11   *Their points being broken – | Down fell their hose.* The joke is lost on a modern audience. *Points* are not only the sharp ends of swords but were also the laces which fastened stockings (*hose*) to doublet.

212   *I followed me* (see the note to line 196)

213   *with a thought* quick as thought

218   *Kendal green.* This was a cloth of green, associated with Kendal in Westmorland, worn by foresters, servants, and country people. Robin Hood's men were said to wear Kendal green, and Robert Armin, who probably played Touchstone in the first productions of *As You Like It*, wrote in his *A Nest of Ninnies*: 'Truth, in plain attire, is the easier known: let fiction mask in Kendal green', suggesting that it was also a garb worn by thieves.

223   *knotty-pated* block-headed (compare note on line 68)

224   *tallow-catch.* This may be a dripping-pan to catch the fat from meat being roasted, or 'keech' (rolled fat used by candle-makers) may be intended by *catch*.

225-6   *Is not the truth the truth?* (a proverbial saying)

233   *strappado* (a torture or punishment in which the victim was strung up by the arms and then dropped suddenly, so jerking the arms from their sockets)

       racks (an instrument of torture by which the victim was slowly stretched)

235   *reasons* (puns on 'raisins')

238   *sanguine coward*. Cowards were proverbially pale – lily-livered – and thus *sanguine coward* is a comic contradiction in terms. *Sanguine* describes Falstaff's drink-flushed complexion.

240   *starveling* thin, lanky, person

       elf-skin mere nothing. Q1 reads *elſkin*. Q 3, Q 4, Q 5, and F, have *elſskin*, with or without a hyphen, but many editors have thought the word should be 'eel-skin', a word that accords with the ensuing descriptions and was used elsewhere by Shakespeare. It has excellent support, therefore. It has also been suggested that the word 'elshin' is intended. An 'elsin' is a northern dialect word for a shoemaker's awl – an appropriate description of Hal, but a very obscure word.

       There is one curiosity about the way that this word is printed in Q1 that has led to the reading *elf-skin* being chosen here. Almost invariably when a double s was required for Q1 a ligatured long s (ſſ) was used. The difference between ſ and f was minute and mistakes sometimes occurred.

       Setting the two letters, ſ and s, required the compositor to make two deliberate choices from his type case. Thus, if *eel-skin* was intended, he has not mistaken a single letter only, but has made a rather complex sequence of errors – a mistaken letter and a reversal of letters. On the other hand, if *elf-skin* was intended, a very simple and likely error has occurred – ſ has been set instead of f. This was probably the result of faulty distribution: that is, ſ could have been put into the compartment reserved for f in the compositor's case when type previously used was being distributed.

       The choice is not an easy one, but as the meaning is sound, it is felt that the implications of the setting of ſ and s should here be taken into account and *elf-skin* selected.

241   *neat's-tongue* ox-tongue

241   *bull's-pizzle* bull's penis (which when dried was used as a whip)

       stock-fish dried cod

243   *standing tuck* (a small rapier standing on its end. A rapier was also said to stand when the blade was no longer resilient.)

251   *with a word* in brief

258   *starting-hole* bolt-hole

259   *apparent* manifest

260   *what trick hast thou now?* The problem here, for critics and performers, is, who is tricking whom? The 'fourth-wall convention', which still constitutes a very large part of our theatrical experience (in which the audience 'overhears' what is going on on the stage, as if the fourth wall of the room had been removed), was not known to the Elizabethans. We know that the Elizabethan comedians directed their attentions directly to the audience, conversed with members of the audience, and even moved among them. The relationship of performers (especially clowns) to audience was similar to that of music-hall performers to audience, and this may, to some extent, have been so for serious scenes also (as at I.2.193–215 in this play. See also the Introduction, page 19).

       Whilst this scene could be played as if the audience 'overheard' what was going on, and the actors assumed that the audience was not there, it has been more recently felt either that the Prince and Poins share the joke with the audience, or that Falstaff does. Falstaff is certainly in a corner when Poins poses this question at line 260 – but the scene can be played so that it is he who has led the Prince and Poins into a verbal ambush (just as they ambushed him physically in II.2). Falstaff is enjoying the situation as much as the Prince and Poins – and the audience.

       It is a commonplace of duo acts of this kind in the nineteenth and twentieth centuries (and their type can be seen in Shakespeare's own plays) that *both* parties appeal directly to the audience. Thus, after the quite magical pause that should follow Poins's question, we with the Prince and Poins are put down, yet, because of our association with Falstaff also, we delight in our discomfiture. The perfection of such a joke as this depends not on wit, but upon the relationships established between performers and audience, and it is these relationships, if re-created by the actors, that make this moment supremely comic time after time. As at II.2.33, Falstaff's enjoyment of the joke is vital (see note to that line), but line 276 shows he is also hurt.

265   *The lion will not touch the true prince* (a belief traceable back to Pliny)

268-9   *thou for a true prince.* That Falstaff, the lion, would not touch Hal proves his legitimacy – and see I.2.138-9, 152-54.

270-71   *Watch tonight, pray tomorrow!* 'Watch' means both to keep watch and to revel or carouse. Once again, Falstaff echoes a Biblical text – 'Watch, and pray, that ye enter not into temptation', Matthew 26.41 – and once again Falstaff perverts the meaning. The joke would have been more obvious, to an Elizabethan audience, if Falstaff was called after the Lollard, Oldcastle.

274   *argument* plot (some plays were preceded in printed editions with an outline of the plot and this was called The Argument)

276   *no more of that* (the joke is now over)

283-4   *royal man.* A noble ('nobleman', line 280) was worth 6s. 8d., and a royal, ten shillings.

287   *What doth gravity out of his bed at midnight?* This is a question, in so far as gravity implied old age, that Falstaff might have asked of himself.

299   *swear truth out of England* swear so fully and so falsely that there would be no place left for truth in England

302   *tickle our noses with spear-grass.* The nose could be made to bleed easily, and fairly painlessly, by irritating the inside of the nostril with one of a variety of grasses. It was done by beggars at one time; it is still done by children. Derrick, in *The Famous Victories of Henry the Fifth* tells how he did this when a soldier:

> *Every day when I went into the field,*
> *I would take a straw and thrust it into my nose*
> *And make my nose bleed.*

305   *that* something

308   *taken with the manner* caught in the act (a legal expression)

309   *fire* (referring to Bardolph's complexion – as does Falstaff, III.3.26–7)

313   *exhalations* fiery meteors

316   *Hot livers, and cold purses* liverishness and an empty purse (because got with drinking)

317   *Choler.* Bardolph maintains he is not to be trifled with.

318   *rightly taken* (1) properly understood; (2) justly arrested
    halter (destined for hanging)

320   *bombast* (1) cotton or wool used for padding (2) high-flown language

324   *thumb-ring* (used in sealing documents)

329   *Amamon* (a devil)
    bastinado beating on the soles of the feet

330   *made Lucifer cuckold* was the reason why horns grew on Lucifer's head

331   *liegeman* subject
    Welsh hook (pike or bill – having no hilt, forming a cross, it could not be sworn on. See note to II.4.202.)

341   *So did he never the sparrow.* Hal's wit is, at times, very like Hotspur's – compare this with the latter's response to Glendower's claim that he 'can call spirits from the vasty deep'. 'But will they come,' says Hotspur, 'when you do call for them?' (III.1.50–52).

342   *good mettle* (1) a good spirit (and so no coward); (2) good metal (which does not run)

346   *cuckoo* (to cuckoo is to repeat incessantly)

350   *blue-caps* Scots (in blue bonnets)

361   *spirit* 'spirited', and perhaps, 'devil'

368   *practise an answer.* This is the play extempore suggested by Falstaff at line 273, but the subject is of Falstaff's choosing. A play is also given in *The Famous Victories of Henry the Fifth* in which John Cobbler plays the Lord Chief Justice and Derrick the young Prince.

371   *state* chair of state

374   *leaden* (and so, useless)

376–7   *an the fire of grace be not quite out of thee.* At I.2.17–18 Falstaff maintains the Prince has none.

379   *in passion* with deep emotion

379–80   *in King Cambyses' vein* after the style of *Cambyses*, Thomas Preston's extravagant but primitive tragedy (1569). Dr Johnson thought Shakespeare may not have known the play at first hand (though he seems to parody its title in *A Midsummer Night's Dream*). Certainly Shakespeare does not imitate its rhymed fourteeners. Falstaff begins in an exaggerated style (lines 384 and 386–7), but with his 'Peace, good pint-pot' he quickly relapses into a form of humour more suitable for him. It is doubtful if an extended parody of Preston's play was ever intended. Lyly is a more likely object of parody and Kyd has been suggested for lines 386–7.

381   *my leg* my bow (to introduce myself)

384   *Weep not.* Preston's *Cambyses* has a stage direction instructing the queen to weep. The Hostess's tears are of laughter, of course.

385   *holds his countenance* keeps a straight face

386   *tristful.* The reading of all the quartos and the Folio is 'trustful'. This emendation comes from the Dering manuscript (see An Account of the Text) but that does not mean the reading has special authority: it is simply

an excellent conjecture which later editors have been glad to accept.

388   *harlotry* (used affectionately, not abusively)

390–91   *tickle-brain* (a cant name at the time for a strong drink)

393–4   *camomile*. The camomile proverbially grew faster the more it was trodden on. The style parodies Lyly's *Euphues*.

397   *trick* characteristic
foolish wanton, roguish

398   *nether* lower
warrant indicate

400   *pointed at* (contemptuously)

400–   *prove a micher, and eat blackberries.* To mitch or mooch
401   was to play truant, especially to gather blackberries. This passage has also been said to be imitative of Lyly.

402   *son* (a quibble on 'sun', the symbol of royalty; see note to I.2.195)

405   *ancient writers*. One ancient writer who stated that 'Who so toucheth pitch, shall be defiled withal' was the author of Ecclesiasticus (13.1) and another, less ancient, was Lyly. The joke lies in giving ancient authority for the most common expression.

408   *in passion* with emotion

412   *portly* stately
corpulent well-made

416   *lewdly* wickedly

417–18   *If then the tree may be known . . . as the fruit by the tree.* This was a popular saying. It occurs in Matthew 12.33 and Luke 6.44.

418   *peremptorily* decisively

426   *for a rabbit-sucker, or a poulter's hare* for (something as slight as) a baby rabbit or a hare hanging in a poulterer's shop

427   *set* seated

434   *ungracious* graceless

436   *tun* 'large barrel' (with a quibble on 'ton weight')

438   *humours* secretions (with the implication of 'diseases')

438   *bolting-hutch* sifting-bin

439   *bombard* large leather wine-vessel

440   *cloak-bag* portmanteau

       Manningtree ox. East Anglia was well-known for its cattle but not Manningtree specifically. Thomas Heywood, however, in his *An Apology for Actors* (1612) states that 'to this day, in divers places in England, there be towns that hold the privilege of their fairs, and other charters by yearly stage-plays, as at Manningtree in Suffolk, and Kendal in the North, and others'. The reference to fairs suggests that such festivities included the roasting of a whole ox – something that might well have had pleasant associations for actors concerned with the plays – and a sequence of morality terms occurs in the next two lines.

441   *pudding* stuffing

441–2 *Vice ... Iniquity ... Ruffian ... Vanity.* These are all names of characters in Morality plays. A *ruffian* (or *ruffin*) was a devil. For the Vice, see note to lines 131–2.

444   *cleanly* deft

       cunning skilful

447   *take me with you* let me know your meaning

455   *saving your reverence* (a formula excusing possible offence)

459   *Pharaoh's lean kine* (Genesis 41)

464–5 *Banish plump Jack, and banish all the world.* As Falstaff ends this speech, the mood of comedy gives way to sentiment – indeed to sentimentality on his part. Perhaps he senses that so far as Hal is concerned, he is expendable. The knocking at the door comes at just the right moment to ensure that an even keel is restored, for as Falstaff angrily says in his next speech, 'I have much to say in the behalf of that Falstaff.'

468   *watch* watchmen, officers to maintain order

472–3 *the devil rides upon a fiddle-stick* what the devil's all the fuss (a proverbial expression)

476   *Dost thou hear, Hal?* This first sentence of a puzzling

speech can refer to two things: Falstaff's wish to say what he has to say 'in the behalf of that Falstaff' (his situation being very like that of Francis at the beginning of the scene when Poins kept interrupting – see note to line 49); and Falstaff's attempt to get Hal to take the arrival of this 'most monstrous watch' seriously. As Falstaff tries to get rid of Bardolph and his unwelcome news (lines 469–70), it is more likely that he is trying, with some desperation, to hold Hal's attention for just a moment longer. If this is so, it suggests the meaning underlying the obscure lines that follow.

476–8 *Never call a true piece of gold a counterfeit. Thou art essentially made without seeming so.* Many interpretations have been offered of these lines. One possibility, quite different from that suggested here, is that Falstaff is begging not to be given away. Some editors have suggested amending *made* to 'mad'.

The first sentence clearly means do not mistake the genuine for the false. The key word in the second sentence (addressed to Hal) is *essentially*. This occurs in *Hamlet*, III.4.187, being opposed to 'craft' (a word associated with *counterfeit*): 'I essentially am not in madness, | But mad in craft.' The opposition in this second line is, again, between the genuine and the false. The whole passage may be explained, however, from within *1 Henry IV*, as a whole, and from this scene in particular. Frequently in the play the word 'true' occurs. In this scene it is used by Falstaff of Hal and of himself. At lines 263–9 we have the business of the lion recognizing a 'true prince' – and this Hal is, with some emphasis – recognized as being. At lines 460–65 Falstaff makes his appeal – not comic, but deeply felt – that 'true Jack Falstaff' (with many other qualities besides) should not be banished.

It is in these lines that we have the essence of Falstaff's plea. He begs that he will not be regarded as anything but true: and as Hal is a true prince (which, however he behaves, essentially he is), he will not neglect (banish) a comrade, for to do so would be the reverse of being true.

This interpretation is in accord with the play as a whole. Hal is seeking his true self and his awareness of this, and ours, is made clear in I.2.193-215, where he compares himself, amongst other things, to 'bright metal on a sullen ground' (line 210). As 'bright metal' he is *essentially made* even if, because his (the sun's) beauty has been smothered from the world, he is *essentially made without seeming so*. (And if the metaphors appear to be mixed in this explication, it might be claimed that gold was thought to be a product of the sun.) See also Hal's answer at III.2.92-3.

481   *I deny your major. If you will deny the sheriff* ... Falstaff has failed to get his message through to Hal – he has been dismissed as 'a natural coward without instinct'. He resorts to an involved pun (on *major* and 'mayor' – the sheriff being his officer) and attempts to use syllogistic logic to answer Hal – he denies his major premiss. But more important than this involved quibbling is the anticipation this moment has of Falstaff's rejection in *2 Henry IV*. Faced with the possibility of arrest Falstaff retains a certain dignity (which he will soon lose): 'If you will deny the sheriff, so; if not, let him enter.'

483   *bringing up* (1) upbringing, (2) being summonsed

485   *arras* (here, the curtain closing off the inner stage from the main playing area)

492   *hue and cry* general pursuit

497   *not here*. This is not strictly 'true'. Falstaff is not in the room because he has hidden behind the arras.

500   *dinner-time*. Dinner was served some time before noon and could last two or three hours.

502   *withal* in addition

511   *Paul's* (St Paul's Cathedral)

524   *ob.* obolus, halfpenny (sometimes modernized in performance)

526   *intolerable* exceedingly great

527   *close* safely, secretly

        at more advantage at a more convenient time

530   *a charge of foot* an infantry company

531   *twelve score* (paces)

532   *advantage* interest

III.1   Shakespeare gives no location but an eighteenth-century editor suggested the Archdeacon's house in Bangor, North Wales, where, according to the historian Holinshed, such a meeting took place.

2   *induction* opening scene (of a play)

     prosperous hope hopes of success

11   *my nativity.* These portents may have been suggested by those that are reported by Holinshed to have occurred at Mortimer's birth. Holinshed also mentions a blazing star which was seen in 1402 and was said to foretell Glendower's success in battle against Lord Grey; this may have suggested to Shakespeare the idea of associating portents with Glendower's birth.

13   *cressets.* A cresset was a metal basket, suspended or carried on a pole, into which were put combustible materials, the result, when set alight, being like a blazing torch. The word here suggests 'blazing stars', perhaps from the star observed in 1402 (see note on line 11).

25   *eruptions* outbreaks (as in the eruption of spots in the course of a disease)

25–30   *oft the teeming earth | Is with a kind of colic pinched ... and topples down | Steeples and moss-grown towers.* This explanation of earthquakes goes back to classical times. It is mentioned by Aristotle and Pliny.

25   *teeming* pregnant, over-full

29 *beldam* grandmother (with a suggestion of witchcraft from the second meaning of *beldam*: hag or witch)

31 *distemperature* disorder

32 *passion* agony
of from

33 *crossings* contradictions

35 *front of heaven* sky

41 *clipped* bound

42 *chides* contends with, beats against

43 *read to* lectured

45 *trace* follow

46 *hold me pace* keep up with me
deep experiments investigations into the depths – the occult

47 *speaks better Welsh.* The surface meaning is obvious but beneath the compliment is a double insult. To 'speak Welsh' was to speak double-Dutch – nonsense; it was also to brag.

55 *Tell truth, and shame the devil.* Hotspur's delight in his use of this proverbial saying is very clear and rather childlike. His humour in these exchanges is not unlike Hal's in his little game with Francis (II.4).

60 *Three times* (1400, 1402, and, antedated here, 1405)
made head raised an army

63 *Bootless* unsuccessful
weather-beaten (according to Holinshed, 'by mists and tempests sent')

65 *scapes* escapes

66 *right* rights, what we claim

67 *threefold order taken* triple entente

70 *hitherto* to this point

76 *indentures tripartite* triple agreement
drawn drawn up

77 *sealed interchangeably* (so that each party to the agreement has a copy signed by the other two)

78 *this night may execute* may be done this evening

83 *father* father-in-law

88   *in my conduct* escorted by me, in my care

92   *Methinks my moiety.* When Hal imitated Hotspur he
        parodied this habit his rival had of delaying his
        response (II.4.106–7).

        moiety share (not necessarily a half)

        Burton (on the river Trent)

94   *cranking* winding

96   *cantle.* All the quartos print 'scantle', which means a
        small portion. The Folio has 'cantle', a segment. The
        Folio's emendation has generally been accepted.
        'Scantle' may have been the result of the final letter of
        'monstrous' being attracted to 'cantle' as the com-
        positor said the line to himself as he set it in type.

98   *smug* smooth

101   *bottom* valley

106   *Gelding* cutting

        continent bank (that which contains)

111   *charge* expenditure

120   *gave the tongue a helpful ornament.* Glendower quibbles.
        When he sang 'an English ditty', he graced it with a
        delightful accent (a defence of his Welsh), set it to
        music ('framed to the harp'), and gave to the English
        language (*tongue*) something of literary worth (*a helpful
        ornament*) – achievements Hotspur could not claim.

124   *metre* metrical, doggerel

125   *canstick* candlestick

128   *mincing* affected (poetic) feet

131   *I do not care.* Hotspur may seem capricious, but his
        attitudes, though they change rapidly, are not un-
        becoming to him by Elizabethan standards. He is at
        one and the same time quixotically generous and
        determined to maintain his rights (as he understands
        them).

138   *Break with* break the news to

142–3   *Sometime he angers me | With telling me.* It is a trifle
        ironic that Hotspur, so free with his views, should
        complain of Glendower's capacity for talking. As

events prove, however, Hotspur's talking is supported by his actions whereas Glendower is 'o'er-ruled by prophecies' (IV.4.18). It is noteworthy that Hotspur, on hearing the news that Glendower has failed them, wastes no breath in bemoaning his absence (IV.1.130–34).

143 *moldwarp* mole

144 *Merlin* (wizard or prophet at King Arthur's court)

147 *couching, ramping* (parodic forms of heraldic terms: couchant – lying; rampant – rearing)

148 *skimble-skamble* nonsense (a word coined by Shakespeare)

149 *faith* (in Christ)

152 *'Hum', and 'Well, go to'* (simulating interest when bored)

156 *windmill* (because noisy and unsteady)

157 *cates* delicacies

160–1 *profited | In strange concealments* proficient in secret arts (compare line 46)

171 *wilful-blame* wilfully blameworthy

175 *blood* spirit

176 *dearest* noblest
grace credit

177 *present* show

178 *want of government* lack of self-control

179 *opinion* conceit

183 *Beguiling* cheating, defrauding

184 *good manners be your speed* may it be good manners that gives you success (in battle). In view of the way in which Worcester beguiles Hotspur by not revealing 'The liberal and kind offer of the King' (V.2.2), this is rather an ironic exchange.

185 *and*. In Elizabethan English *and* could connect an affirmation and a command. Another instance occurs at V.4.33.

190 *my aunt Percy*. The Mortimer who was Glendower's son-in-law was Lady Percy's brother; the Mortimer

who was proclaimed heir to the throne was Lady Percy's nephew – but he did not marry Glendower's daughter. The family relationship is described in notes to I.3.79 and 83.

191 (stage direction) *Glendower speaks to her in Welsh*. It has been suggested that when the play was first performed, a Welsh singing boy was available to Shakespeare's company.

193 *harlotry*. As at II.4.388, *harlotry* is not used here to imply prostitution. It is intended affectionately, if slightly deprecatingly, as if to say Glendower's daughter is a silly little wretch, a misery.

195 *swelling heavens* eyes filled with tears

196 *I am too perfect in* I understand only too well

197 *should I answer thee* (by weeping also – were it not shameful)

199 *feeling disputation* dialogue of feelings (not speech)

202 *highly penned* high flown

204 *division* (a rapid passage of short notes based on a simple theme)

207 *wanton rushes*. Rushes covered the floor (and also the stage in all probability), and these have been spread wantonly – without restraint.

210 *crown* give absolute power to

214 *heavenly-harnessed team* sun (from the team of horses driven by Helios, the sun god)

217 *book* indentures tripartite (mentioned in line 76)

218–19 *those musicians that shall play to you | Hang in the air a thousand leagues from hence*. The musicians who are to provide the music are spirits, like those which Prospero requires to give *Some heavenly music* (*The Tempest*, V.1.52).

221 *thou art perfect in lying down* (with sexual innuendo)

225 *he is so humorous*. The punctuation of Q1 at the end of lines 224 and 225 (given in this text) does not make it clear whether the devil (*he*) is humorous because he speaks Welsh (a comical language to learn in Hotspur's

opinion), or because of the association of humour and music with the devil (compare II.4.472-3 – 'the devil rides upon a fiddle-stick'). Q6 (1622) made the matter clear by punctuating with a full stop after 'Welsh' (line 224). This is attractive (though that quarto has no special authority) as an emendation, but it has not been used here because, whether intended or not, the punctuation given us in Q1 suggests the way Hotspur's mind moves from one association to another. Lady Percy, it will be noted, takes up the association of *humorous* and 'musician', punning on the first word to give 'humours' – whims (see note to IV.1.31).

229   *Lie still, ye thief, and hear the lady sing in Welsh.* This banter delightfully expresses Lady Percy's love for her husband (see also the note to II.3.93-4).

230   *brach.* Properly, this is a hound that hunts by scent; loosely it means a 'bitch', and is used as a term of abuse. Hotspur is surely using a word that has all the appearances of being Welsh (though it is not) as a kind of joke – a rather more subtle one than he usually makes. The phrase 'Lady the brach' occurs in *King Lear* (I.4.111), and 'brach' within a list of dogs at III.6.68 in that same play.

233   *still* silent

234   *'tis a woman's fault* (to be unable to remain quiet or still)

241-2   *you swear like a comfit-maker's wife.* Just as Hal parodied Hotspur in II.4, so now Hotspur mimics his wife. The relationship of the humour used by Hal and Hotspur is discussed in the Introduction. 'Comfits' were sugar-plums – crystallized fruits.

243   *mend* amend

245   *sarcenet* (light as) silk

246   *Finsbury.* In Shakespeare's day, a favourite walk and place of recreation was Finsbury Fields. It was the sort of entertainment enjoyed by sober citizens – or so it is

implied. The joke is not so much at Lady Percy's expense (though it fits the context well enough if one allows for the anachronism), as an allusion for the enjoyment of the audience for whom it would be local and topical. This is an example of a character stepping out of his role, though not to the same extent as Falstaff does in recounting the events at Gad's Hill (see the note to II.4.260).

247   *a lady* an aristocrat (a plebeian concept, surely, and hardly appropriate to Hotspur)

249   *protest* protestation
       pepper-gingerbread. The precise meaning is not clear – perhaps 'mealy-mouthed' with a touch of pepper, a touch of 'acid', is the nearest equivalent. Whatever the exact meaning, Hotspur's protest comes across vividly.

250   *velvet-guards* velvet trimmings (that is, those who wear them – citizens in their finery)

253–4 *'Tis the next way to turn tailor, or be redbreast teacher.* Hotspur offers mock encouragement, realizing Lady Percy will not sing: 'It's the best way to fit yourself to be a tailor, or to become a teacher of robins'. Tailors, like weavers (see II.4.128–9) and robins, were held to be good singers.

258   *By this* (time)
       book agreement
       but just

III.2.1 *give us leave* (to be alone)
6   *doom* judgement
8   *passages* events, incidents
9–11   *thou art only marked . . . To punish my mistreadings.* The meaning here is ambiguous. The passage can mean that Hal will suffer for Henry's sins (Richard's deposition) or that Henry is already being punished for his sins by the manner of Hal's behaviour. The second meaning

is probably intended. There seems no justification on this occasion for arguing that both meanings are meant.

12   *inordinate* (1) immoderate; (2) out of order (unworthy of your high rank)

13   *bare* wretched

      lewd base

      attempts exploits

14   *rude* uncivilized

15   *withal* with (and at line 21)

17   *hold their level with* put themselves on a level with

19   *Quit* acquit myself of

20   *doubtless* certain

22   *extenuation* mitigation

23   *many tales devised* much malicious gossip

25   *pickthanks* talebearers (the word is derived from Holinshed)

28   *Find pardon on my true submission.* Hal asks forgiveness for what he has truly done especially as he is guiltless of many things said against him.

30   *affections* inclinations

      hold a wing take a course (a term from falconry)

31   *from* away from

32   *rudely lost.* Shakespeare omits the reason here, although it is mentioned in all the sources, including *The Famous Victories of Henry the Fifth*, and by Falstaff in *2 Henry IV*, when he says to the Lord Chief Justice, 'For the box o' the ear that the prince gave you, he gave it like a rude Prince, and you took it like a sensible lord' (I.2.182–3). It is noticeable that 'rude' (uncivilized) is used on each occasion.

39   *Had I so lavish of my presence been.* It was not thought proper for a king to show himself over-frequently to his people.

40   *common-hackneyed.* One part of this word duplicates the other; in combination the result is forceful and individual. Henry's account of his behaviour does not tally with that given by Richard in *Richard II* where,

with a variety of detail, he is said to court the common people, seeming 'to dive into their hearts | With humble and familiar courtesy' (I.4.25–6).

43   *possession* the possessor (King Richard)

45   *likelihood* (of having a future)

50   *I stole all courtesy from heaven* I assumed a divine graciousness. The word *stole* is not without significance. Although Henry is being shown in a favourable light here, he did steal Richard's throne.

54   *Even in the presence of the crownèd King.* The allusion is probably to the entry of Bolingbroke (Henry) and Richard into London, described in *Richard II*, V.2, by York.

56   *pontifical* (as worn by a Pope or bishop)

60   *skipping* frivolous. Richard's faults are, not surprisingly, exaggerated by Henry.

61   *rash* quickly lighted

       bavin faggot used for kindling (and soon burnt out)

62   *carded his state.* To 'card' wool is to tease out impurities and to straighten the fibres by means of a comb-like device. It is not, as has sometimes been suggested, a process in which various qualities of fibre are mixed (hence implying that the King debased himself by associating with inferiors), but essentially a cleansing and straightening process. Carding of the mixing kind was used for shuffling cards, but as this fault is described in the line that follows ('Mingled his royalty with capering fools'), there is no need to repeat it. The word *carded* here means, surely, 'tortured' – tore at, or scratched, his state – a form of torture practised in the period. The textile association of *carded* presumably led Shakespeare to think of mingling. Another textile processing term is used at III.2.137 – 'scour'.

65   *countenance* authority

       against his name to the detriment of his reputation

66   *push* pushing and shoving

67   *comparative* dealer in insults (see also I.2.80)

69   *Enfeoffed* surrendered
       popularity the common people

77   *community* familiarity

79   *sun-like majesty*. The sun is a traditional symbol of
       royalty (see note to I.2.195). Its association here with
       'cloudy men' (line 83), hostile to the sun, is similar to
       the association of the sun with 'the base contagious
       clouds' in I.2.195–6.

87   *vile participation* (low companions)

91   *foolish tenderness* tears

94   *As thou art to this hour was Richard.* The likeness of Hal
       to Richard may not seem obvious, but it evidently
       struck Shakespeare. In *Richard II*, when Henry
       anxiously asked after Hal he described him as a 'young
       wanton and effeminate boy' (V.3.10). In one of Shake-
       speare's sources for that play, and this one, Samuel
       Daniel's *The First Four Books of the Civil Wars Between
       the Two Houses of Lancaster and York* (1595), Richard II
       is called 'This wanton young effeminate'.

97   *to boot* as well

98   *worthy interest* right by worth

100   *colour* semblance

101   *harness* armed men

102   *Turns head* (1) turns his eyes; (2) turns the army he has
       raised

103   *And being no more in debt to years than thou.* Hotspur
       was actually older than Henry IV, Hal's father (see
       note to I.1.86–7).

109   *chief majority* pre-eminence

112   *Thrice.* The battles were Otterburn (at which the
       English were defeated and Hotspur was captured;
       Hal was then aged one), Nesbit (see note to I.1.55),
       and Holmedon. Douglas's father was killed by Hotspur
       at Otterburn.

116   *To fill . . . up* to increase, to enlarge

120   *Capitulate* sign agreements
       are up (in arms)

123 *dearest.* The first meaning is 'most precious' but there is also a pun on *dearest*: 'direst'.

124 *vassal* base, abject

125 *start of spleen* fit of pique

126 *To fight against me under Percy's pay.* This very serious charge had no foundation at the time but it is possible that Shakespeare had in mind a reported usurpation of the crown by Hal in 1412, a decade later. There is a dramatic moment in *2 Henry IV* when Hal, believing his father to be dead, puts the crown on his head, only to be bitterly rebuked by Henry:

> *I stay too long by thee, I weary thee.*
> *Dost thou so hunger for my empty chair*
> *That thou wilt needs invest thee with mine honours*
> *Before thy hour be ripe?*   IV.5.92-5

See also V.4.50-56 of this play.

136 *favours* features

141 *unthought-of* poorly thought-of, despised

147 *factor* agent

151 *worship of his time* honour of his lifetime

156 *intemperance* wild behaviour. F substitutes 'intemperature', which is an attractive reading (for it means both 'licentiousness' and 'distempered condition') but, as is argued in An Account of the Text, has no authority.

159 *parcel* portion

161 *charge* a command

   sovereign trust (1) a most important command; (2) the King's wholehearted trust

164 *Lord Mortimer of Scotland.* This is yet another, but a different, confusion concerning the Mortimers, who were Lords of the Welsh Marches (or Borders). George Dunbar was Earl of the Scottish Marches (see note introducing II.3).

167 *head* army

172 *advertisement* news

175-6 *Harry, you | Shall march through Gloucestershire.* This would require a journey by a secondary route. Shakespeare, or Hal, forgets this plan, for Hal meets Falstaff in IV.2 near Coventry on the main Shrewsbury road.

177 *Our business valued* our affairs put in order

180 *him* himself

III.3 As the Hostess enters after line 50, we are evidently in the tavern in Eastcheap.

2 *last action* (at Gad's Hill, or possibly the engagement with Hal in II.4)

 bate lose weight

4 *old apple-john* (an apple noted for its long-keeping qualities. Although the flesh remained sound, the skin shrivelled.)

5 *suddenly* at once

 am in some liking (1) feel like doing so; (2) still have some flesh on me

5-6 *out of heart* (1) dispirited; (2) in poor condition

6 *no strength* (of body, and, of purpose)

7 *An* if

8 *peppercorn* mere nothing (as in 'a peppercorn rent')

 brewer's horse (notoriously worn out)

11 *fretful* (1) anxious; (2) fretted (worn)

13 *there is it* there it is

18-19 *in good compass* within bounds

19-20 *out of all compass* (with a glance at his girth)

25 *admiral* flagship

27 *Knight of the Burning Lamp* (a parody of Amadis, Knight of the Burning Sword, a chivalric figure. Beaumont parodies him in his *The Knight of the Burning Pestle*.)

29-30 *as good use of it as many a man doth of a death's-head.* This seems to be ambiguous, perhaps deliberately so. Rings were engraved with a skull and these served as a reminder of death ('*memento mori*'). But they were regularly worn by prostitutes, of which many a man makes use.

31   *Dives* (the rich man who feasted whilst Lazarus starved – Luke 16; see also IV.2.24)

35   *God's angel*. The allusion is probably to the story of Moses and the Burning Bush in which, it is said, 'the angel of the Lord appeared unto him in a flame of fire' (Exodus 3.2).

    given over (to Satan)

39   *ignis fatuus* fool's fire, will o'the wisp

    ball of wildfire firework (and possibly, erysipelas – a skin disease)

40   *purchase* value

    triumph illumination for a festival

42   *links* small flaming torches

44   *drunk me* (an archaic construction; modern English does not require 'me')

44–5   *good cheap* cheaply

46   *salamander* (fabulous lizard that lives in and on fire)

48   *I would my face were in your belly* (proverbial retort)

51   *dame Partlet* (a traditional name for a hen, and so a fussy woman. 'Pertelote' is the name of the hen in Chaucer's *Nun's Priest's Tale*.)

58   *shaved*. In addition to its usual meaning, 'shaved' could mean 'cheated' and 'to have caught syphilis' (which was believed to lead to baldness).

60   *you are a woman* (and thus unreliable if not untrustworthy)

68   *Dowlas* (cheap linen from Doulas in Brittany)

69   *bolters* (cloths used for sieving)

70   *holland* (fine linen, and rather over-priced at eight shillings an ell)

71   *ell* (in England, 45 inches)

72   *by-drinkings* drinks between meals

78   *denier* (one-tenth of a penny)

79   *younker*. An alternative name for the prodigal in the parable of the prodigal son was 'the younger'.

81   *mark* (13s. 4d.)

84   *Jack* knave

86   (stage direction) *playing upon his truncheon like a fife.*
Presumably when Falstaff says in line 85 that he would
cudgel Hal, he imitates the action. When Hal enters,
Falstaff rapidly and comically changes his 'business' to
meet the new situation.

87   *door* quarter

89   *Newgate fashion* two by two (as prisoners)

111-12 *stewed prune* prostitute

112   *drawn fox.* The meaning is not clear; perhaps the joke
has been lost to us. It has been explained as a fox drawn
from cover and so relying upon cunning for its life; a
disembowelled fox; a dead fox used to give a false trail;
and a drawn sword (so named because of the figure of a
wolf engraved on the blade which was mistaken for a
fox).

113-14 *Maid Marian may be the deputy's wife of the ward to
thee.* The deputy of a ward was a highly respectable
citizen, and his wife was expected to be so also. Maid
Marian's reputation was very low, however, and thus
Falstaff says that compared to the Hostess, Maid
Marian was a highly respectable woman.

116   *What thing* (a sexual quibble)

117   *no thing* (another sexual quibble)

126   *where to have her* (with sexual quibble)

147   *The King himself is to be feared as the lion.* The lion, like
the sun, was a symbol of royalty (see note to I.2.195).

149   *I pray God my girdle break* (a proverbial saying)

155   *embossed rascal.* There are probably puns on both
words. *Embossed* can mean (1) swollen; (2) slavering
like a hunted deer; *rascal* is (1) a knave; (2) a lean,
inferior deer.

157-8 *sugar-candy to make thee long-winded.* Even in Shakespeare's day sugar was prescribed to aid stamina –
particularly that of fighting cocks!

159   *injuries* (things whose loss you complain of as injuries.

The use of *injuries* with this meaning makes possible a pun on 'wrong' in line 160.)

167   *by* according to

168   *Hostess, I forgive thee.* Doubtless Dame Partlet will be so flustered by now that she will feel gratified at being forgiven for what is Falstaff's fault.

171   *still* now

177–8   *double labour* (taking it and returning it)

182   *with unwashed hands* without wasting any time

184   *charge of foot* company of infantry (see II.4.530)

196   *the Temple hall* Inner Temple Hall (a popular meeting-place)

199   *furniture* furnishing, equipment

203   *I could wish this tavern were my drum.* This has not been wholly satisfactorily explained. It has been suggested that there is a pun on *tavern* and 'taborn', a kind of drum; or that Falstaff wishes the tavern were the only drum he must follow, which, as it stands, is not very close although the sense is reasonable.

There seem to be two other possibilities. A *drum* was at this time a small party of soldiers sent, with a drummer, to discuss terms with an enemy. Falstaff might feel that any military party discussing terms might for preference meet at a tavern. Secondly, Falstaff says *my drum* – Jack's Drum. Jack Drum's Entertainment was a rowdy reception – a fair description of a battle, and of the behaviour of Falstaff and company in the tavern (as, for example, when the Sheriff arrives in II.4). Shakespeare uses the expression John Drum's entertainment in *All's Well that Ends Well* (III.6.33) and Marston wrote a play called *Jack Drum's Entertainment*, published in 1600.

IV.1   The scene is set in the camp of the rebels at Shrewsbury.

2   *fine* refined

3   *attribution* (of praise)
4   *stamp* stamping, coinage
5   *general current* widely accepted (and see the note on
     the use of *current* at II.3.97)
6   *defy* distrust
7   *soothers* flatterers
     braver finer
9   *task* test
     approve me put me to the proof
11   *ground* earth
12   *beard* come face to face (literally, 'pull by the beard',
     and particularly 'beard the lion')
13   *I can but thank you.* Hotspur's reply is delayed – a trick
     imitated by Hal (see note to II.4.101–107) – but here
     with some reason as he responds naturally to the Mes-
     senger's entry.
16   *he is grievous sick.* Northumberland's illness occurred
     earlier. It is mentioned by Holinshed immediately
     after his account of how Worcester, 'that had the
     government of the Prince of Wales' conveyed himself
     'in secret manner' out of the Prince's house. Shake-
     speare brings news of Northumberland's illness to
     light just before the battle of Shrewsbury, so bringing
     out his son's impetuosity and courage, and perhaps
     suggesting that the father was as devious as the son was
     outspoken. His reasons for not sending a force to
     support his son (lines 30–8) are not very convincing.
     Whereas Shakespeare refashions history for dramatic
     effect in this instance, he makes no use of the fact,
     available in the same section of the same source, that
     Worcester 'had the government' of Hal – except pos-
     sibly to pick up the word 'government' (command) for
     line 19.
20   *His letters bear his mind, not I, my lord.* This reply,
     what Touchstone might have called 'the Retort
     Courteous' (*As You Like It*, V.4.70), is not as deferen-
     tial in tone as one would expect from a mere mes-

senger – especially the carrier of bad tidings. The Messenger ought, perhaps, to be a member of the Percy household, a squire. In the quartos and the Folio, *bear* is given as 'bears'. Though a plural subject sometimes did have a verb in the singular in Elizabethan English, this has been emended here.

24   *feared* feared for

30   *'Tis catching hither* it will infect us here

31   *inward sickness –* . The quartos merely have a comma after *sickness*. Clearly the sense cannot run on to the next line. It is conceivable that a line has been lost, but the text as we have it is more likely a representation of the way in which Hotspur's thoughts run ahead of what he says (see also the note to III.1.225).

32   *deputation* others acting as his deputy

33   *drawn* drawn in, involved
    meet appropriate

35   *removed* not closely connected

36   *bold advertisement* (either 'confident advice', or 'instruction to be resolute')

37   *conjunction* forces so far joined together
    on go on

44   *present want* absence now

45   *more* greater
    find it (to be)

47   *main* (quibbling on 'stake' in a game of chance, and 'army')

48   *nice* delicate

50   *very bottom* whole extent
    soul essence (possibly with quibble on 'sole', the 'bottom' of the shoe, and the 'singleness' of such hope – but such is Shakespeare's potentiality for quibbling that we are inclined to see puns where none were intended and where they may be inappropriate)

51   *very list* extreme limit

54   *reversion* inheritance (prospect) to look forward to

56   *of retirement* into which to retreat

58–9   *look big | Upon* threaten

59   *maidenhead* first trial

61   *hair* appearance

62   *Brooks* permits

64   *mere* downright

66   *apprehension* idea, belief

67   *fearful* timorous

69   *offering side* side offering a challenge. 'Offering' is spelt
       'offring' in Q1 to make it, strictly, a two-syllable word.
       It has been spelt in full here, the speaker being
       expected to adjust the stress to suit his own style of
       speech (see also the note to I.1.8).

70   *strict arbitrement* impartial adjudication. Worcester's
       behaviour at the opening of V.2 accords with the
       opinion expressed here.

71   *loop* loop-hole

73   *draws* draws aside

74   *a kind of fear* (in us)

75   *strain too far* exaggerate

77   *opinion* repute

78   *dare* risk

80   *make a head* raise (such) a force

83   *joints* limbs

92   *intended* on the point of setting out

95   *nimble-footed.* Hal was reported in the histories to be
       particularly fleet of foot
       madcap (see I.2.140–41)

96   *daffed* tossed aside (compare 'doffed')

98–9   *All plumed like estridges that with the wind | Bated, like
       eagles having lately bathed.* These lines introduce a
       passage rich in images. Vernon's speech is no more
       representative of character than the Queen's speech in
       Hamlet that begins 'There is a willow grows aslant a
       brook' (IV.7.167). Vernon's words evoke that spirit
       of pride, honour, royalty, and ceremony, which is
       appropriate to this occasion. The moment here is one

of chivalric challenge. It will be contrasted by Shakespeare with its opposite, Falstaff's consideration of honour, his 'killing' of the dead Hotspur, and his comment on the 'grinning honour as Sir Walter hath' (V.3.59) (see also the Introduction). These two lines of Vernon's speech have been called the 'chief crux of the text' by John Dover Wilson and a number of emendations have been proposed. Two of the most interesting are the substitution of 'wing' for *with* and a much more radical rearrangement involving the omission of *estridges*, which, it is suggested, Shakespeare had failed to cancel clearly during revision. This would give the single line, 'All plumed like eagles having lately bathed', instead of the two lines printed in this edition (and Q1). The first proposal is helpful, but not essential; the second, though attractive, requires the omission of a particularly appropriate and colourful image, the Prince of Wales's plumes (ostrich feathers) ruffled (*Bated*) in the breeze. *Bated* can mean refreshed (exactly as in the dialect noun, 'bait', for food between main meals) but it is applied to food, not the refreshment that comes from bathing. *Estridges* could be goshawks, though this seems unlikely here. The passage may have been inspired by descriptions in Thomas Nashe's *The Unfortunate Traveller*, Spenser's *Faerie Queene* (I.xi.33–4), and most interestingly George Chapman's *De Guiana Carmen Epicum* (1596) where the following lines occur as Raleigh is about to leave on his second expedition to Guiana:

> *where round about*
> *His bating colours English valour swarms . . .*
> *And now a wind as forward as their spirits,*
> *Sets their glad feet on smooth* Guiana's *breast . . .*
> *And there doth plenty crown their wealthy fields,*
> *There* Learning *eats no more his thriftless books,*
> *Nor* Valour *estridge-like his iron arms.*

100 *coats* surcoats (worn over the armour and usually
     having the knight's arms depicted thereon)
     images effigies (of saints or warriors)

104 *beaver* (part of a helmet protecting the lower jaw)

105 *cuishes* cuisses, thigh-armour

107 *vaulted with such ease.* To jump, fully armoured, into
     the saddle was a feat requiring great strength and
     agility.

109 *turn and wind* turn and wheel-about (terms in horse-
     manship)

110 *witch* bewitch

111-12 *Worse than the sun in March, | This praise doth nourish
     agues.* The sun in March was thought to be strong
     enough to assist in the breeding of fevers without
     dispelling them. Some contemporary references relate
     to this action of the sun on the bodily humours, but the
     expression may also be related to the effect of the sun
     on marshland, for there, sun of this strength would
     encourage the marsh vapours to rise and propagate but
     would not be strong enough to dry up the marsh.
     (Compare *King Lear*: 'You fen-sucked fogs, drawn by
     the powerful sun', II.4.169.)

113 *like sacrifices in their trim.* Decked like this, they are
     as beasts for sacrifice.

114 *fire-eyed maid of smoky war* (Bellona, goddess of war.
     Macbeth was described by Shakespeare as 'Bellona's
     bridegroom' (*Macbeth*, I.2.56))

116 *Mars* (Roman god of war)

118 *this rich reprisal.* 'Reprisal' means 'prize'. The phrase
     is also appropriate to describe the style of Hotspur's
     rhetoric in reply to Vernon's description of Hal's
     chivalric company. The language in this speech is of
     blood, mail, smoke, and sacrifice. The images in
     Vernon's speech are altogether different; indeed, they
     are *'full of spirit as the month of May'* (line 101) as
     opposed to Hotspur's *'Worse than the sun in March'*
     (line 111).

123   *corpse*. In Q1 the spelling 'coarse' is used (for 'corse'), indicative of the Elizabethan pronunciation of this word.

126   *He cannot draw his power this fourteen days* he cannot collect his army together for a fortnight. Hotspur is now let down again, yet there is no outburst from him as there is when he describes the tedium of Glendower's conversation (III.1.142–58). In Holinshed's chronicle, the Welsh are said to be present at the battle, but in Daniel's poem on the civil war (see note to III.2.94) it is said that 'The swift approach and unexpected speed' of Henry's advance did not give time for the Welsh forces to reach Shrewsbury. Shakespeare evidently follows Daniel's account at this point and the reason is plain – Hotspur is further isolated.

129   *battle* battle array

130   *thirty thousand*. It is not possible to take too certainly estimates of numbers involved in medieval battles. Hotspur was said by Holinshed to have had 14,000 men, but his chronicle does not give a number for the King's army; another chronicle does give a figure of 30,000, and Hall gives a figure of 40,000 for those engaged on both sides.

132   *powers of us* forces we have
        serve suffice

134   *Die all, die merrily* if die we must, let it be cheerfully
135   *out of* free from

IV.2.3   *Sutton Coldfield* (to the north-east of Birmingham, well off the Coventry–Shrewsbury route)

5   *Lay out* use your own money

6   *an angel*. An *angel* was a coin with the Archangel Michael stamped on it and worth between 6s. 8d. and ten shillings – eleven or twelve shillings being a journeyman's weekly wage at the time.

8   *answer the coinage* be answerable for making money
that way ('coining' money on bottles)

9   *Peto.* At III.3.195 Hal tells Peto they have thirty miles
to ride together. It may seem (as it did to Dr Johnson)
that as Peto is with Falstaff here, some other name
(such as Poins's) should be substituted at III.3.195.
As, however, Hal was to travel through Gloucestershire (III.2.175–6) but appears in this scene, it is clear
that the plans have been changed, wittingly or not, by
Shakespeare.

12   *soused gurnet* preserved gurnet (a small fish with a big
head)

      misused the King's press misapplied the commission to
draft men (compare the expression 'press-gang')

14–15   *I press me none but good householders.* Falstaff's description of his technique is amusing roguery, but it must
have struck audiences of the time as not wholly comic.
The satire on the practice of pressing men (very common in the 1590s) might have been taken as an 'act', a
turn, in its own right and accepted as comic social
comment. Such turns were not uncommon in Elizabethan drama (for example, Launcelot Gobbo's mono-
logue in *The Merchant of Venice*, II.2) but Shakespeare,
unlike many of his colleagues, very soon begins to
integrate these in his plays (as is evident in the example
from *The Merchant of Venice*). If, however, we are to
see this account of pressing as integrated wholly within
the play, and thus being an outcome of Falstaff's
character (rather than a comic vehicle for the comedian), then it must reflect on the character himself
and this seems to be happening here. Here we have
a characteristic of Falstaff which an audience aware of
the implications of pressing would not find wholly to
its liking. The process begun at II.4.476–8 (and see
note thereon) is now put into effect, subtly but
distinctly. (See also Introduction, pages 33–4.)

15   *good* substantial (with money to buy themselves out)

17   *commodity*. Falstaff speaks of his men as merchandise which he can trade in order to make a profit.
     warm well-to-do
     slaves (contemptuous for 'subjects')

19   *caliver* light musket

20   *toasts-and-butter* milksops

23   *ancients* ensigns (of which the word is a corruption)

24   *gentlemen of companies* (gentlemen volunteers who held no formal rank – and see note to I.2.26.)

24–5   *Lazarus in the painted cloth*. Falstaff has already referred to the parable of Dives and Lazarus (III.3.31) and it is, once again, an instance of Falstaff's store of Biblical knowledge. 'Painted cloth' was a very inferior form of tapestry. (See note to line 33, below.)

27   *unjust* dishonest

27–8   *younger sons to younger brothers* (having no prospect of inheritance)

28   *revolted* runaway (see II.4.45–7)
     trade-fallen out of work

29   *cankers* parasites
     long peace (considered to be unhealthy – as if the state needed its blood let in accordance with the current medical practice)

30   *fazed* frayed

33   *prodigals*. Another Biblical reference from Falstaff, this time to the best known of all parables. The prodigal son, when he had spent all his money, was reduced to eating the food he had to serve the pigs. Shakespeare uses the word 'husks'. This is found in the Geneva Bible, not the Bishops' Bible (where 'ceddes' is used), which he seems to have been most familiar with (and from which Biblical quotations in this Commentary are taken). Falstaff also refers to the parable of the prodigal son in *2 Henry IV*, II.1.140.

34   *draff* pig-swill

40   *out of prison*. The practice of releasing prisoners to serve in the armed forces still occurs in some countries.

It had been permitted in London in 1596, just before
1 Henry IV was first performed, to provide men for
the expedition to Cadiz.

46   *find linen ... on every hedge*. Linen was put out to dry
by draping it over hedges (a practice still employed
by gipsies).

47   *blown* (1) short-winded; (2) swollen

    Jack (besides Falstaff's name, a contemptuous word
for 'fellow' and also the name for a soldier's quilted
jacket)

48–9   *What a devil dost thou in Warwickshire?* Falstaff quickly
asks Hal (perhaps bearing in mind the original arrangement – III.2.175–6 – though Falstaff was not present
on the occasion that this was revealed to the audience),
before Hal can ask him what he's up to.

58   *steal cream*. A pun on 'stale cream' has been suggested
here.

61   *Mine, Hal, mine*. The absence of any shame here
(despite his earlier assertion that he will not march
through Coventry with such a rabble), indeed, the
positive pride, is quite outrageous.

63   *to toss* (on pikes, as in *3 Henry VI*, I.1.244: 'The
soldiers should have tossed me on their pikes')

63–4   *food for powder*. Falstaff's lack of concern for his men
is surely more than a reflection of the attitude of
captains to their men in Elizabethan times – a greater
concern for their men's pay than their lives. This is no
comic turn in isolation (see the note on lines 14–15,
above) but an attitude that draws a little sympathy away
from Falstaff. Were he not a comic figure he could not
but appear despicable here; the dramatic conventions
of comedy protect him from the full implications of
what he says.

71–2   *three fingers in the ribs*. A finger measured three-
quarters of an inch and thus Falstaff's ribs are well
covered with flesh. In *The Merchant of Venice* there is
a contrary use of the relationship of ribs and fingers.

Launcelot refers to his being badly fed by saying, 'you may tell every finger I have with my ribs' (II.2.99), and traditionally he makes his blind father feel his fingers spread over his chest.

IV.3	The scene is set in Hotspur's camp at Shrewsbury.
3	*supply* reinforcements
10	*well-respected* well-considered
17	*of such great leading* who are such experienced generals
22	*pride and mettle* spirit
26	*journey-bated* weakened by travel
29	*stay* wait
30	*I come with gracious offers from the King.* The King's ambassador was the Abbot of Shrewsbury but, as in the first scene of the play, Blunt's role is enlarged (see note to I.1.63). From Hotspur's response, Blunt is clearly regarded highly by the rebels as well as by Henry. Thus his death, and Falstaff's reaction to it (see V.3.58–9), are built up to be more than incidental.
31	*respect* attention
36	*quality* party (with no reference to 'worth')
38	*defend* forbid
	still always
39	*limit* bounds of allegiance
41	*charge* official duty
42	*griefs* injuries
	whereupon wherefore
43	*conjure* call up
51	*suggestion* temptation (*suggestion* being a more sinister word than it now is)
52–3	*The King is kind ... when to pay.* These lines are neatly phrased by Hotspur to give just the right satiric impression. Whether the injuries Hotspur feels he has suffered are sufficient to justify rebellion or not, he here makes, very coolly and satirically, an exposé of

228

Henry's usurpation of Richard's throne. Blunt's response – 'Tut, I came not to hear this' – could be as much embarrassment as awareness that this was not the reason for Hotspur's present feelings of injury.

62   *sue his livery* beg for his inheritance following his father's death. ('As I was banished, I was banished Hereford; | But as I come, I come for Lancaster', *Richard II*, II.3.113–14).

          beg his peace (from Richard)

64   *in kind heart and pity moved.* Northumberland's heart was moved solely by self-interest.

68   *more and less* high and low

          with cap and knee cap in hand and on bended knee

70   *Attended* waited for

73   *golden* richly dressed

75   *Steps me* (an archaic construction; 'me' is no longer required)

          his vow (to seek no more than the inheritance to which he was entitled)

79   *strait* overstrict

82   *face* appearance assumed for the occasion

83   *seeming brow* front, semblance

85–6   *cut me off the heads | Of all the favourites.* This refers to the execution of Bushy, Green, and Wiltshire in *Richard II* (the two first-named in III.1). Bolingbroke had no right to order these executions; he was already assuming Richard's prerogative. The word *me* would be omitted in modern English; it does not imply that the heads were cut off to please Hotspur.

87   *In deputation* as his deputies

88   *personal* personally engaged

92   *in the neck of* immediately after

          tasked taxed (a technical term for a tax of one-fifteenth)

93   *his kinsman March.* See note to I.3.83.

95   *engaged* held hostage

98   *intelligence* use of spies

99   *Rated* berated, dismissed with abuse. This refers to the

dismissal of Worcester, I.3.14–20. Hal, of course, had also been 'rated' – III.2.32–3.

100 *In rage dismissed my father from the court.* The King's words at I.3.120–22 are hardly in rage.

103 *head of safety* army with which to protect ourselves
     withal in addition

105 *indirect* 'not of the true line of descent', and also 'morally crooked'

108 *impawned* pledged (by exchange of hostages)

111 *purposes* proposals

113 *And may be so we shall.* Hotspur's conciliatory tone is surprising. Although it accords with Holinshed, that is not the reason for Shakespeare's use of it. Henry is not without fault (as he himself knows, III.2.4–11). His deception in the course of usurping Richard's throne is recounted not only here but also in *2 Henry IV* – 'God knows, my son, | By what by-paths and indirect crooked ways | I met this crown' (IV.5.184–6) – and even by Hal himself in *Henry V*: 'Not today, O Lord, | O not today, think not upon the fault | My father made in compassing the crown!' (IV.1.285–7). This is not just the opposition of right and wrong. Henry's faults were very serious and the implications of his usurpation of Richard's throne were well known in Shakespeare's day. It still left the problem unresolved as to whether it was permissible to rebel against a sovereign, as Hotspur is doing. Shakespeare, however, in addition to making clear Henry's guilt, also brings out two elements from the chronicles that favour the character of Hotspur. First, his willingness to reflect (here), and secondly, Worcester's deception of Hotspur (V.2).

IV.4 The scene is presumably set in York. Sir Michael (Mighell in Q1) is not known to history. 'Sir' was a courtesy title for priests, and a priest might well be the Archbishop's messenger, or Sir Michael might be a knight. The scene serves to heighten the desperate state in which Hotspur finds himself. There would not, of course, have been any point in Shakespeare keeping secret the outcome of the battle: an Elizabethan audience would know only too well who had won.

1   *brief* letter

2   *Lord Marshal* (Thomas Mowbray, Duke of Norfolk)

3   *my cousin Scroop.* It is uncertain to which of several Scroops this refers. The Sir Stephen Scrope (members of the family spelt their name differently) who tells Richard II of his younger brother's execution by Bolingbroke at Bristol (referred to at I.3.265) seems likely. It could, however, be Sir Henry Scroop, executed as a traitor in *Henry V*, II.2.

7   *tenor* purport

10   *bide the touch* be put to the test

15   *first proportion* greatest magnitude

17   *rated sinew* valued source of strength

18   *o'er-ruled by prophecies.* Shakespeare here maligns Glendower. According to Holinshed, the Welsh were at Shrewsbury, but, as mentioned in the note on IV.1.126, Daniel states they did not reach Shrewsbury in time owing to the King's rapid advance.

20   *instant* immediate

31   *corrivals* associates

       dear noble (as at I.1.62)

35   *prevent* forestall

38   *our confederacy* our united opposition

V.1   The scene is the King's Camp at Shrewsbury.

3   *distemperature* cosmic disorder

4   *his* (the sun's)

6   *Foretells a tempest and a blustering day.* The relation of cosmic to human affairs was frequently observed by the Elizabethans and occurs often in Shakespeare.

13   *our old limbs*. Henry was younger than Hotspur (see note to I.1.86–7).

17   *obedient orb* sphere of loyal obedience (the idea being that the planet circles the earth, which most people in Shakespeare's day believed to be fixed)

19   *exhaled* dragged from rightful course

20   *prodigy of fear* fearful omen

26   *dislike* discord

28   *Rebellion lay in his way, and he found it.* Falstaff's witticism puts Worcester's 'protest' (line 25) perfectly in its place, as Hal's affectionate 'chewet' indicates.

29   *chewet* (1) jackdaw (a chatterer); (2) minced meat dressed with butter (both applicable to Falstaff)

32   *remember* remind

34–5   *For you my staff of office did I break | In Richard's time.* This event is recorded by Holinshed and, though Worcester does not himself appear, it is mentioned twice in *Richard II* (II.2.58–9 and II.3.26–7). The Percies' case has already been presented in detail by Hotspur in IV.3 and described in I.3.146–74. That it is now described a third time suggests the importance attached by Shakespeare to Henry's mode of accession. Lines 41–5 are particularly noteworthy, repeating what Hotspur said at IV.3.60–63. Worcester's interest was no more selfless than was Northumberland's, needless to say.

44   *new-fallen* newly fallen due to you

50   *injuries* abuses
       wanton time period of misgovernment

57   *gripe* seize
       sway rule (of the whole country)

60   *gull, bird* nestling

69   *dangerous countenance* threatening looks

71   *younger enterprise* earlier undertaking (his claim to his inheritance)

72   *articulate* formulated item by item

74   *face.* The meaning here seems to be to cover (as with

one fabric by another) – to put a different face on things, rather than simply to adorn.

75 *colour* (the colour of the facing, with also the metaphorical implication of misrepresentation)

77 *rub the elbow* hug themselves with pleasure, arms crossed. Joy was believed to make the elbows itch.

78 *innovation* revolution

80 *water-colours.* Painting in water-colours was not considered permanent – they might easily be washed off. 'Impaint', in this same line, is the first recorded use of this word. The effect of 'Such water-colours to impaint his cause' must have been striking when used here.

his its

81 *moody* sullen

88 *set off his head* removed from his account, not counted against him

89 *braver* finer

100 *in a single fight.* There is no reference in any source to such a challenge but it accords with the chivalric tone that Shakespeare is setting here and in Vernon's description of Hal (IV.1.97–110).

105 *cousin's.* 'Cousin' did not in Shakespeare's time necessarily imply the precise family relationship which the word denotes to us (and see note to I.1.90).

106 *grace* pardon

111 *wait on us* are at hand

114 *We offer fair.* As Holinshed says: 'the King had condescended unto all that was reasonable at his hands to be required, and seemed to humble himself more than was meet for his estate'.

122 *bestride me* (stand over Falstaff to protect him)

123 *a Colossus.* A colossus is a statue considerably larger than life size and there were a number in the ancient world. *The* Colossus, however, was that of Helios at Rhodes, which was over 100 feet high. It was destroyed by an earthquake after standing for fifty-six years,

about 224 B.C., but many Elizabethans believed that its legs still stood over the entrance to the harbour.

124   *Say thy prayers, and farewell.* Hal's abruptness is understandable in the circumstances, but its degree is, perhaps, a little surprising.

125   *I would 'twere bed-time, Hal, and all well.* One of the most human touches in all Shakespeare. The Prince in his reply takes the sense of *bed-time* to be debt-time (a similar quibble occurs at I.3.183–4).

129   *pricks* spurs

130   *prick me off* select me for death (compare, select by picking with a pin)

131   *set to a leg* set a broken leg

132   *grief* pain

137   *insensible* not perceptible to the senses

138–9   *Detraction* slander

139   *suffer* allow

140   *scutcheon* funeral hatchment (a square or lozenge-shaped tablet)

       catechism. This describes the question and answer technique which Falstaff has just used. Falstaff's 'theory of honour' is now, rather ironically, shown in practice. (See also the Introduction, pages 23–4.)

V.2   The scene is the rebels' camp at Shrewsbury.

1   *my nephew must not know.* Worcester's deception of Hotspur is recounted by Holinshed. Honour is, indeed, 'a mere scutcheon'!

6   *still* always

11   *trick* trait

12   *or . . . or* either . . . or

18   *an adopted name of privilege* a nickname licensing him (to be rash)

19   *a spleen* an impulse

20   *live* are active

22   *taken* caught (as in 'take cold')

28   *Deliver up my Lord of Westmorland.* Westmorland was evidently the 'surety for a safe return' of Worcester and Vernon (IV.3.109). He is now to be released. It has been suggested, as we are not told that Westmorland is to be held hostage, that a passage has been omitted, by accident or through revision. It is at least as possible that Shakespeare is using a short-cut to avoid cluttering the action with unimportant details. (See note to I.3.259.)

32   *Douglas.* Strictly speaking, line 32 has only nine syllables, but, if it were desired that the iambic metre be preserved exactly, *Douglas* could be pronounced as three syllables. The situation is the reverse of that discussed at I.1.8. Rhythm in Shakespeare, and indeed in much English verse, is more subtle than counting syllables will allow.

34   *seeming* semblance of

38   *forswearing* denying by a false oath

43   *engaged* held as a hostage (as Mortimer at IV.3.95)

48   *draw short breath* become short-winded (by exertion in battle). Short of breath to the point of death is also implied.

50   *showed his tasking* offered he the challenge

52   *urged* proposed

54   *proof* trial

55   *duties of a man* praises due a man

59   *dispraising praise valued with you* disparaging praise itself as compared to you yourself, the object of praise

61   *blushing cital of himself.* Either, he gave a modest recital of his own merits, or, in his recital of his own merits he blushingly called himself to account.

64   *instantly* simultaneously

66   *envy* ill-will

67   *owe* own

71   *liberty* reckless freedom

74   *That* so that

76–8   *Better consider what you have to do | Than I that have not well the gift of tongue | Can lift your blood up with persuasion* you are better able to consider for yourselves what you have to do than I am able, by gifts of oratory, to inspire you. The tortuous expression of Hotspur's meaning here might suggest he did lack *the gift of tongue* were it not that elsewhere he hardly strikes one as being tongue-tied. The highly compressed style here may occur by chance, or it might, perhaps, be intended as a humorous touch. He does, nevertheless, make a modest address to his followers in lines 90–100. This has a half-comic beginning which supports the suggestion of humour in these three lines.

82–4   *To spend that shortness basely were too long . . . ending at the arrival of an hour* if life lasted but an hour, it would be too long if it were spent basely

83   *dial's point* finger of a clock

90   *cuts me from my tale* stops me talking

91   *I profess not talking* talking is not my profession

91–2   *Only this – | Let each man do his best.* The effect of bathos here is at once comic and touching.

94   *withal* with

96   *Esperance!* This was the Percy battle-cry (see also the note to II.3.74).

99   *heaven to earth* odds of infinity to nothing

V.3   Although the rest of the play is divided into three scenes, the place and time are not differentiated. What is said in the opening comment to I.1 applies here with particular force.

21   *Semblably furnished* seemingly armed

22   *A fool go with thy soul.* Q1 has 'Ah foole, goe with thy soule', but the emended form, proposed in the eighteenth century, seems to give what was intended, as this makes a popular colloquial formula – 'the name of fool go with you'.

25   *coats* surcoats (see note to IV.1.100)

29   *stand full fairly for the day* are a fair way to victory

30   *shot-free* (1) unwounded; (2) without paying the bill

31   *scoring* (1) charging to an account; (2) cutting (wounding)

33   *Here's no vanity*. All (in life) is vanity, but here in death there is no vanity. Another Biblical reference by Falstaff (to Ecclesiastes 12.8).

35   *led* (but not necessarily from the front – 'I have led them to a place where they might be peppered')

37-8   *the town's end* (to beg near the town gates)

39   *What* why (exclamation)

43   *Lend me thy sword*. In Q1, 'thy sword' is printed as prose in the same line as 'Whose deaths are yet unrevenged. I prethee.' The sudden shift to a line of prose is awkward, though most editors accept it – it is not, of course, exceptional. The arrangement in this edition makes a slightly smoother transition to Falstaff's prose, but the result cannot be called remarkable poetry. (See also the note to II.2.102–108.)

45   *Turk Gregory*. The Turks had a reputation for ferocity. Two popes have been suggested as the Gregory referred to, Gregory VII, who reigned in the eleventh century, and, much more convincingly, Gregory XIII, 1572–85, who not only was credited with encouraging the Massacre of St Bartholomew and plots to murder Elizabeth I, but, with Nero and the Grand Turk, appeared in a coloured print called *The Three Tyrants of the World*, being sold in the streets of London in Shakespeare's time.

46   *paid* killed

52   *is it in the case?* (instead of primed, ready for use)

53   *'tis hot* (with great use)

56   *pierce* (pronounced 'perce')

58   *carbonado* (rasher for grilling)

59   *such grinning honour*. See note to IV.3.30.

61   *there's an end* (of life, or, the subject)

V.4.4   *make up* go to the front

5   *retirement* retreat

amaze dismay

12   *stained* (1) blood-stained; (2) disgraced (by defeat)

23   *mettle* spirit

24   *Hydra's heads.* The Hydra was a many-headed monster, eventually killed by Hercules, which grew two heads for each one cut off.

26   *those colours* (the King's)

29   *shadows* imitations

30   *very* true

33   *assay* try

41   *It is the Prince of Wales that threatens thee.* Hal's part in the battle was small, though he seems to have been wounded and refused to leave the field (see lines 10–11).

42   *Who never promiseth but he means to pay.* This is surely an echo of I.2.206–8, especially the second line: 'And pay the debt I never promisèd'.

47   *opinion* reputation

48   *makest some tender of* hast some regard for

50–51   *they did me too much injury | That ever said I hearkened for your death.* There was no ground for such accusations at this time – but see note to III.2.126.

51   *hearkened for* desired

53   *insulting* contemptuous, exultant

57   *Make up* advance

64   *Two stars keep not their motion in one sphere.* According to Ptolemaic astronomy, each star had its own course.

65   *brook* endure

68–9   *would to God | Thy name in arms were now as great as mine.* It was a principle of chivalric combat that a knight only fought another of equal rank. Hal's rank is above Percy's, but not the honour he has won. Hotspur's statement is not as self-regarding as it sounds to us. In *Richard II* Aumerle makes much the same point when insulted by Bagot:

> *Shall I so much dishonour my fair stars*
> *On equal terms to give him chastisement?*
>
> IV.1.21–2

74   *Well said* well done!

75   *boy's* child's

80–82 *But thoughts, the slaves of life, and life, time's fool, | And time, that takes survey of all the world, | Must have a stop* (thoughts, life, and eventually, time itself, must all end)

82   *I could prophesy.* Prophecy was associated with dying men. Gaunt, in *Richard II*, thought himself 'a prophet new inspired' (II.1.31).

87   *Ill-weaved ambition.* Poorly woven cloth shrank easily.

89   *bound* boundary

92   *stout* valiant

93   *sensible of* able to respond to

94   *dear a show* warm a display

95   *favours.* In Hal's case these would seem to be the plumes from his helmet, which were mentioned by Vernon at IV.1.98 (see note). In a tournament a favour was usually a scarf or glove, worn by a knight as a sign of a lady's favour. It has been argued that such a favour is intended here, on the grounds that Hal's badge, the three ostrich feathers, was not well known in Shakespeare's time.

104   *heavy* (a pun – Falstaff's flesh is compared with Hotspur's *stout* spirit, line 92)

107   *dearer.* The pun here is obvious – 'more loved' and 'more noble' – and it is clear that there are many who have fallen (Sir Walter Blunt, for example) who are more noble than Falstaff. But do we expect any of them, even Sir Walter, to be more loved by Hal? The ironical banter of the opening of the speech (so similar in tone to that exchanged by Hotspur and Lady Percy) is certainly affectionate and the implication of 'I could have better spared a better man' perfectly sums up Hal's affection for Falstaff and his realization

of Falstaff's shortcomings. Possibly, as Dr Johnson complained, a pun was irresistible to Shakespeare and we ought not to attach too great significance to this apparent lowering of Falstaff in Hal's affections. (See also the note to IV.2.14–15, and Introduction, pages 33–4.)

108   *Embowelled* disembowelled (for embalming). A sequence of puns involving hunting terms begins here. Falstaff has just been called 'a deer' (line 106), and deer, on being killed, were disembowelled. When Hal leaves Falstaff to lie 'in blood' he means, in his own blood, but he uses a term which, in hunting, meant 'in full vigour' – and as Falstaff is feigning, this happens to be true. The expression 'to powder' (line 111) meant 'to pickle' and refers to the deer's flesh.

109   (stage direction) *Falstaff riseth up.* Hal's speech over Falstaff is sufficiently serious and deeply-felt to suggest that Falstaff might have seemed to be truly dead to an audience as well as to Hal. The stage direction after line 75 is ambiguous: *he fighteth with Falstaff, who falls down as if he were dead.* Falstaff's rising up here should not follow immediately on Hal's exit. There ought to be a pause because, whether a modern audience believes him to be dead or not (and many members of a modern audience will know he is feigning), his coming to life is a moment of comedy of which an actor can make much. It is comparable to the situation in II.4.261 when, even if we know what Falstaff's answer is to be, we await it with anxiety and receive it with delight.

112–3 *that hot termagant Scot* (Douglas)

113   *scot and lot* in full (with a pun on 'Scot')

119   *part* quality (not 'portion')

124–5 *Nothing confutes me but eyes* no one can prove me wrong but an eye-witness (and there is none here, except the audience who Falstaff assumes will take his part)

126   *thigh.* Why Falstaff should choose the thigh as a place to wound Hotspur is puzzling. The thighs would be cov-

ered with 'cuishes' (Hal's are referred to at IV.1.105), and, indeed, at the time of Shrewsbury all the front of a man in armour was fully protected. Whilst Shakespeare could hardly be expected to know the details of the armour used two centuries before he wrote *1 Henry IV*, the armour he could have seen would, if anything, have been even more elaborate. Hotspur's 'mangled face' is uppermost (line 95) and thus it would seem that the action required – and presumably carried out in the original production in Shakespeare's own time – would be for Falstaff to turn the body over and stab it in the only unprotected place – the top of the thigh, the bottom – 'protected' by being sat on when the knight was on horseback. If the actor deliberated over speaking the word *thigh* as he stabbed, the effect would be gruesomely comic and it might thus remove, through the convention of comedy, the full implications of Falstaff's dishonourable act. What follows is certainly in the vein of comedy. (See also the notes to IV.2.14–15 and IV.2.63–4, and that to line 150, below.)

128   *fleshed* used for the first time. John of Lancaster was then only 13. The attention given him at the end of *1 Henry IV* has been thought by some critics to be a preparation for his part, as Bedford, in *2 Henry IV*. If that is so it is one piece of evidence to indicate that Shakespeare had a second part of *Henry IV* in mind when writing this part (but see Introduction, pages 10–11).

137   *Jack* knave

149–50 *I'll take it upon my death* (an oath of particular solemnity)

150   *thigh.* Falstaff repeats the place of wounding and, if the argument on its meaning in line 126 is correct, this would again be comic – more comic than before, indeed, for the unlikely case of killing a man by stabbing in such a place would be very obvious.

156   *a lie* (of yours)

157   *happiest terms* most favourable expressions of support

159   *highest* (part of the ground)

161   *I'll follow, as they say, for reward.* This is another quibble based on hunting. The hounds are said to *follow* and they are given as *reward* portions of the deer that has been brought down.

163   *purge* (1) repent; (2) take laxatives

V.5.1   *rebuke* violent check

2   *Ill-spirited* evil-minded

      did not we send grace. Compare 'will they take the offer of our grace' – pardon – at V.1.106.

6   *Three knights* (ten, in Holinshed)

15   *pause upon* postpone taking a decision

20   *Upon the foot of fear* with the speed of panic

36   *bend you* you direct your course

      dearest best

41   *his* its

43-4   *And since this business so fair is done | Let us not leave till all our own be won.* This does not read like the end of *Henry IV* as Shakespeare conceived it: it almost invites our attention to a second part.

43   *fair* successfully

AN ACCOUNT OF THE TEXT

WHEN we read a book in a certain edition we expect every copy of that edition to be identical. If a dozen people were each to use a copy of this edition of *1 Henry IV* for study or in preparing a production of the play, they would rightly expect the same words to appear in the same places in each person's copy. The content of books can change from edition to edition, and that of newspapers invariably does, but sometimes books will go through edition after edition without any changes being made, other than the date of the edition, repeating even errors that are obvious.

This edition of Shakespeare's play differs from versions prepared by other editors. The arrangement of the contents and the editorial comment will be expected to be different, but it may come as a surprise that the words of the play itself are sometimes different from those in other editions. The text given here is similar to that in the edition prepared by A. R. Humphreys in 1960, rather less like that published in 1946 by John Dover Wilson, and quite different from the version printed in the collected edition of Shakespeare's plays published nine years after his death. Some of the changes reflect different approaches to modernization. The 1598 edition prints *coarse* at IV.1.123 but the Arden editor spells this 'corse' whereas it is fully modernized to 'corpse' in this edition. Some changes are the result of different ways of adapting Elizabethan punctuation to modern needs. Only occasionally is meaning affected in *1 Henry IV*. All editors find it necessary to change the names of the speakers at II.4.168, 169, 171, and 175, from those given in 1598. Many editors consider that 'Oneyres' (II.1.77) needs amendment. This kind of variation is not the product of editorial pedantry. Each editor has tried to provide his readers with what

Shakespeare intended to be his *First Part of King Henry the Fourth* in a way that will be comprehensible to them. But the editor has then to work out what Shakespeare did intend. *1 Henry IV*, like many plays of the period, was published in different versions that might or might not represent its author's intention and copies of the same edition read differently in places because in Shakespeare's time printing often began before proofs were read.

As our knowledge of Shakespeare's plays, and the ways in which they were printed, has grown, it has become possible, despite many frustrations and uncertainties, to present texts which are believed to be closer to what Shakespeare wrote than those published a decade or a century ago, or even than those published in his own lifetime. This is not as surprising as it might seem, for the texts of works by modern authors are not always printed as they have directed.

Obviously an editor's problem is more difficult when he cannot know at first hand what an author intended. Nowadays most authors have some say in the printing of their work. What they say may not be noted, or the author may have said different things on different occasions so that the resulting editions are not always readily reconcilable, or the author may not have noticed errors made in printing or reproduced from his original.

It cannot be taken for granted that an author saw his work through the press in Shakespeare's day and it has long been asserted that most dramatists, and Shakespeare especially, had little control over the printing of their work. So inaccurate are even the best early editions of some of Shakespeare's plays that scholars have felt reluctant to believe that such a genius could have been so careless of his reputation. One contemporary of Shakespeare, Thomas Heywood, in an epistle printed with his play *The English Traveller* in 1633, stated that actors were averse to the publication of those of his plays which were still in the repertoire because they 'think it against their peculiar profit to have them come into print'. In the prologue to his delightfully named play, *If You Know Not Me You Know Nobody*, in 1637, he maintained that a quarter of a century earlier this play had been pirated (published without authority): 'some by Stenography drew the plot: put it in print: (scarce one word true)'. Evidence of this kind, and our knowledge that the law of copyright did not then protect authors to the extent it does now, have given the impression that dramatists had little control over the publication of their plays.

On the other hand, Thomas Heywood also tells us, in an address to the reader published in 1608 with his play *The Rape of Lucrece*, that some playwrights sold their work twice, first to a company of actors and then to a printer. In recent years close examination of various kinds of evidence, including plays themselves, has shown that more dramatists than was once thought likely read proofs of their plays and sometimes even added material to them for the benefit of their readers. Thus, quite recently, it has been suggested that Shakespeare too might have been more active in the publication of his plays than was once thought.

It seems to me that the printer's copy used for the publication of *1 Henry IV* in 1598 was in Shakespeare's handwriting and that he may have slightly revised it for this purpose. There is no evidence that he did more than that.

The first complete version of *1 Henry IV* that has come down to us is the first Quarto, of 1598 (Q1). It is called a quarto because the individual sheets used to make up the book were each folded twice to give four leaves (eight pages). A century ago, in 1867, it was reported that a single sheet of a slightly earlier version had been found in the binding of an Italian grammar published over three hundred years earlier (though obviously bound later). This fragment is called Q0. From the similarity of type used it seems to have been printed by the same printer, Peter Short, as Q1. Q1 has one line more on each page than Q0 and these extra lines made it possible to print Q1 much more economically, saving not only two leaves required for these extra lines but also the paper for the blank leaves that would usually be used with these additional pages. For these and other reasons Q1 is thought to be a reprint of Q0.

Each of the succeeding five quartos was printed from its predecessor and one cannot take very seriously the claim on the title page of Q2 that it has been 'Newly corrected by *W. Shakespeare*'. Then, in 1623, Shakespeare's plays were gathered together and printed in what has come to be called the Folio. Later quartos introduced colloquial contractions, and the Folio introduces, among other things, Act divisions, the purging of oaths (in belated accordance with an Act of Parliament passed in 1606), and a very small number of interesting amendments. In addition, 'Bardolph' usually replaced 'Bardol'. The only other text of the period is a handwritten version, the Dering Manuscript, which is made up from both parts of *Henry IV*, evidently for a private performance.

It is known that some literary works were prepared by their authors in different versions on, or for, different occasions. We know that Thomas Middleton, a contemporary of Shakespeare, wrote different versions of his play *A Game at Chess*; these versions, in his own handwriting, have come down to us. Furthermore, these versions coexist – one does not replace the other.

It has recently been argued from evidence of this kind that different versions of words and lines in Shakespeare's plays may be Shakespearian – that though some variant forms result from the errors of scribes or the men who set the type, we ought to take into account the possibility that Shakespeare, like Middleton and others, may have produced more than one 'final' version of his work. If this argument is correct, then an editor has to choose between correct and incorrect readings and also between different authorial versions. When looked at in isolation the choice between these readings may be slight but cumulatively the effect can be significant. For example, the tone of *1 Henry IV* differs quite surprisingly if an editor (or producer) chooses colloquial instead of formal readings.

Some editors have considered that when the text for the Folio was prepared, Q5 (upon which it was certainly based) was corrected from the prompt book that had been used in the Globe Theatre. If this were so, it is very surprising that so *few* changes were made. Indeed, all the changes introduced could have been made without reference to any other manuscript. If the prompt-book had been used, we should expect amplified stage directions; the supply of those missing (rather than their *omission*); the correction of long-standing errors; and perhaps the restoration of *fat* at II.2.109, a word omitted in all editions after Q0. It has been argued that Shakespeare would naturally have written colloquially (especially in prose passages) and that a pedantic scribe or compositor was responsible for expanding many colloquialisms. But there is no necessity for even such a line as 'All is one for that' (II.4.150) to be made colloquial, for it is at least as dramatically effective in its context that *All* should be stressed as it is to say 'All's one for that'. If such pedantry were practised it is remarkable that so many colloquial contractions were allowed to stand and even in the Folio there are many places where contractions are not used. Furthermore, these colloquial contractions do not all appear for the first time in the Folio but are introduced gradually, quarto by quarto. It seems more likely that as compositors said lines over to themselves – carrying them in their heads as they set the type – they themselves colloquialized the lines. Contractions, incidentally, require less work to set, and speed is always an attraction to compositors.

As it stands, Q1 does not read like an acting script. It lacks, for example, certain entrances and exits; a few, if unimportant, speech prefixes are inexact; and there are references to non-existent characters. It is likely that from Shakespeare's manuscript he, or someone else, prepared a version for use as the theatrical prompt-book, tidying up details in order to make the play suitable for performance. This copy would be sent to the Master of the Revels, Edmund Tilney, who was required to authorize plays for performance – that is, act as censor. Although the manuscript believed to have been used for the first edition of the play was not entirely suitable for performance as it stood, it was in very much better order than is usually the case in copy of this kind – much better than that used for *2 Henry IV* for example.

We are here in the field of conjecture (as is everyone endeavouring to solve this problem), but it may be helpful to imagine what occurred when objections were raised to the use of the name of Oldcastle in *1 Henry IV* (see Introduction, page 29), and perhaps also to the use of the names 'Harvey' and 'Russell' which seem originally to have been used for 'Bardolph' and 'Peto'. ('Harvey' and 'Russell' survive in Q1 at I.2.160.) There existed a prompt-book manuscript and the manuscript on which it was based. Changes had to be made in the prompt-book at once and this task would, it seems to me, have been given to the author, who might be expected to provide alternative names and would be the person most familiar with the text, and thus most able to make the necessary changes rapidly. Later, when printing was proposed, a manuscript would have to be provided. Even if the play was not then being performed, it is unlikely that the prompt-book would be released, because it would contain the precious authorization for performance; and, in any case, the text we have is not prepared for performance. In order to avoid giving offence by the use of the name 'Oldcastle' it would be necessary to amend the earlier manuscript or to make a copy of either the manuscript or the prompt-book. This work could have been done by a scribe or by Shakespeare.

A scribe, one imagines, would need the prompt-book before him to see what changes were necessary, and these would be hard to miss if they stood out like the emendations in the prompt-book of Massinger's *Believe as You List* (which has come down to us). It is not unreasonable to suggest that if a scribe had collated this manuscript with the prompt-book, though he would doubtless have made errors, he might have been expected to make a more thorough job of the entries and exits than is the case. I imagine, therefore, that Shakespeare himself made the emendations in his own manuscript and, simultaneously, tidied up most of the speech prefixes. That is, he changed chiefly what was obvious (for example, speech prefixes) but missed what wasn't, such as the prefix *Per.* (*Percy*) instead of *Hot.* (*Hotspur*) in IV.1, the reference to Harvey and Russell at I.2.160, the three speeches attributed to Russell in II.4 and the entries and exits already lacking.

Thus I believe (for there is no certainty) that the manuscript used in 1598 by Peter Short, the printer, was in Shakespeare's handwriting and that there is a reasonable likelihood that he revised it slightly for publication; and, furthermore, that no later edition, nor the Dering Manuscript, has any authority, though these versions contain occasional acceptable guesses. It seems to me improbable that the existence of full and elided expressions represents alternative readings both having Shakespeare's authority.

How far can we rely upon Peter Short's workmanship? There are two emendations that appear in the Folio ('President' – for 'precedent' – at II.4.32 and 'cantle' at III.1.96) and one in the Dering Manuscript ('tristful' at II.4.386) that every editor is grateful for. Some editors make use of more readings from editions published after Q1 than do others, but on the whole Q1 gives the impression of being a very reliable edition. Its printer, Peter Short, was very respectable. He printed Foxe's *Acts and Monuments* for the Company of Stationers, and a number of works by St Augustine, Bede, and Thomas à Kempis; by Lodge, Drayton, and Garnier; music by Farnaby, Morley, and Dowland; Daniel's *Civil Wars* (a source of *1 Henry IV*); Meres's *Palladis Tamia* (which quotes a line from *1 Henry IV*, though they were published in the same year); as well as two plays with Shakespearian associations, *The Taming of a Shrew* (in two editions) and *The True Tragedy of Richard Duke of York*; and editions of Shakespeare's *Venus and Adonis* and *The Rape of Lucrece*.

In the past decade or so editors have devoted particular attention to what went on in Elizabethan printing-houses. Efforts have been made by a variety of techniques to identify the work and habits of those who set type, the aim being to evolve techniques that are objective and demonstrable in order that the editor's subjective impressions shall not unduly influence his decisions. The application of such techniques to Q1 of *1 Henry IV* virtually proves what might be guessed from the publication of a second edition (Q1) within a few months of the first (Q0), and it also reveals an unusual printing procedure.

There are still words in English which may, allowably, be spelt in different ways. In consequence printing houses must decide whether, for example, they will favour endings in '-ise' or '-ize', and whether they will spell 'judgement' as 'judgment'. In Elizabethan times spelling was far more variable. In Q1 of *1 Henry IV* we have, for example, *tongue*, *toung*, and *tong*. It is sometimes possible to distinguish between the men who set type by examining the way they spelt. There are many difficulties; some compositors did not stick to preferred spellings; some altered spellings to make words fit the length of line required; sometimes they adopted spellings from the copy they were setting, especially in line-for-line reprints like Q1.

The problem is made difficult, wellnigh impossible indeed, in *1 Henry IV* because we have only eight pages of Q0 (too small a sample in this case to make precise discrimination possible) and Q1 reveals a bewildering variation of spellings. In the part we can check, we can see that whoever set Q1 changed *enough* in Q0 to *inough* on two occasions; changed *tongue* to *toung*, *all* to *al* – and *al* to *all*! Six times *-ie* endings were changed to *-y* endings – and six times exactly the opposite change was made. Either one or two men could have set Q1 so far as the evidence of spelling alone is concerned. What is clear is that though spellings were altered, Q1 follows Q0 remarkably faithfully by the standards of Elizabethan dramatic printing. A slight error is corrected (*my* is changed to *mine*) and one word, *fat* at II.2.109, is erroneously omitted.

Of the other editorial techniques applied, only one produced useful information. At the top of each page of Q1 of *1 Henry IV* the play's title is given in the form *The History | of Henry the fourth* (spelt in a variety of ways). It was customary for such 'running titles' to be transferred, after they had been used with one set of type, to another set of pages. Whereas the type for the text had to be broken up to be used again, the type for running titles could be kept standing. In Q1 of *1 Henry IV* four pages of type were printed simultaneously on *one side* of a large sheet of paper. This required four running titles – two for *The History* and two for *of Henry the fourth*. After the first four pages had been printed on one side of the large sheet, the four pages that backed on to them had to be printed on the other side. This, when folded twice, gave eight pages of text (four leaves). It was (and is) possible to use the same running titles for both sides of the sheet, but it seems likely that it was more economical of time to arrange two sets of four running titles, each set forming a 'skeleton'. Recent studies of printed books of the late Elizabethan period have indicated that normal practice was for these skeletons to be used alternately.

It so happens that in Q1 not only are the running titles spelt in different ways but some of the pieces of type can be individually identified and it is thus possible to demonstrate that Q1 uses eight titles, making two distinct skeletons. But, instead of being used alternately, one is used twice, then the other occurs twice, and so on. As the whole point of making up two skeletons is to use them alternately, why did Short's men do this?

In all the other plays Short printed before 1598, whether quartos or octavos, only one skeleton is used for each text. Though the evidence is slight, a single skeleton seems to have been used for the fragment we have of Q0. The effect of using two skeletons in this manner in Q1 is as if *two* compositors had set the type, each one using a single skeleton for the pages he set, and each man setting an alternate eight pages. What we normally expect when two men set type for a quarto is the use of four skeletons (as for *Hamlet* in 1604). The implications are modest but support an editor's reliance on Q0 and Q1.

It will be remembered that Q0 and Q1 do not show as much colloquial elision as later quartos and the Folio and that it has been agreed by some editors the lack of colloquialism in Q1 was caused by a pedantic compositor. Certainly we can say that Q1 follows Q0 exactly. Furthermore, lines where colloquial elision occurs in later quartos and the Folio, where past forms of verbs are wrongly left unelided, and lines in Q1 which might have been adapted to suit the metre, are evenly distributed between the two men conjectured to have set Q1. We can reasonably assume that what we have in Q1 almost certainly represents the copy provided for these two compositors – that is, Q0. Unfortunately we cannot extract as much information as we should like about Q0 from the fragment that has come down to us. We can but wonder if whoever set the type was as accurate as his colleagues who set Q1, if, indeed, he was not one of them.

That Short took the, for him, unusual step of putting two men to set the type for Q1 confirms what we might guess: that there was a heavy demand for the play and he was anxious to publish it quickly. (It is the only play by Shakespeare of which two editions were published in the same year – and a third appeared in the following year.) Yet the evidence we have shows no sign of carelessness or undue haste on the part of the compositors. It would seem that Short's compositors were competent craftsmen who followed their copy with care – much more than can be said for the compositor who set the greater part of *1 Henry IV* in the Folio. Until further evidence comes to light we must put our trust in the 1598 editions of *1 Henry IV*, and we may do so, I believe, with some confidence.

COLLATIONS

The lists that follow are *selective*. Except where a passage has been relineated for the first time in this edition, relineation (usually of prose to verse) is not noted; nor are changes in punctuation, and minor variants that are undisputed. The long s used in printing the early texts (ʃ) is replaced here by modern s (except where long s affects the reading).

I

The first word or phrase is that given in this edition; the word or phrase after the square bracket is what is given by Q1, in its original spelling. Most of the changes are modern forms of archaic words.

I.i.   4 strands] stronds
        43 corpses] corpes

I.2. 33 moon. As for proof? Now,] moone, as for proofe.
           Now
      136 Who I? Rob? I a thief?] Who I rob, I a thiefe?
           (*Most editors read* Who, I rob? I a thief?)

I.3. 13 helped] holpe
      43 corpse] coarse (*and. at* IV.1.123)

II.1. 18 Christian] christen
      56 Weald] wilde
      77 O-yeas] Oneyres (*see Commentary*)

II.2. 0 Peto *omitted from this entry and added, with*
          Bardolph, *at line 46 stage direction* (*see Commentary*)

II.3. 94 Kate?] Kate (*see Commentary*)

III.2. 59 won] wan

III.3. 132 owed] ought

IV.2. 3 Sutton Coldfield] Sutton cop-hill

V.3. 42 Whose deaths ... prithee] *taken as verse;* Lend
          me *follows* preethe *in* Q1.

2

The following readings have been adopted from editions other
than Q0 and Q1. Only the more interesting changes, and any
that could be considered significant from the early quartos and
the Folio, are included. The first word or phrase is that given
in this text. It is followed by a square bracket and sometimes
the source of the emendation. Usually where no source is named
the emendation is the work of an eighteenth-century editor, e.g.
Capell, Theobald, Hanmer, or Steevens. The second word or
phrase quoted is the reading of Q1 unless a statement to the
contrary appears.

I.1.   0 *Sir Walter Blunt*] *added from Dering Ms.*
      30 Therefor] *A. R. Humphreys;* Therefore
      62 a dear] deere
   75-6 In faith, | It is] In faith it is. *spoken by King*
I.2. 79 similes] Q5; smiles

253

I.2.   80   sweet] sweer (*the error in* Q1 *not noted elsewhere*)

160   Falstaff] Falstalffe (*and frequently*)

Bardolph, Peto] Harvey Rossill (*see An Account of the Text, page* 248)

I.3.   95   tongue for] tongue: for

199   HOTSPUR] Q5; *omitted from* Q0 *and* Q1

260   granted. (*To Northumberland*) You my lord,] granted you my Lord.

II.2.   12   square] squire

109   fat] *omitted from the Folio and from all early quartos except* Q0

II.3.   50   thee] the

72   A roan] Q3; Roane

II.4.   6   bass string] *G. L. Kittredge*; base string

7   Christian] Q5; christen

32   precedent] F (President); present

168   PRINCE HAL] Prince F; Gad.

169, 171, 175 GADSHILL] Gad. F; Ross. (*see An Account of the Text, page* 248)

240   elf-skin] Q3 (elfskin); elfskin Q1; *many editors emend the reading of* Q1 *to* eel-skin – *see Commentary.*

386   tristful] *Dering Ms.*; trustful

394   yet] Q3; so

III.1.   96   cantle] F; scantle

III.3.   56   tithe] tight

IV.1.   20   I, my lord] I my mind

55   is] F; tis

108   dropped] Q2 (dropt); drop

126   cannot] Q5; can

127   yet] Q5; it

V.2.   3   undone] Q5; vnder one

V.3.   22   A fool] Ah foole

36   ragamuffins] rag of Muffins

V.4.   67   Nor] F; Now

91   thee] the

164   nobleman] Q4; noble man

The short list that follows gives a few of the more interesting readings that have not been adopted in this edition. The Commentary at II.1.77 and II.4.240 might also be consulted in this connexion. The reading of the present text is given first.

I.1.   16   allies] all eyes Q4
I.3.   233   wasp-stung] waspe-tongue Q2
II.2.   34   my] Q0; mine Q1
II.4.   122   lime in it] in't *uncorrected Folio;* lime *corrected Folio. The Folio compositor missed out the word* lime *when he set this passage and the result was nonsense. To make sense (but not quite that of the original) without re-adjusting all the type that followed in order to take in an extra word,* in't *was simply replaced by* lime.
         333   O, Glendower] Q2; O Glendower Q1; Owen Glendower *Dering Ms.*
III.2.   156   intemperance] intemperature F

Claimants to the Throne of England after the deposition of Richard II

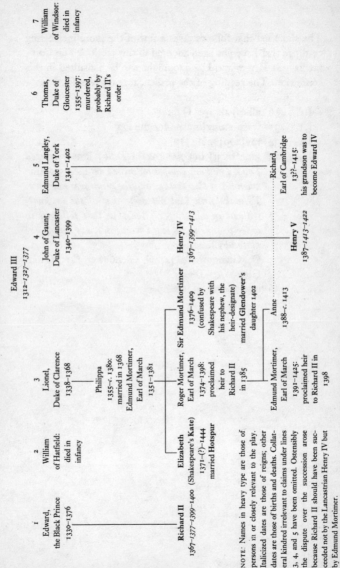

Edward III
1312–1327–1377

1
Edward,
the Black Prince
1330–1376

Richard II
1367–1377–1399–1400

2
William
of Hatfield:
died in
infancy

3
Lionel,
Duke of Clarence
1338–1368

Philippa
1355–c. 1380:
married in 1368
Edmund Mortimer,
Earl of March
1351–1381

Roger Mortimer, Sir Edmund Mortimer
Earl of March   1376–1409
1374?–1398:   (confused by
proclaimed   Shakespeare with
heir to   his nephew, the
Richard II   heir-designate)
in 1385   married Glendower's
                      daughter 1402

Elizabeth   Anne
1371–(?)–1444   1388–c. 1413
married Hotspur

Edmund Mortimer,
Earl of March
1391–1425:
proclaimed heir
to Richard II
in 1398

4
John of Gaunt,
Duke of Lancaster
1340–1399

Henry IV
1367–1399–1413

Henry V
1387–1413–1422

5
Edmund Langley,
Duke of York
1341–1402

Richard,
Earl of Cambridge
13??–1415:
his grandson was to
become Edward IV

6
Thomas,
Duke of Gloucester
1355–1397:
murdered, probably by
Richard II's
order

7
William
of Windsor:
died in
infancy

NOTE: Names in heavy type are those of persons in or closely relevant to the play. Italicized dates are those of reigns; other dates are those of births and deaths. Collateral kindred irrelevant to claims under lines 3, 4, and 5 have been omitted. Ostensibly the dispute over the succession arose because Richard II should have been succeeded not by the Lancastrian Henry IV but by Edmund Mortimer.